Property of —

Bea J. Waterbury
3 Ginger Hill Ln
Toledo, Oh 43623

A COOK'S GUIDE TO GROWING HERBS, GREENS, AND AROMATICS

A
GROWING HER

COOK'S GUIDE TO

BS, GREENS, AND

AROMATICS

by Millie Owen

Illustrations by Karl Stuecklen

Alfred A. Knopf · New York · 1978

THIS IS A BORZOI BOOK
PUBLISHED BY ALFRED A. KNOPF, INC.

Copyright © 1978 by Mildred Ziegler Owen

Artwork Copyright © 1978 by Karl Stuecklen

All rights reserved under International and Pan-American
Copyright Conventions. Published in the United States by
Alfred A. Knopf, Inc., New York, and simultaneously in Canada
by Random House of Canada Limited, Toronto. Distributed by
Random House, Inc., New York.

Library of Congress Cataloging in Publication Data
Owen, Millie [date]
A cook's guide to growing herbs, greens, and aromatics.
1. Herb gardening.   2. Cookery (herbs)   3. Greens,
edible.   I. Title.
SB351.H509   1978   641.3′5   77-20368
ISBN 0-394-73454-8

Manufactured in the United States of America
First Edition

FOR WAYNE AND GRIFF

CONTENTS

PART II

ACKNOWLEDGMENTS

Judith B. Jones, my editor, inspired this book, and I am grateful for her friendship and guidance.

Karl Stuecklen's contribution has been immense. I greatly appreciate his sensitive expertise in illustrating plants.

Many other people made it all possible and aided in various ways: my grandparents, Anna and Henry Hertzler and Mattie and Will Ziegler; my parents, Osie and Ralph Ziegler; my teacher Eva Carper, and other friends and relatives in Denbigh, Virginia.

Numerous cooks, seed growers, herb societies, horticulturists, and other gardeners have shared so much that I wish I could give detailed credit to all of them. I can only say that I hope our combined efforts will make life more pleasurable for everyone.

Ann Turner, head librarian at Norwich University, was most helpful in supplying me with sources. Many local herb growers shared seeds and plants and advice, and I especially thank neighbor Kassie Dreyer. Other neighbors, Bernice Pierson and Judy Viele, alleviated my domestic duties so I could type.

My friend Emily Grace Shenk and my brother Don Ziegler, who went over the manuscript, added style and accuracy. So did my husband, Wayne, who invented and tested many of the recipes. Griffith, our son, while admiring and eating and tearing up plants, confirmed my belief that people of all ages enjoy herbs and greens and aromatics.

Thanks to all of you.

MILLIE OWEN
Northfield, Vermont
Spring 1977

INTRODUCTION
land and space

When we moved from Manhattan to Vermont, for the first time in years we had land and space—almost everything we needed to grow things. In addition, we had a brook to sprout watercress, woods to explore for fiddleheads, sunny windows to give light to indoor basil.

When I set out my first tarragon plant, I knew little about soil and climate and pests. I did remember from my childhood in rural Virginia most of what my parents had taught me about greens and wild plants, but I still needed a lot of practical advice about the many new things I wanted to try. The dozens of gardening books I consulted made it all sound so easy. The herbals concentrated on cures for warts, tales about the Virgin Mary hanging her sky-blue cloak on a rosemary bush, and what to put under your pillow to attract a lover. But folklore wasn't useful when the slugs found the asparagus, and home remedies didn't cure sickly dill. So I found that I really had to learn by trial and error.

I took notes, learned from my mistakes, and grew more confident with each triumph. It took me almost eight years. Now I realize how much time, frustration, wasted energy, and expense I would have saved if I had had this very book to guide me. In fact, that is why I decided to write it. I hope its practical information will get you off to a good start and help you enjoy your bounty much more quickly than I ever could.

I was pleased to learn that most of my plants contained many vitamins but few calories, so I've tried to put down the specific nutrient content of herbs rather than remedies for obesity and flatulence. I have given practical advice on how to plant and harvest rather than suggesting that leaves should be gathered with a golden sickle under a full moon. I've shared what I've learned about keeping plants happy, nursing the sick ones, and fighting pests without

Sunny windows to give light to

give light to indoor basil

We had a brook to sprout water cress,
Woods to explore for fiddleheads,

using harmful chemicals. Since I have tended plants both indoors and out, I think I've run into just about every problem you're likely to have, and I've offered solutions. If, like me, you enjoy exploring the country and sampling what nature offers freely, this book should serve as a guide to foraging for wild things. There are all sorts of ideas here for preserving herbs, and I have put down my favorite recipes for using herbs and greens and aromatics in the most delectable ways.

At first I was simply curious about how sorrel tasted, when to pick milkweed, how to make full use of a burgeoning crop of basil. Now, all these things have become a way of life. This is bound to happen to anyone who loves food, particularly to good cooks who cherish the value of fresh flavors. When I look at a new Chinese or Indian recipe that calls for fresh coriander, I'm glad I don't have to search out a Chinatown and pay 79¢ for a small limp bunch. If I'm trying one of those new, healthful French recipes that calls for braising a roast on a bed of aromatics (vegetables like shallots, celery, and carrots that add flavor and aroma to foods), I know it's going to turn out that much better because my aromatics are plucked straight from the garden. We hardly use salt anymore because of all the new tastes that have awakened our palates.

As a child, I savored country greens and wild asparagus. Later, in the city, I was pleased to find that I could grow parsley and chives indoors. Now that I'm back to country living, I'm sharing with you all the pleasures I've experienced in growing and eating herbs, greens, and aromatics. Whatever age you are, whether you live in the country or the city, join me in the joys of fresh foods—they're what this book is all about.

PART I

GROWING HERBS, GREENS, AND AROMATICS OUTDOORS

 # trellises for:

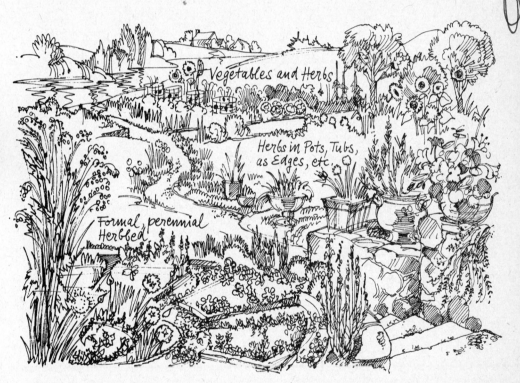

Vegetables and Herbs

Herbs in Pots, Tubs, as Edges, etc.

Formal, perennial Herbbed

It doesn't take a lot of space to grow a few herbs and greens outdoors, and even the city-bound can often do it. If your apartment has wide enough sills, you can install window boxes or a tray with pots or a built-in planter. Perhaps you have a balcony or some yard space. If so, you can set a small area aside for greens,

Asparagus Beds

lettuces, herbs, and other tidy plants. If you have just enough soil outside your door for a limited garden, be sure to combine the vegetables and herbs that give you the greatest reward for the least space: for instance, Malabar spinach, nasturtiums, and cucumbers on trellises; an asparagus bed; shallots and garlic between pepper plants; onions among lettuces and greens; marigolds wherever there's an empty spot.

When you have acres of land to cultivate, your possibilities are limited only by your appetite, time, and budget. Secretly I would love to have a huge formal herb bed, but until I retire or can afford a gardener, I am content to scatter herbs and greens all over our five acres (more or less, as local deeds are worded): in the permanent perennial herb garden, among flowers, in the vegetable garden, bordering the asparagus patches, in neglected corners, out in the fields, and along the brook.

Where to Plant Herbs and Greens

Most herbs and greens prefer sunny, well-drained soil, although some will do well in partial shade or any old kind of dirt. Look carefully through Part II for the preferences of individual plants for soil, light, and water, then consider the appropriate places you have for growing them.

Some herbs and greens are perennial—they continue growing year after year. You may want to put them in a permanent bed apart from biennials, which live for two years, and annuals, which bloom and die the year they are planted.

Think of convenience before you plant. If you're going to use herbs primarily for cooking, plant them as near the kitchen as possible, or plant annuals in the vegetable garden, where they're handy to pick along with your other crops. For instance, I like basil with tomato dishes, dill with cucumbers, and savory with beans, so I plant these herbs and vegetables together.

Check the size of mature plants and arrange them accordingly. Give them adequate space, and place taller ones in the background. Many smaller herbs and greens can be used as borders in flower beds.

It is not necessary to put all plants that like rich soil in one bed, and those that like acid soil in another area. Make pockets of the desired soil by digging up a small area, replacing the dirt with an appropriate mixture, and seeding or transplanting whatever will thrive there.

Combining plants with contrasting colors and foliage can make your arrangement diverse and artistic. Plant gray herbs near greener herbs and greens, those with lacy leaves alongside shrubby ones.

But use your own imagination in making your collection of herbs and greens unique. Here are some ideas to get you thinking:

An herb bed for the bees and the birds (as well as yourself) might include borage, lavender, sage, thyme, and savory—because bees love their flowers—along with plants whose seeds birds savor: lovage, lamb's-quarters, dill, sunflowers. Just keep the herbs away from your catnip, to avoid conflict between felines and birds.

Make a purple bed combining purple basil, purple cabbage, purple cauliflower, purple beans, ruby lettuce, and eggplant. Or plant variations of gray with wormwood, horehound, and lavender.

If all you have is a spot that gets little sun, try mints, chervil, parsley, violets, lemon balm, lettuces, spinach, and watercress.

You might make a garden that includes the most fragrant herbs, or one with as many biblical herbs as possible, or one combining herbs mentioned in Shakespeare's plays.

Herbs that crawl along the ground—creeping thymes, prostrate rosemary, Corsican mint—can be used as ground covers on banks or be planted between stepping stones on a walkway.

Use shrubby herbs such as rosemary, winter savory, lavender, and wormwood as hedges that can be trimmed or let sprawl.

Grow herbs in planters or tubs or hanging baskets outdoors. Consider containers that can be moved indoors in winter.

Don't neglect the flower beds. Chives are beautiful when they bloom among iris and delphiniums. Creeping thyme adapts well to rock gardens. Many herbs have flowers that are pretty enough to be an accent in any flower garden: dill, borage, rocket, sage, and bergamot mint are some examples. Curly kale and ruby lettuce are attractive edible border plants.

Go ahead and try things. Use leftover seeds or thinned seedlings in any spot you can find. You may be surprised at how well some plants thrive in unusual locations or poor soils.

My local Greenhouse

Where to Get Your Plants

All herbs and greens except tarragon and garlic can be grown from seeds. Seeds are inexpensive and fairly easy to acquire: check your local seed racks for common herbs and greens, and order others from the sources I've listed in the back of this book.

I'm not sure why seed companies are so generous when they pack herbs. They often put a thousand seeds in one package. You don't have to plant all of them, and it's better to sow thinly, as is usually directed on the packet, than to spend time thinning plants later. Most seeds keep well for a few years if they're stored in a cool, dry place. Or you can share them with friends.

Follow package directions or see Part II for when and how to plant seeds outdoors. In general, herbs and greens can be planted as soon as the ground warms up in spring. They should be covered with soil to about twice their diameter. Since many of them have tiny seeds, that means barely covering them with fine soil.

Start plants from seeds indoors if you're eager to start harvesting (see page 20), but don't get so eager that you have flats of crowded seedlings without warm soil to transplant them into. See Part II for specifics about how well individual herbs and greens transplant.

If your local nursery carries the plants, you can get a head start by setting out healthy herbs, greens, and lettuces. They'll be more expensive than seeds, but you can often start harvesting right away. Some nurseries also mail herb plants, leek seedlings, shallots, and onion sets.

If you're new to an area or are just starting out growing herbs, try to locate your resident herb lovers (I got leads from my local greenhouse). Herb growers are without exception generous, warm, and helpful people who delight in sharing their knowledge and their extra plants. Getting perennials from them, which have been grown in your own area, is the most practical and pleasurable way to start a permanent herb bed. Soon you'll find that you too are ready to share extra seedlings, cuttings, tips, books, magazines, and recipes.

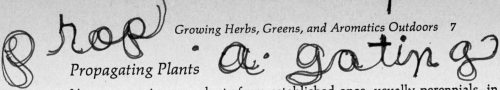

Propagating Plants

You can acquire new plants from established ones, usually perennials, in several ways:

Cuttings, or "slips," are simple to root. Select plant tips with strong growth. With scissors or a knife, cut just below a leaf bud (a node) 2 to 4 inches down from the tip. Strip leaves from the bottom inch of stem, and dip the stem in a hormone powder (available at greenhouses) if you want quick growth.

Some slips root easily if you simply put them in a glass of water. Basil (surprise, since it's an annual!) sprouts roots quickly in water, and mints and watercress also root rapidly if they're simply kept moist.

But the fastest and most reliable way of rooting most slips is to create a greenhouse for them. Place the stems of the cuttings in moist sand, peat moss, or vermiculite. Slip them into a plastic bag, or invert a glass over the cuttings. Put them in a place with good light but not direct sunlight. Remove the cover occasionally to admit fresh air, and add water if the soil dries out. Most herbs will root in about a month; some with especially woody stems, such as rosemary, may take several months.

Root cuttings can be made from plants whose roots send up new stems. Dig gently until you find a large root. Cut a piece of it 1 to 3 inches long. Fill a container with soil, place the root cutting on top, cover it with about ½ inch of soil, and water thoroughly. Cover with newspaper or glass, place in a shady place, and keep moist. When the roots send up shoots, remove the covering and transplant into appropriate soil.

Layering is often simpler than making cuttings, and many herbs layer themselves outdoors when their stems fall over and root. Look for tarragon, sage, and especially wormwood that have self-rooted, but layer perennials yourself if you want extra plants. Select a healthy branch near the ground and bend it down to touch the soil. Find a section just below a leaf node, about a foot from the stem tip, and scrape away a bit of the underside of the stem. Loosen the soil under the stem section and secure that part to the ground with a hairpin or a piece of wire. Mound soil on top, water well, and add a mulch of leaves or compost. Place a brick or stone on top. Roots will probably form in six weeks. Carefully remove soil, and if roots are well established, sever the stem from its parent and transplant the new roots.

Stem Cuttings

Sterile Soil

Root Cuttings

Layering

Division

🌿*Root divisions* can be made from large perennials that have more than one main stem. Early spring and fall are the best times to divide roots. You can cut with a sharp knife through roots and soil and lift separate divisions or dig the entire plant and gently separate root sections. Replant sections immediately and water them well.

A few other plants discussed in Part II can be propagated in other ways. Tarragon produces offsets, little shoots like suckers, around the base of the plant. You can cut them away along with some roots and transplant them. Shallots, garlic, and some onions produce cloves within the bulb that are separated for replanting.

Weeds and Mulch

"Weeds" are inherently neither good nor bad. They are simply plants that grow where they're not supposed to grow.

Weeding herbs on your hands and knees, if you have lots of time, can be a pleasure—you can sniff herb fragrance and munch some leaves as you go along. Most of us, however, would prefer to use our time doing other things, and that is why I strongly recommend a mulch for your herbs and greens. It conserves moisture, prevents rain splash, keeps the soil from becoming too hot, adds nutrients, and greatly reduces weed growth.

Mulch does not eliminate all weeding. If you plant seeds you have to keep the seeded area open to the sun until the plants are well up. Meanwhile, you may be sure, the weeds will be growing as fast as the seedlings. Start weeding and thinning your plants as soon as possible, and keep at it until you can push mulch closely around the stems.

Black plastic "mulch" is an exception: you can cut holes in the plastic and set plants or sow seeds in them. Black plastic is expensive, but if you buy the right kind—6 to 8 mils—it is effective and lasts several seasons. Select mulch on the basis of accessibility and aesthetics. Find out if a mulch material is available free or cheap in your area. Look for such by-products as chopped sugar cane, hop vines, peanut hulls, sawdust, or shavings. Try to get your neighbors' raked leaves or lawn clippings or spoiled hay. Gather leaf mold or marsh hay or seaweed.

We've found a newspaper and hay mulch excellent for the vegetable and annual herb garden. My husband, Wayne, separates the *Times* pages to four layers, dips them in the brook until they are soaked, spreads them on the garden between rows, then covers them with a thick layer of hay. As the plants grow, we push the hay closely around them. This means we don't have to till lime and fertilizer into the whole garden; we work it only into the areas being seeded. In the fall we push the hay over the rows and put some compost on top. By spring everything is partially decomposed, the rows are ready to sow after the hay is pushed back, and it's time to put down more newspaper layers and hay.

I've used sawdust and hay in the perennial herb bed. Sawdust is so acidic, however, that generous amounts of lime should be added to it before it is applied in a thick layer. It weathers to a nice gray color.

We've used other mulches over the years, and here are some notes on them:

Lawn clippings are excellent, especially around plants that grow close together—the fine texture of the grass makes it easy to push the mulch around the stems. It is seldom possible to collect enough grass clippings for your whole garden; so I use grass selectively, spreading it thin around onions, dill, and seedlings. If you pile damp clippings more than a few inches high, they rot and smell awful.

Peat moss is expensive but attractive. It dries out quickly and is acidic. I use it and pine bark around acid-loving plants.

Leaf mold from the woods is also acidic, but it's free. It takes a lot of it to stop weed growth—in fact, it often contains weed seeds, and that is why I have jack-in-the-pulpits and other nice wild plants in some of my gardens.

Leaves raked up in fall should be shredded or composted for a few weeks before being used as a mulch. Don't just pile them on the garden—they'll become a sodden mass—but you can spread them over an area you plan to till in the spring.

Weeds make good mulch if they are thoroughly dried out, so they don't revive when they're piled. Avoid using witchgrass and quackgrass—nothing kills them. Some gardeners actually use live weeds such as purslane as a "mulch," letting the plants creep over the ground and shade the soil to retain moisture. I don't recommend it.

Partially decomposed compost can be used as a mulch. It is generally not pretty, but it is good for the soil as it breaks down further. I cover it with hay. I've also pushed vegetable wastes directly from the kitchen as well as weeds under the hay mulch, à la Ruth Stout, rather than composting them. I won't go into the details of composting here, although of course I recommend it. Check Catharine O. Foster, *The Organic Gardener*, for more information, or for specific questions write to the Connecticut Agricultural Experiment Station in New Haven, which specializes in composting waste matter for soil improvement.

Companion Planting

Many organic gardeners advocate companion planting, the intermixture of plants for mutual benefit or pest control. Pungent herbs are an important part of companion planting. Dill is grown near tomatoes as a trap plant; tomato worms supposedly concentrate on the dill and spare the tomatoes. Chives are said to chase aphids, marigolds repel nematodes, and so on.

I've tried planting many of these recommended varieties together, and the method often seems to be beneficial. There is scientific evidence for its validity, but it's hard to apply the scientific method to one's own failures and successes. Would the plants have done just as well if they hadn't been placed together? Did the dill simply attract tomato worms to the garden? Anyway, I'd prefer that the tomato worms eat the tomato leaves and stay away from my dill.

The greatest value of companion planting, I think, is its stress on

diversity. One is tempted to plant traditional tidy rows, with each variety lined up together. Mixing plants is often better. Under the bower of leaves of big plants such as peppers you can grow lettuces and greens that don't mind some shade. If predators destroy the cabbage, you'll still have those onions you planted between them. Radishes planted around zucchini hills may repel cucumber beetles, but the radishes also profit from the rich soil and moisture, and they're ready to pull before the squash takes over.

Scatter short rows or clusters of herbs and greens and other vegetables around the garden; if one area is attacked, another is often spared. It's even been suggested that predators are disoriented by the barrage of chemical stimuli from a mixture of plants. If you're interested in more information on companion planting, write to Rodale Press, Emmaus, Pennsylvania 18049.

Pests, Diseases, and Predators Outdoors

They won't all attack at once, even though some years they seem to marshal forces. Pests and diseases are rarely the problem outdoors that they are indoors, since plants grown in the sun and watered by rain are doing what comes naturally to them, and Mother Nature has a balance that usually protects them if we don't tamper too much.

First, take defensive measures, basically the good cultural practices recommended in this chapter, to create healthy plants that can ward off problems.

Attract birds by planting shrubs with berries they like and feeding them in winter. They'll reward you in summer by eating millions of insects. Toads may not be beautiful, but they eat larvae that destroy your plants. Ladybugs and praying mantises, which you can now order from many sources, eat scales, mealybugs, aphids, and other insects.

When you have to go on the offensive, start with a homemade spray that is abhorrent to many pests but not poisonous to humans or wildlife. Place a few garlic cloves and several hot red peppers in your blender container, add 2 cups of water, and blend until finely ground. Hold your face at a distance when you remove the lid and strain the mixture. Dilute with 1 quart of water. Put in a

Japanese Beetle

Cabbage Worm

Cabbage Butterfly

Aphids *Enlarged*

Earwig

Slug

Cutworm and Grub

Nematodes (Enlarged)

sprayer, and use within a week (or freeze, then thaw as needed). You can also make the mixture using a garlic press and powdered cayenne pepper if you don't have a blender. Be careful not to get the hot pepper in your eyes, keep the spray away from children, and wash your hands after using it.

Botanical sprays such as rotenone and pyrethrum are relatively safe compared to most pesticides, but use them as directed. I do not recommend putting chemical pesticides on edible herbs and greens. If you think you must use them, follow directions very carefully.

Here are some creatures that may try to beat you to your crop and some ways to combat them:

Aphids come in several colors, but the ones you'll usually encounter are green or black. They're indiscriminate in their tastes, sucking the life out of almost any tender growth. If plant leaves curl, develop black mold, or have ants crawling over them, look for insects about ⅛ inch long on the new growth. Aphids leave a secretion, called honeydew, on which mold grows, and ants milk the aphids for this honeydew. Cut off and destroy badly infested growth, then blast the remaining foliage with water. If aphids persist, apply a garlic and hot pepper spray (see above) or order some ladybugs. In desperation, use rotenone or pyrethrum. But aphids are usually more of a nuisance than a serious problem on the herbs and greens mentioned in this book.

Slugs are those slimy fat blobs that make you wonder if Someone didn't diversify a bit too much in creating creeping things. Cowardly, slugs hide under trash during the day; vengefully, they slide out at night to eat holes in your favorite vegetables. Giving them beer seems too merciful a killing, but they will crawl into saucers of stale beer and drown. Use lettuce or cabbage leaves, potato slices, lengths of board, or overturned grapefruit shells for traps. At daybreak, slugs will hide underneath, and you can collect and destroy them. Sprinkle flour or sand around plants; slugs slide along on slime, and anything that is powdery or sandy impedes them. Salt sprinkled directly on slugs kills them, but too much salt is not good for soil, so invest in slug tweezers and a jar of kerosene. When slugs are ruining your first tender asparagus, you're willing to go out at dawn to do them in one at a time. It's not the most felicitous way to start the day, but there's a certain satisfaction in that plop, plop, as the slugs get their just desserts.

Nematodes are tiny worms that attack root vegetables. The best way to combat them outdoors is to plant marigolds, whose roots are poisonous to nematodes. Lime and fish fertilizer are also repellent to nematodes.

Cabbageworms may be a problem on horseradish and cabbage-related greens. You can pick them off, but they're often hard to see, since their green color blends with the crops they attack. Shaking salt on the leaves is somewhat effective, but avoid overuse of salt in the garden. Watch for white cabbage butterflies fluttering around the garden. Although they're pretty, they lay the eggs that turn into cabbageworms, so go at them with a butterfly net or tennis racket. For bad infestations check seed catalogs or garden centers for *Bacillus thüringiensis* (sold as Biotrol, Thuricide, or Dipel), a bacterium that attacks cabbageworms.

Japanese beetles haven't migrated as far north as my garden, but I am assured by southern friends that milky spore disease (marketed as Doom) is effective in killing the grubs. Or hire a neighborhood child to pick off the beetles (I used to be paid a penny apiece for this job, but no doubt rates have gone up).

Cutworms chew the stems of seedlings. If you notice toppled young plants with chewed stems, dig in the soil around them and look for fat grubs. Destroy them, or they'll go on to other plants. Preventive measures for cutworms include sinking cardboard collars (or paper cups with the bottoms cut out) around seedlings, mulching with wood ashes, and planting onions between rows.

Funguses, wilts, blights, and rots are numerous and difficult to diagnose. They are usually a problem in very wet weather. Check seed catalogs for disease-resistant plant varieties. Water plants in the morning to avoid wet foliage at night, when fungus and rot flourish in the damp. If you have persistent problems, contact your agricultural agent for identification of the disease and help in dealing with it.

Animal predators can be far more difficult to deal with. If you live in the country, you are fortunate indeed if your garden has been ignored by predatory wildlife. The best solution is to sink a fine-mesh fence several feet into the ground to stop the moles, mice, and woodchucks, 8 feet in the air to block the deer, and screen across the top to deter the birds, but few of us can afford that. Since our vegetable garden is near the woods, we've never had a summer in which some animal hasn't crept out to destroy, and I wish I knew what to do short of killing wild creatures. Fortunately, they don't attack all at once, and we often have enough to share.

Our county agent gives us bloodmeal every summer to deter the deer. I'm convinced that they eat it for dessert, but it's good for the soil anyway. Try laying chicken wire across areas at the edge of the garden where deer usually enter; apparently they don't like to catch their feet in it. Deer don't care about my herbs, but they love lettuces and greens, which can be protected with a wire-mesh tent.

Woodchucks, or groundhogs, are also deterred by wire protectors—sometimes. I find myself thinking that woodchucks deserve to be composted. Rabbits are something else—only cruel or very hungry people would kill Flopsy, Mopsy, and Cottontail. Lure them away from the garden by setting out rabbit food, or catch them in humane traps and set them free miles down the road (and hope that your neighbors aren't following suit), or place a chicken-wire fence around the vegetables that rabbits especially savor.

Moles make tunnels that push up the soil; mice lazily use those tunnels; neither are all bad. Moles eat grubs and aerate the soil, mice won't bother your herbs, and who could kill Stuart Little? Well, cats could, and they'll get Mr. Mole too. If moles and mice are really bothering you, push mothballs into their tunnels and tramp the soil back in place. Plant daffodils—their bulbs deter rodents, and their flowers will make springtime even more joyous.

Be as gentle as possible—people, animals, insects, and plants all share the earth and air. Your plants may have holes or a few worms. Be grateful: they're not plastic, they haven't been bombarded with chemicals, and they're fresh and good.

GROWING HERBS AND GREENS INDOORS

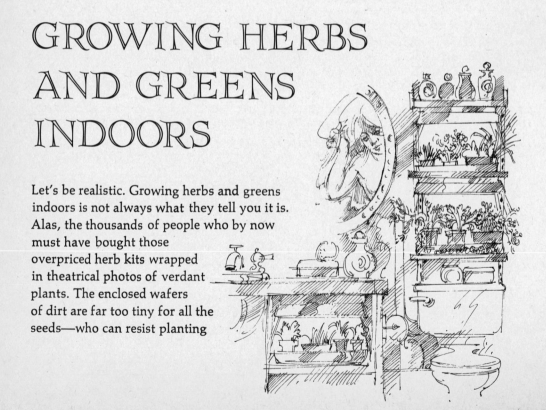

Let's be realistic. Growing herbs and greens indoors is not always what they tell you it is. Alas, the thousands of people who by now must have bought those overpriced herb kits wrapped in theatrical photos of verdant plants. The enclosed wafers of dirt are far too tiny for all the seeds—who can resist planting

them all?—and over the weeks the would-be herb gardener gets only some first-hand observation of nature's laws as the thyme fails to germinate, the dill spindles up and falls over in resignation, and the parsley becomes jaundiced from its nutritional deficiencies.

So there are problems. Herbs grown indoors need adequate soil. Most of them like supplemental plant food. They may become infected by some disease or pest, although everyone told you that herbs' pungent oils make them trouble-proof. And, even if herbs and greens have all the benefits, they may, in protest against something vague you can't remedy, become scraggly or less green or quietly dead.

Clearly, you can't expect perfection. But do it anyway. Freshly grown things are infinitely better than dried: they taste greener, they smell better, their varied foliages are pleasant to look at, and they remind you that summer will return.

Most herbs would much prefer to be back in their native outdoor climate, washed by rain and warmed by sun, but you can make them happy with surrogate benefits, which I'll explain. First, which ones to start with.

How to Start Growing Herbs and Greens Indoors

The best way to decide what to grow indoors is by the process of elimination. Even if you have a full-scale greenhouse and a full-time gardener, you can't grow everything.

Start by looking through the herbs and greens I discuss in detail in Part II. Note those you especially like or think you'd like to try, eliminating those that can't be grown indoors.

Think of your purpose for growing herbs and greens. Do you want them mostly for cooking? For fragrance? For decoration? For experimentation and simply out of curiosity?

Some herbs are good dried (I like dried oregano and tarragon in winter dishes). Some, parsley and watercress especially, are widely available in stores and markets. You might want to grow only those herbs and greens that you most like fresh and can't get elsewhere.

Consider your space and light. Do you have room to grow whole flats of lettuces and spinach? Certain herbs are smaller and tidier than others. Some do well under less light. Check the descriptions and eliminate those least appropriate for the space and light you have available.

The time you have to care for indoor plants is an important consideration. It's best to start with a few plants, tend them well, and be rewarded by good growth. You can then add more as free minutes permit. If you begin with more than you can handle, you'll likely be disappointed and tempted to give up.

Some herbs and greens are easier to grow than others. Tarragon and rosemary require careful attention to watering; dill and mints tend to get spindly. You may want to start with plants that require less effort, such as chives, parsley, and chervil.

The plants I like to include indoors each winter are: basil (green and purple), chervil, chives, dill, marigolds, marjoram, nasturtiums, parsley, hot red peppers, rosemary, sage, winter savory, tarragon, and some sort of thyme. These are plenty to care for, since I want several pots of some of them, but I add others for experiment or fun, depending on how much space and time I have left.

Where to Get Herbs and Greens for Growing Indoors

After you've decided what you want to grow, you have to get plants.

If you've never grown herbs or greens indoors, the easiest way to start is to go to a nursery and select plants. Somebody else has done the hard part—seeding, potting, and nurturing—and you have healthy, tidy plants that you can start harvesting right away. This gives you self-confidence, and if you can't grow plants outdoors, it means you don't waste a whole packet of seeds when you want only one pot of something. And greenhouse plants won't have the shock of moving into your warm house from an outdoor climate.

Unfortunately, many nurseries do not carry herbs, or if they do, they confine their selection to parsley, chives, and rosemary, with perhaps a few annuals in spring. Ask your local nurseryman to start the ones you like. You may have to pay an extra fee, but it's worth it if you have limited facilities and time. Search out local herb lovers for plants as well.

If you can't get plants locally, you may have to order them by mail. It's a bit risky, plants and the postal system being what they are, and fewer nurseries specializing in herbs now seem willing to mail and guarantee plants. See the list of sources in the back of the book for some who will.

If you have an outdoor garden, you can pot up small herbs and young lettuces and greens to bring inside. Do this on a cloudy day, and have clean pots, sterile potting soil, and buckets of mild soapy water and clean water handy. Dig plants carefully and hold the root ball in one hand while you dip the plant foliage in soapy water, then swish it in rinse water. Gently rinse the roots in clean water to remove soil. Replant them in a pot immediately, and water the soil well. Trim any foliage that looks scraggly, so you have a tidy plant that can put forth new growth indoors.

Wherever you get your plants, it's a good idea to quarantine them from other houseplants for a few weeks to be sure they're not harboring insects or diseases.

Many herbs, especially perennials, can be propagated by cuttings, layerings, or root divisions. I've discussed how to do it on pages 7–9 and indicated appropriate plants in Part II. One of these methods can be used to acquire small indoor plants from large outdoor herbs. Don't try to dig up huge plants and jam their extensive root systems into pots.

Seeds may be the only way to get certain herbs and greens, especially annuals. Sowing seeds indoors is easy and inexpensive unless you want to complicate it with fancy apparatus. All you need are the seeds (see source list in back of book for where to get unusual aromatics, herbs, and greens), sterile soil or a soilless potting mixture, water, and light. Check seed catalogs for all the types of pellets, pans, pots, and growing kits available for starting seeds and try what appeals to you, or simply use milk cartons with one side cut out, egg cartons, or old aluminum pans. Fill the container with soil, sow seeds thinly, and cover to the depth recommended on the packet. Water thoroughly, but be careful not to wash out seeds. Label the container, and slip it into a plastic bag. Place it 3 to 5 inches under plant lights or in a sunny window. Remove plastic when seeds germinate. When the seedlings have two sets of leaves, transplant them to pots or thin them. (If you plan to set seedlings outdoors, harden them off to face the changing environment by placing them in a shady area outdoors for several hours a day for a week or in a coldframe for a few days before transplanting.)

Where and in What to Put Your Herbs and Greens

Your home and your budget largely determine the location of your herbs and greens. You're lucky if you have a heated sunporch, and it's wonderful if you can afford an elaborate system of plant lights. In any case, your imagination and ingenuity will make a big difference in the effectiveness of your arrangement of herbs and greens. Where you grow plants depends a great deal on your source of light, but once that is determined consider these ideas for making your indoor garden special:

Many herbs, even if they grow upright outdoors, tend to sprawl indoors, especially if they don't have the benefit of artificial lights. Any plant that starts to trail is adaptable to a hanging basket. Many containers and hangers are available these days. Arrange several in a sunny window and try any of these herbs in them: creeping thymes, rosemary, nasturtiums, mints, marjoram.

Group short, small herbs and greens with taller, bigger ones or with other indoor plants that are showier. Plant small herbs around the base of indoor trees. Blend colors by including purple basil, nasturtiums, and marigolds with grayish or green herbs and lettuces.

Although some herbs are rather insignificant-looking, each is attractive in its own way, especially in the proper setting. Look for containers whose colors complement plant foliage and shape. Hide boring clay or plastic pots by slipping them into cache-pots or straw baskets. Try unusual containers that fit your décor: kettles, buckets, bowls, bottles. My herbs grow fine in cut-off bottles—practically free if you have a bottle-cutting kit. Drainage is important, but a drainage hole is not essential if you put several inches of pebbles in the bottom of the container before you add soil.

An old glass fish tank or bowl or a large jar or bottle can be used to make a terrarium for herbs. Simply set potted plants on pebbles in the tank and cover it with glass, or use your imagination in planting an arrangement in any covered glass container large enough to hold plants. Terrariums do well under plant lights or in a spot that receives reflected light—never direct sunlight.

Arrange potted greens and herbs on a large lazy Susan you can easily rotate so plants don't lean in one direction toward sunlight. You can move the whole arrangement to the table for a centerpiece.

A window box or built-in planter increases your growing area. Make or buy one to fit the space you have in front of a sunny window. With artificial lights, you can put it anywhere in the house. You might use it as a room divider or in the foyer. Be sure it has a waterproof liner if you want to plant directly in it or set pots in it with drainage holes and no saucers. You can place a layer of pebbles or peat moss in the bottom.

Look in crafts and plant shops for all the beautiful and unusual items that are constantly coming on the market with the increasing interest in indoor

plants. But be alert to ways you can enhance your plant display and enjoyment less expensively and by yourself. My husband glued wine bottles together side by side with epoxy to make a sturdy green plant stand. Inexpensive colorful plastic storage cubes can be stacked as high as you like and arranged in various ways to form a planter or a stand. Maybe your child has outgrown his cradle or crib or high chair, but it's a nice piece of furniture and you want to keep it. Use it to hold plants.

Make your indoor garden a reflection of your own good taste by its individuality and your choice of good things that go into it.

Soil

Herbs and greens vary greatly in their soil preferences, and perhaps the only generalization is that all do best in a growing medium that drains well yet holds moisture. While ordinary garden dirt suits many plants outdoors, it is often inferior for potting plants. It tends to pack down and dry out. It inevitably contains disease organisms, insect pests, and weed seeds that will flourish in a warm indoor environment.

 Make your own basic potting-soil mixture of one part sterile potting soil, one part perlite, one part fine peat moss, and one part vermiculite. You needn't be rigid or commercial about all this. Sterilize soil from your garden by adding 1 cup of water to each gallon of soil and baking it in the oven at 180° F. or boiling it for about half an hour. Let it cool and dry out for 24 hours before using. You can use sand from the beach, the brook, or the kids' sandbox instead of perlite. Crumbled leaf mold from the woods or compost heap, sterilized as you do soil, is a good substitute for peat moss. Clean cat litter, which is simply hard-fired clay, is cheaper than vermiculite and serves the same purpose: it helps hold water around plant roots.

To this basic mixture you should add acid or alkaline ingredients according to the individual needs of your plants. Potting soil isn't really as complicated as it's often made out to be. Certain plants require acidity (or sourness) in their growing medium in order to utilize minerals. Others will not thrive unless the soil is alkaline (or sweet). Many plants are indifferent: they grow healthily in almost anything.

I specify in Part II whether a plant is acid-loving, prefers alkaline soil, or is content with neutral soil. The basic mixture I've suggested here for indoor gardening contains peat moss, which tends to acidify, and therefore you should add several tablespoons of some form of lime to each quart of the mixture before potting plants that are not acid-loving. The lime can be limestone chips, powdered lime, or ground eggshells (let the shells dry, then spin them in the blender).

A few plants prefer poor soil and won't respond well to fertilizer of any sort, but many herbs and greens grown indoors under plant lights need extra nutrients because they're working overtime in an artificial environment—more light than they get outdoors, less soil for their roots to feed from, and leaching of minerals when they're watered.

Parsley, lettuces, and mints are among those that like rich soil and produce greener, more nutritious, and healthier growth if they're given supplemental shots of nitrogen, phosphorus, and potassium, abbreviated as NPK (the numbers on the fertilizer container indicate percentages in that order). Fertilizers can be confusing: deciding what to use for which plant, the amount to apply, and the frequency of application could occupy much of one's time. Don't worry about it too much if your plants are healthy, and don't try to lay in a supply of all the different liquid and granular combinations. Whatever fertilizer you use, do check directions carefully, and don't overdo it.

I like fish emulsion. It smells a bit fishy, an attraction to cats and other predators (some creature once dug up all the fish-emulsion-fertilized tomatoes and herbs I planted out in spring), but indoor plants flourish if you use it at about one-tenth the strength recommended on the bottle every time you water. It's liquid, so you don't have to spend time dissolving granules; it's an organic product that won't burn plants the way many chemical fertilizers do if used carelessly; it's high in nitrogen, needed by many greens and herbs; and it contains essential trace elements necessary to good plant growth.

Light

There was a time when herbs and greens needed sunlight to thrive. Today they can flourish in a closet. Artificial lights for plants are a boon for apartment dwellers, but they also have many benefits for those of us who have long gray winters and toddlers with grabby fingers.

Most herbs grow well in a spot where they get full morning or afternoon sun. But let's face it: many herbs grown indoors are not showy plants, and a row of them on the windowsill often simply looks cluttered or uninteresting. I prefer to put larger plants and trees in the window areas and group most of my herbs and greens under plant lights in less conspicuous places.

If you're starting out with growing plants under lights, I strongly suggest that you begin in the bathroom. Bathrooms often have wasted spaces—perhaps under the sink or above the toilet. Bathrooms have the humidity herbs and greens like, and they're handy places to water and mist plants. And, if you arrange your light garden attractively, it can add to your bathroom décor.

A logical place for plant lights is in the kitchen, where herbs will be convenient to pick while you cook, but their great advantage is that you can put them anywhere—on a library shelf, in a cupboard, in a false fireplace opening—from basement to attic.

Plant lights, whether fluorescent or incandescent, are widely available and inexpensive. The profusion of brand names and sizes can make a choice confusing. I suggest starting with a 4-foot fixture with a reflector; it holds two 40-watt fluorescent tubes. Buy the so-called full-spectrum lights, which are most suitable for green plants. But first measure the space you have for plants, then visit a garden center or store that sells lights and look at all the possibilities. A sympathetic salesperson can give many suggestions for what will work best in your space and for your purposes and advise you on installation and decoration. Avoid the expensive piece of "furniture" with shelves and lights built in—unless you really like the way it looks or plan to hide it. I've never seen one of those industrial-looking plant stands that was attractive, and your creativity in designing your own light garden will make it distinctive.

Numerous books are devoted entirely to gardening under lights, and you might want to check some of them for more details, or consult the Indoor Light Gardening Society, which has chapters in major cities.

Once your lights are installed, place your potted herbs and greens under them on a tray with pebbles beneath the plants. For plants that love sun and for seedlings, the leaves can be as close as 3 inches to the light bulbs. Herbs that do well in partial shade outdoors can be placed as much as a foot below the lights or at the ends of the tubes, where the light quality is weaker. This creates a problem if you have plants of varying heights. Boost the ones you want closer to the light by setting them on appropriate-sized objects, such as upside-down flower pots, or trim the tops off herbs that are too tall. Plants get elongated if they are too far from the source of light. Their leaves curl if they're too close.

Leave plant lights on fourteen to sixteen hours a day. You can buy an automatic timer to turn them on and off, but it's an unnecessary expense unless you have to be away frequently. Don't make my mistake of assuming that if lots of light is good, more must be better. I lost a flat of herb seedlings because weeks of constant light caused them to shoot up and bloom long before the foliage developed well. Plants need dark periods to rest too.

And if you don't have sunny windows or plant lights? A few herbs will do fairly well without full sunlight. Try chervil, lemon balm, and mint in a sunless window or an area with reflected sunlight.

You'll get used to the light needs of your indoor plants. Sometimes they just don't seem to thrive in one area of the house. Try moving them to another spot where there is more or less light. And rotate them frequently so they won't get lopsided as they lean toward sunlight.

Water

Most of us associate "watering" with providing moisture to a plant's roots. Especially for the indoor gardener, giving herbs and greens moisture is more complicated than pouring water on the soil around them.

A plant outdoors is usually watered by rain. Think of all the benefits rain provides: a shower on the plant's foliage, a bath for its roots, and humidity in the air around it. Think of how good you feel when you walk in wet grass after a warm spring shower. When a plant is brought indoors, it's no wonder if it feels deprived and fails to flourish as it did outdoors.

Most houses, especially in winter, are filled with hot, dry, stagnant air. Many people overwater or underwater their plants—understandable when one is busy or has many plants of different varieties. And washing plant leaves is time consuming, one of those tasks you can put off until tomorrow.

Humidity is important to herbs and greens. Most of them like it, just as most people feel better when there's enough moisture in the air for them to breathe comfortably. If your house has a humidifier you don't have to worry overmuch about your plants' breathing. If the air is dry, consider growing herbs and greens in your bathroom, laundry room, or kitchen, spots that are relatively humid. Or grow them in a terrarium or under glass or plastic to retain moisture. Create a nearby source of humidity by filling a deep tray with pebbles or sand or bricks, and nearly covering them with water. Place plant pots on top, without letting their bases touch the water. Keep adding water as it evaporates. It's easier, though less effective, to arrange attractive containers, such as vases or bottles, among the plants and keep them filled with water. An old-time method of adding humidity to rooms is to set pots of water on the wood stove or radiators.

A mister is valuable to the herb grower. It's your way of giving plants a rain substitute that cleans their pores of dust, provides water through their leaves, and adds humidity to the air. You can buy fancy expensive misters, including battery-operated ones. Don't bother. The cheap plastic ones work fine, and you can recycle the sort of spray-cleaner bottle that has a nozzle (not the aerosol kind, of course). Use water at room temperature to spray plant foliage about once a week. Protect walls or other surfaces that might be damaged by water: hold newspaper behind or beneath the plant, or carry pots to the bathtub.

Certain herbs, such as sage and rosemary, are shaped so that they can be held on their sides under running water or dipped into a sinkful of water—a more effective cleaning than the mister, since you can wet all sides of the leaves and get at insects the mister misses. I've tried putting plants in the bathtub and turning on the shower, but it's messy—soil splashes out, and the pots get sopping wet. A sink sprayer with a fine mist that wets mostly the foliage is more effective.

Watering plants indoors involves diligence more than expert know-how. Few people need an electronic moisture meter to tell them if plants are too dry or too wet. Use your eyes and fingers. If leaves are drooping and soil is dry to the touch, add water until you think the soil is damp from top to bottom. If water runs through into the saucer at the bottom and stands there for more than an hour, drain it off. When water stands for days on top of the soil, you may have drowned the plant or the roots may have become diseased. It might be too late to rescue it, but try: gently uproot the plant, wash its roots, cut off any that are rotted or diseased, and repot in fresh soil immediately.

Give your plants a daily check, and tend to their individual watering needs. Herbs and greens that do well in moist spots outdoors need more frequent watering than thyme and other herbs that hail from hot, dry climates; herbs with fleshy roots, such as tarragon, rot if overwatered. Plants in small pots dry out more quickly than those in large pots. Humusy soils retain moisture longer than sandy ones. High heat and low humidity cause faster water evaporation. Plastic pots hold moisture longer than clay pots. Consider all these aspects and the specific recommendations on watering discussed under the individual herbs and greens in Part II before you routinely splash vague amounts on everything every few days.

Whenever I get lazy about watering I regret it, and I've been lazy or preoccupied or careless often enough to have to resort to last-ditch efforts for plants that I valued. First, mist or wash the leaves. If the pot has a drainage hole, place the pot in the sink and run lukewarm water almost up to its top. When enough moisture has been drawn up from the bottom so that it appears on the soil surface, remove the pot and put it in a shady spot for a few days. The plant sometimes recuperates, but if it doesn't, it's always a reminder to pay more attention to watering.

One consolation: if an herb dies from lack of water, you can sometimes at least salvage the leaves that have dried on the stalks. I've done this several times with rosemary, an herb especially sensitive to drying out. Before you throw out the dead plant, strip off the leaves and pack them in jars. Now wasn't that obliging of the plant to handle the drying all by itself?

Air

My friend Sally Pellman has repeatedly told me that plants suffer most indoors from lack of fresh air. I'm convinced she's right, since I long to throw open the windows in midwinter when I feel I can breathe no more smoky, stale, dry air. That could be disastrous for the plants, which can't stand extreme temperature changes, and it would be little comfort when the fuel bill came.

Fresh, circulating air is important for plants because it supplies oxygen, necessary for their growth, and it blows away disease organisms that might otherwise land on the plant and germinate. Whenever you can open windows and doors to let outside air in comfortably, do so for your plants' health and yours. Be careful not to blast plants with sudden drafts, however; if it's cold outdoors, you might open a window in a room that has no plants so the fresh air will reach them gradually.

Some kitchens, bathrooms, and laundry rooms have vent fans which at least move the air. If you live in the North, consider growing your herbs and greens in these rooms in winter.

Space your plants so air can circulate around their leaves. They may not get claustrophobia if they're jammed together, but they will suffer from competition for air.

In climates where you can't thoroughly air out the house for months, pay special attention to keeping plant leaves clean and providing as much humidity as possible. This will help compensate for lack of fresh air.

Temperature

Too much is made of "ideal" temperatures for various indoor plants. If you're comfortable in the house, your herbs and greens are likely to be too; if you're feeling a bit chilly, they may be chuckling with pleasure, since most of them don't like hot temperatures year-round. Thus, the energy crisis is beneficial in some ways; and many of us take it into account when we grow herbs and greens indoors.

While plants withstand considerable changes in temperature outdoors, a certain pattern in their growth is affected by temperature. They work at photosynthesis, the production of carbohydrates, in the light and warmth of the sun during the day. In the cooler night temperatures they utilize the carbohydrates for growth. You can save on your fuel bill and create a more natural environment for your plants if you turn the thermostat down when you go to bed.

Herbs and greens will grow quite well in indoor temperatures lower than those of most houses in winter, and so will most people. We live in a drafty old house, and I am sensitive to cold, but the cost of fuel is so horrendous that I've learned to live with keeping the thermostat at 65° or lower and wearing more clothes. Even the tender herbs have not suffered, and lettuces thrive on cooler temperatures.

Some herbs and most greens and lettuces are so happy with cool temperatures that you can grow them in a closed-off unheated room that has plenty of sunlight or plant lights. As long as the temperature doesn't go much below freezing, you can grow such hardy herbs as chives, mints, parsley, winter savory, tarragon, and thyme.

Pests and Diseases

Pests are my greatest frustration in growing herbs and greens indoors. I think I've done everything right—soil, light, water—and suddenly there is an insect invasion.

Sooner or later you are likely to encounter one of the insects or diseases described below, no matter how you obtain plants. Greenhouse plants are notorious sources of pests. Plants you bring in from outdoors often harbor insects. And seeds can carry disease or insect eggs.

Organic gardeners don't use most pesticides, but even people who have no objections to treating plants with poisonous chemicals certainly don't want to put them on herbs and greens they're going to eat. Nobody should ever use systemic pesticides on edible plants. I don't even like to use rotenone and pyrethrum, natural pesticides approved by most organic gardeners, on my indoor plants. So it is important to keep plants healthy and strong against invasion, avoid conditions conducive to infestation, and take immediate measures when pests or diseases appear. Here are some general suggestions and tips, which I've elaborated on in previous sections.

Plants from greenhouses or nurseries should be isolated for a few weeks to be sure they're pest-free and won't contaminate other plants.

Wash plants brought in from outdoors, checking for pests.

Use sterile potting soil and clean pots.

Maintain good humidity in the house.

Don't crowd plants—they need air circulation.

Gently stir soil surface occasionally to aerate it.

If possible, grow plants in different parts of the house, or plant several different ones in one large pot. What attacks one type of plant in one location may spare those elsewhere or different species.

Check plants, especially underleaves, often and quarantine those that are ailing.

Mist or wash plant foliage weekly.

If trouble strikes anyway, here are the most probable causes and some ways to deal with them.

Aphids are usually brought in on plants that have been outdoors (see page 13). Inspect plants, especially new growth, before you bring them

inside. Wash off any aphids with soapy water, then rinse well. Remove any damaged growth. Aphids wash off fairly easily and shouldn't be much of a problem indoors.

Fungus diseases, rot, viruses, and bacterial infections are generally avoidable if you maintain a healthful environment for your herbs and greens. If mildew, mold, rust, black spots, or rot appears, check the preceding discussions on soil, light, water, air, and temperature. You may be overwatering, crowding plants too much, giving them improper soil, or who knows? Plants do get infections that are as difficult to diagnose as a specific virus is in human beings. Don't blame yourself. Isolate the ailing plant to see if it recovers. If it dies, chuck it out along with its soil and try again.

Mites are almost too small to see, but they can do a lot of damage. If plant leaves turn pale yellow or have pale speckled areas, then drop off, suspect mites. Look under the leaves for fine webs, or a sprinkling that looks like paprika. If you find either, act fast, or the plant will soon be covered with webs swarming with minute red, green, or yellowish creatures that look like little crabs if you inspect them under a magnifying glass. Red spider mites destroyed several of my red pepper plants before I learned that mites hate water. Spraying them with a blast of cold water or immersing the plants in water daily for several days takes care of most of them. And remember that mites thrive in dry, stale air; increasing humidity and air circulation reduces mite infestations.

Mealybugs are, I think, the most loathsome of indoor pests and the most difficult to eradicate. As soon as you see cottony-looking specks on a plant's leaves or stems, get it away from other plants right away. The cushiony clusters contain eggs that will turn into grayish oval flat scales about ⅛ inch long. I've never seen a mealybug move, but somehow they travel rapidly from plant to plant—they must hold races after I've gone to bed. They suck plant juices, causing stunted growth, and eventually they kill the plant.

Mealybugs prefer woody-stemmed plants. They're particularly fond of sage and rosemary. When I see them, I'm tempted to just throw the plant out. You can pick them off by hand—fairly effective if you keep at it—but I can't stand to touch them. You can kill them by touching every single mealybug and egg cluster with a cotton-tipped stick dipped in some form of alcohol—vodka, nail-polish remover, perfume—but you probably don't want to eat the residue from some of these substances, and it's hard to get all the insects on a large plant. I wash the entire plant in sudsy water to which I've added a splash of rubbing alcohol and rinse it thoroughly under a strong stream of water, repeating every few days for a few weeks. Even this may not work if the plant is badly infested. Mealybugs are tough. They hang on by a sticky substance, and they must be able to breathe under water. I once submerged a sage plant for hours in sudsy water, and the mealybugs were unfazed. Neither rotenone nor pyrethrum is effective. Malathion is, but never use it on herbs and greens you're going to eat. Discouraging, isn't it? May you be spared these rascals, and if they invade, may any or all of the above procedures be more helpful to you than they are to me. I've tried a lot of things on mealybugs, and the best advice is: catch them early and keep battling.

Scale insects are often mistaken for mealybugs, and they are related. The ones likely to turn up on your herbs are brown, tan, or gray, up to ⅛ inch long, usually hard-shelled, and round or oval. Different species attack leaves, stems, or both. Some lay eggs in white sacs similar to those of mealybugs. Scales aren't likely to be a great problem for the grower of indoor herbs and greens, but if they appear, try the treatments suggested for mealybugs.

Whiteflies are 1/16 inch long with four wings when they are adults.

The young ones are scalelike. They usually arrive on plants from greenhouses or outdoors. They especially like basil, so be alert when you bring in plants or cuttings. You'll recognize whiteflies by the little clouds of specks that flutter out when the plant is disturbed and by a sticky substance on the leaves that often contains growths of sooty mold. Whiteflies suck plant juices, cause leaves to yellow and drop, and are a problem to get rid of: they are as elusive as the snowflakes they resemble. You pick up the plant and the flies scatter. Pop a large bag over the plant, take it outdoors, and remove the bag. If it's warm enough, wash the foliage outside with a strong stream of water from the hose, wetting both sides of the leaves and rubbing them between your fingers. If it's too cold, shake the plant leaves to dislodge remaining insects, then bring the plant inside and wash it thoroughly in soapy water. Rinse well. Repeat every few days for two weeks, meanwhile keeping the infested plant isolated from others.

If you bring in unsterilized soil or unwashed plants from outdoors you are asking for trouble from any of numerous organisms. Some, such as earthworms, are beneficial in the garden, but you don't want them in the house, nor will they be happy in a confined pot. Nematodes, very tiny worms of several kinds, are a nuisance to vegetables and anathema to your indoor plants. They are impossible to eradicate without very poisonous nematocides. When a plant is sickly without apparent cause, look for small nodules on the roots or check the leaves with a strong magnifying glass for wriggling eel-like worms. If either is present, get rid of both plant and soil immediately. Thrips are tiny black insects that look like fine bits of thread. They suck plant juices, leaving papery scars. To get rid of them, wash foliage frequently. Springtails, nearly invisible, scurry on damp soil surfaces and chew tender parts of plants. Let the soil dry out, then water it well with a mixture of 1 tablespoon chlorine bleach to 1 gallon of water. But nematodes, thrips, and springtails are not common, and you should never have to identify or treat them if you're thoughtful about your plants' needs. I've had to deal with some of them only because I started out with little experience and was innocently careless.

All this may sound as though herbs and greens grown indoors have a great many needs and problems. Actually, they have as much will to live as you have. Don't be discouraged by the few that don't make it. Remember, we who grow plants in our homes are not commercial nurserymen or horticulturists. We don't have the benefits of a sophisticated greenhouse or the hours to nurture our plants full time. We're growing herbs and greens for our pleasure. And the first time you make a salad of the plants you've grown yourself you'll realize what a great pleasure it is.

FORAGING FOR WILD GREENS AND HERBS

Searching for wild food is a pleasure. I find it good for the soul merely to walk purposelessly through fields, along streams, and in woods, but when I'm looking for edibles my tramp has the added interest of exploration. Things one ordinarily overlooks—small plants underfoot, berries hanging high overhead, mushrooms pushing through leaf mold—are potentially my dinner.

Identifying wild food is educational. You learn about plant families and relationships. As you observe leaf patterns, note whether a plant is annual or perennial, when it appears in spring and when it tastes best, your knowledge of botany expands and your interest in all plant life—maybe all of nature—increases.

Experimenting with wild food is challenging and full of surprises. As you taste new flavors, your taste buds awaken and become more discriminating. Each new food is unique, to be appreciated for itself, but you start to think in similes and contrasts as you invent your own recipes: these milkweed shoots are a bit like asparagus; this wild sorrel is a good substitute for garden sorrel, but it's more acidic; lamb's-quarters tastes even better than spinach.

Because the flavors of wild plants are new, you don't consider them in clichéd terms of preparation; you taste and combine and revise. You look for recipes in which you can substitute wild greens for cultivated ones. For instance, we found that fresh green noodles made from dandelions tasted better and were greener than those made from spinach.

The joys of discovery, knowledge, and good eating are supplemented by the nutrition and inexpensiveness of wild foods. Many wild greens are extraordinarily high in vitamins and minerals compared to cultivated greens. And wild things are free—if you don't consider time as money. Foraging requires time, but remember you also spend time and money when you go to the grocery store or plant a garden.

Some people worry that they may be accidentally poisoned by wild plants. Mushrooms, of course, should be picked with extreme caution, but you're not likely to be poisoned by wild greens and herbs. Do a little research before you go exploring for your supper. Take Euell Gibbons's pocket-sized *Stalking* books with you if you're unsure about identifying wild things. Toxic substances exist in the house and cultivated gardens as well as in the wild, so familiarize yourself with plants if you have children to care for. Teach them to avoid all wild mushrooms, but let them taste flowers and greens that are safe and good. I learned a great deal from the Poison Control Center after my child ate asparagus berries: immediate advice on the telephone was followed by supplemental information in the mail. Since I now know more about which plants are delicious and which ones fatal, I'm more confident when I'm around exploring children.

Taking a child into fields and woods is wonderful and enlightening. Children pick up sensory data that adults miss, and they are curious about what they see and taste and smell. In the process you have a chance to teach them about the history and geology of your area, about conservation, about nutrition, about the relationships between wild and cultivated plants. I remember so much of what my mother taught me about wildlife when I was a young child that I'm convinced young minds retain what is naturally fascinating to them, especially if an adult's excitement accompanies their discoveries.

In Part II I discuss only the wild herbs and greens that are easily accessible and that I really like. I have had to omit several good things simply because I haven't tried them often or recently enough to give competent advice. For instance, two that I've enjoyed in the past but haven't had access to in years are chickweed and sassafras.

When we were young, my brother and I used to gobble up the chickweed we found around trees at the edge of the woods in Denbigh, Virginia. Since chickweed grows in many varieties around the world, I don't know why it hasn't crept onto our property here in Vermont. It generally spreads over rich soil and has pale-green tiny leaves with a mild, slightly acidic flavor. Add it to salads or steam it if you can find it.

I love sassafras tea, hot or iced, but I'm dependent on my southern relatives for fresh sassafras roots, which I've never found here. Look for shrubby trees with mittenlike leaves. Dig up some roots, break and sniff them, and if you've ever had sassafras tea, you'll know they're the right thing. Gibbons compares their aroma to root beer and gives a full description and recipes in *Stalking the Wild Asparagus*.

There are other wild things that I've omitted because I think they're too much trouble to gather and prepare (such as nettles and burdock) or because I haven't yet developed a taste for them (cattails and jewelweed). Don't let my experience or tastes deter you from trying them. When you first start to learn about something, be it sorrel, snails, sex, or Scotch, your initial reaction may be negative. Subsequent experiences may produce a different reaction or even an addiction.

The wild herbs and greens I've gathered are usually cleaner than those I buy in the store, but be somewhat cautious about picking wild foods along roadsides and in vacant lots where they may have been sprayed with weed-killers or be contaminated with animal or bird feces. In general, rinse wild greens if they appear dusty or have insects on them, and steam them or cook them immediately in the least amount of water possible to preserve their nutrients—or eat them raw, of course. As you experiment, your tastes will tell you how to vary preparation according to the variety and age of the vegetable.

Consider other ways of using wild herbs and greens that you've grown fond of. You can sprout the seeds of dandelion, milkweed, lamb's-quarters, and wild onions as you do bean sprouts, and add them to salads or stir-fried dishes. Most greens freeze well. Many can be dried.

Keep trying things—you may find it so enjoyable that you give up cultivating plants and become a full-time stalker of wild greens and herbs.

PRESERVING HERBS

Your outdoor gardens and your foraging are likely to produce more herbs and greens than you can use fresh daily. Even your indoor plants may bear so bountifully that you can't keep up with them. To ensure a delicious variety of herb flavors year-round without wasting any of your crop, you can preserve the foliage in various ways.

Some basics before you start:

Herb flavors are generally strongest just before the plants flower.

Pick healthy growth and discard damaged leaves.

Gather herbs and greens in the morning—after the dew has dried but before the sun gets hot.

If necessary, wash and dry herbs and greens before preserving them.

Freezing

My favorite way of preserving many herbs and greens is to freeze them with other foods. When winter comes, there in the freezer nestle green beans with summer savory, herby tomato sauce, spinach lasagne, pesto, and other good things already flavored with fresh-tasting herbs.

Unfortunately, summer is so short and demanding that many of us do not have time to make up complicated dishes to freeze. Start simply:

Add a few rosemary sprigs to each corn packet, some chopped dill to the broccoli or peas, marjoram and oregano to squash. Do try to freeze some pesto and end-of-the-herb-garden tomato sauce (see recipes). Then, if you have time, try some of the other recipes throughout the book that I've noted freeze well.

Chives, dill, marjoram, mints, oregano, parsley, and tarragon can be frozen in small packets to use as needed. Place sprigs or chopped leaves in small plastic bags or fold them into squares of plastic wrap. Seal and label them. Add whatever you need, unthawed, to the dish you are cooking. Frozen herbs

become limp when they thaw, so they are not satisfactory in salads, but you can chop them into salad dressings or blend them into mayonnaise.

Herbs and greens can be spun in the blender with water to cover, then frozen in ice-cube trays. Break out cubes, pack them in plastic bags, and label. A mixture of herbs is good done this way—you can pull out as many cubes as you want to add to soup or tomato juice or sauces.

Freeze mint or lemon balm leaves and borage or violet flowers in containers filled with water to make decorative ice cakes for punch bowls or mint tea.

Get a head start on stuffing for the holidays by freezing a seasoning mix when everything is fresh in the garden. Chop onions and celery (or lovage) fine in the combination you like in stuffing. Add herbs to taste: parsley, sage, marjoram, savory, and thyme. Freeze in small containers. Thaw and add to bread crumbs when you're ready to stuff the bird.

For methods of freezing greens and wild vegetables and for recipes, see specific entries in Part II.

Canning

Except for pickles and jellies, I find canning laborious and generally an unsatisfactory way to preserve the flavor of herbs and greens. If you like to can, however, you will find that herbs add interest and flavor to the jars you pack: can beets with rosemary, pears with mint, sauerkraut with dill. Canned tomato sauce with herbs is good, and a combination of vegetables and herbs makes a fine soup base.

Drying

Dried herbs take up little space, they're convenient to have near the kitchen stove, and you may have to make do with them if you don't have a freezer or indoor herb garden. No dried herbs taste quite like fresh ones, but many have a flavor that is just as good in a different way.

The recipes in this book call for fresh herbs. In many of them you can substitute dried herbs, using one-third to one-half the amount specified—use your taste to tell you how much. Dried herbs vary greatly in potency, depending on the herb itself and how long it has been stored.

The problem of storage is intensified when you buy dried herbs. It is almost impossible to determine how long they've been sitting around since they were picked. If you have a choice, frequent stores that seem to have a good turnover in herb sales. Look for dried herbs that *look* fresh, with good color. When in doubt, I don't hesitate to unscrew jars and sniff the aroma. And I complain to the manager when herbs are brown and smell like hay and don't have pull dates.

Do an annual spring cleaning of your herb rack, using the same look-and-sniff method you use in the store. If any herbs smell like hay, that's what they may taste like when added to food. However, hay is not a bad smell, and there may be enough essence left to rescue for certain purposes. Empty all the stale herbs into a saucepan. Cover with water, bring to a boil, steep for a while, and sniff again. If you get a good fragrance, freeze the mixture in ice-cube trays to add to vegetable soup or stews. This may sound like an indiscriminate use of herbs; it needn't be. At least, it probably won't hurt the soup, and it's better than continuing to use a certain number of tablespoons of an herb that's too far gone to do what it's supposed to.

The major purpose in drying herbs is to eliminate the moisture as quickly as possible while retaining the oils that give the leaves color and flavor.

As soon as herbs are dry, strip off the leaves, keeping them as whole as possible. Save dried twigs for use on the charcoal grill or to throw in the fireplace for fragrance. Pack leaves in airtight jars, and store them out of sunlight.

Hanging long-stemmed herbs is the easiest method of drying. Gather a small bouquet, rinse only if leaves are dusty, and tie the ends of the stems together. Hang them upside down in a shady place that has good air circulation. To protect them from sunlight or dust, hang the bundles inside brown paper bags punched with ventilating holes. In one to two weeks, leaves should be dry enough to remove from stalks. If they can be easily crumbled, they're ready to pack in jars.

Screen drying is suitable for small herbs, large single leaves, and seed heads. Use old window screens or stretch cheesecloth over picture frames—anything that allows air to circulate freely. Place a single layer of herbs on the screen (if you place another screen on top, it makes it easy to invert entire layer). Put herbs in a dry, shady place. Turn after a few days so they will dry evenly. They generally dry in about a week.

A clothes dryer is efficient for drying herbs in a hurry, although it is a relatively expensive way to do it (and you shouldn't try to save expense by drying herbs along with clothes, unless you like herb-scented clothes). Because the dryer tosses the herbs and removes moisture from them quickly, they become uniformly dry and retain much of their color. Use leaves only, since stems take longer to dry. Pack clean herbs loosely in clean nylon stockings or large squares of cheesecloth or nylon net bags. Secure tightly so leaves will not fall out. Dry on moderate heat cycle. In my dryer it takes about 2 hours to get most herbs crisply dry. Sage leaves and some mints take longer, and I usually spread them on cheesecloth for a day to dry further. Tarragon and chervil come out of the dryer with fresh flavor and color.

Oven drying also uses fuel, but it works. Place clean leaves in a single layer on trays in a 100° F. oven. Check them frequently, and remove as soon as they are brittle. Freshly picked herbs that don't need washing can be placed in a hotter oven, about 400° F., with the door ajar. They will dry in 5 to 10 minutes, but you must watch them carefully to prevent burning. Herb sprigs placed between paper towels in a microwave oven will dry in 2 to 3 minutes.

Silica gel drying is more amusing as an experiment than practical for drying a large amount of herbs. I tried it just for fun and got lovely green fresh-tasting dried parsley and chervil sprigs. Silica gel, the substance used to preserve color in dried flowers, is available at greenhouses. Follow the directions that come with it, *except:* don't allow edible herbs to touch the silica gel (although it's nontoxic, it's sandy). Put the silica in a cake tin or other sealable container. Place several layers of cheesecloth or a perforated metal rack above the silica, and arrange a layer of clean herb leaves on top. Seal container tightly. Check every day, and remove herbs when brittle. Most will dry in three days. One container of silica gel costs several dollars, and you can't dry many herbs at a time, but it can be used over and over if dried out as directed on the package.

Other Ways to Preserve Herbs

Herb butters are good in any dish that uses herbs and butter—which means they have thousands of possible uses. They make nice gifts packed in crocks or other attractive containers. Herbs that are easily chopped by hand, such as dill and chives, can be creamed into soft butter. It's easier to spin other herb leaves or greens in the blender with melted butter, salted or unsalted, until they are finely chopped. Or use a food processor, and you needn't melt butter. In general, use about ½ cup roughly chopped herbs or greens to ½ cup butter. Add some lemon juice, a few drops of Tabasco, or grated cheese for variations. Most refrigerated herb butters will stay fresh-tasting for up to a month, and they can be frozen. Add herb butters to vegetables, pairing flavors: savory butter with lima beans, tarragon butter with asparagus, sorrel butter with potatoes. Top poached eggs with spinach butter. Brush an herb butter on grilled meat, fish, or hot bread. Melt it into sauces. Cream it into cheeses. You'll find herb butter disappearing so fast that it's a good idea to make up a big batch at a time.

Herb vinegars add subtle flavor to salad dressings and sauces. I like rice-wine vinegar with dill, purple basil, tarragon, chervil, and shallots, to use with delicate lettuces and greens. Cider or red-wine vinegar is fine for robust herbs such as rosemary, sage, and oregano, to use for salads with pungent greens. Garlic is good in any vinegar. Try a variety of vinegars and herbs to make an interesting row on your shelf or to use as gifts. To make flavored vinegar, fill a glass jar with clean herbs. I usually just twist a handful of herbs, stems and all, to release their oils, then drop them into the vinegar. Or I mix the tough leaves and stems left over from making salads or green mayonnaise—basil, parsley, tarragon, chives, or dill. For garlic or shallot vinegar, spin several whole cloves in the blender with each cup of vinegar. Let herb vinegars stand in a warm spot for a few weeks, then strain liquid into clean bottles. Fresh sprigs of herbs can now be added to the bottles to identify the vinegar and make it prettier.

Herb oils are made the same way as vinegars and can be used similarly in salads. Garlic oil is especially good for stir-frying and adding to marinades. Choose oils that complement the herbs—light peanut oil for tarragon, olive oil for garlic and rosemary.

Herb mustards can be as mild or tangy as you like. Try adding *fines herbes* to Dijon mustard, or ground horseradish and chopped sage to lusty German mustards. Pep up bland American mustards by blending them with a handful of mixed herbs. Make your own special mustard blend: stir enough white-wine vinegar into dry mustard to make a paste. Add a little sugar and salt

to taste, then finely chopped herbs, minced garlic or shallots, grated horseradish, or hot peppers. Experiment with combinations until you have the taste you like and one appropriate to the food you're serving the mustard with.

Salt layering works on the principle that salt removes moisture from herb leaves. I dislike the use of so much salt, but it's an effective way to preserve certain herbs whose leaves are very moist or oily. If you want to try it, pour a thin layer of kosher salt in a jar, add a layer of clean dry leaves, then another layer of salt, and continue alternating layers to fill jar. Press down firmly, cover, and store in a dark place. Wash leaves when you remove them to use, or take their saltiness into account when you season dishes. See Basil, Part II, for a method of salt and cheese layering.

Herb salts, homemade, are slightly to be preferred to commercial ones. I don't like either, but you might. Crush very dry minced herb leaves with an equal amount of salt in a mortar, or whirl them together in the blender. Spread mixture on cookie sheets, and dry for an hour in a 200° oven.

Herb cheeses flavored with your own fresh herbs are distinctly better than any you can buy. They're really special if you make your own cheese (see recipe). Add finely chopped herbs to cream cheese, Boursault, cottage cheese, or cheese spreads. Let herb cheeses stand at least several hours to develop their flavor.

Herb jellies and syrups are made for gifts at our house, since we rarely eat sweet things. See the recipe for mint and crab-apple jelly and the suggestions there, as well as the entry on violets in Part II. You can enhance many ordinary jellies, jams, and syrups by using herb infusions as part of the liquid called for in recipes. Lemon balm is good with apple jelly, sage with cider jelly, mints with wine jelly.

Herb liqueurs, cordials, and wines can be made from scratch, but it's a bit complicated. I suggest you steep herb leaves in your favorite spirits for a few days, then strain the liquid. Repeat the process if you want a stronger herb flavor, and add sugar or honey if you like. Check books on winemaking for how to do it the hard way.

USING FRESH MIXED HERBS

Many foods are best prepared simply, with just one herb to accent their flavor. Although I believe in using herbs generously, one can be so profligate in mixing flavors that the ingredients cancel one another out. With care, however, a mixture of several herbs and greens can be a delight of balances. Get to know flavors by using herbs singly at first; when you're familiar with their characteristics you can experiment with blending several.

In Part II, I give recipes using specific herbs and greens; following are some ideas for using mixtures in which no particular herb is predominant or for which you can interchange various herbs and greens.

Herbs can be loosely characterized as fine or robust, and this should be taken into account when you cook and mix them. In general, robust herbs—

sage, sorrel, savory, marjoram, oregano—go well with hearty foods. They retain their flavor even if cooked a long time. Fine herbs—basil, chervil, tarragon, dill—are more delicate in flavor and often should be added to dishes just before serving. There are exceptions, of course, and no flat rules. Your taste and growing herb-consciousness will tell you how to vary and combine.

You don't need fancy kitchen equipment, but a few items are useful if you use lots of fresh herbs and greens and aromatics. A blender saves a great deal of hand chopping and mincing, and it purées soups and beverages in a hurry. I often call for its use in recipes in this book. A food mill can also come in handy; you can vary the texture of chopped herbs and greens by changing blades, and any residue is milled out. A food processor is perfect for chopping and blending herbs and greens. A mortar and pestle are useful for grinding dried herbs, but you can also rub them to crush them in your palm.

Although I've tried to give all details possible to aid you in growing and using the specific herbs and greens in Part II, I'm assuming a certain amount of knowledge on your part as a cook. This is not a basic cookbook. Herb lovers tend to be cookbook lovers, and I assume you know or can look up how to make clarified butter and certain basic sauces and pastries. So make mayonnaise your own way and add chopped herbs; blend herbs with your favorite vinaigrette; add herbs to your brown sauce or bread recipe. Take the ideas here and make them your own.

The recipes in this book are not complicated. Summer is a busy time in the country, and summer is when our herbs and greens are most prolific. Most of these recipes were tested, retested, and simplified between guests and gardening. They call for fresh herbs and greens and the finest other ingredients available to complement their flavors.

Herb Vinaigrette

I make herb vinaigrette in the blender by combining a handful of herbs with 1 part vinegar or lemon juice to 3 parts oil. Depending on the greens to be dressed, I go on to add garlic or shallots or nasturtium "capers" to the sauce.

Vinaigrette is the basic dressing for mixed green salads, and I discuss it under Lettuces in Part II. As you become familiar with various herbs, greens, lettuces, and aromatics, you will increasingly enjoy pairing them in different combinations. Here is the essential recipe for enough vinaigrette to dress a large green salad for four to six people. Use vinegar in salads that contain greens with a strong flavor—watercress, sorrel, dandelions—and add a bit of mustard or Tabasco if you like. For delicate lettuces, I prefer lemon juice and such gentle herbs as basil and tarragon. MAKES 1 GENEROUS CUP

¼ cup vinegar or lemon juice
¾ cup oil

½ cup roughly chopped herbs
Salt and pepper

Combine vinegar or lemon juice, oil, and herbs in blender, and blend at high speed until mixture is smooth. Or chop herbs fine, beat them into vinegar or lemon juice, and gradually beat oil in with a fork. Season to taste.

depending on the herb potency

Green Herb Dip

Herbed dips and spreads are easy to whip up, and the possible combinations are endless. Depending on the potency of the herbs and aromatics you use, you can add some milk product (cream cheese, cottage cheese, yogurt, heavy cream, butter, grated hard cheese, crumbled soft cheese) to this basic recipe. Experiment to make the consistency and flavor you like for dipping fresh vegetables and chips or for spreading on bread. MAKES ABOUT 4 CUPS

1½ cups chopped mixed herbs and
greens (such as spinach, lamb's-
quarters, nasturtium leaves,
dandelion leaves, parsley, chives,
dill, watercress, horseradish)

4 shallot cloves
1 cup mayonnaise
1 cup sour cream
¼ cup lemon juice

Place all ingredients in blender container in the order listed. Blend, pushing mixture down around the sides if necessary, until herbs and greens are finely chopped. (Or you can finely chop herbs, greens, and shallots by hand, or put them in a food processor, then add to remaining ingredients.) Chill for several hours for flavors to blend.

Violets and nasturtiums

I think Mama missed her sisters. she had to stand by herself till she almost couldn't be with them late of the HAD missed BEING part of their every day for too long, maybe that's one that's one part. without them

A Bowl of Herbs with Mezze

Rarely are herbs served all by themselves, and few people taste their diverse fresh flavors unaccompanied by sauce or broth.

Claudia Roden suggests serving a bowl of fresh herbs along with mezze, Middle Eastern appetizers. I'd often arranged herb bouquets, but until I read her *Book of Middle Eastern Food*, I'd never thought of urging guests to have an herb tasting, just as one would have a cheese or wine tasting.

Mrs. Roden offers an array of ideas for mezze, ranging from simple fresh vegetables to stuffed pastries. For the bowl of herbs, she suggests starting with parsley, mint, chives, cress, dill, coriander, tarragon, and scallions. Add any other herbs and greens and lettuces you like. Include purple basil, violets, and nasturtiums for color variation. Think of combinations you like in food: sage sprigs with Cheddar cheese, dill with cold shrimp and sliced cucumbers, basil with cherry tomatoes, parsley with almost anything, and make arrangements in separate bowls if you like.

Wash sprigs, shake them dry, and arrange them attractively with their stems in a bowl of crushed ice. Provide knives so guests can chop herbs over their buffet dishes, or suggest that they nibble them along with appetizers.

Green Mayonnaise and a Bonus

The way I usually make green mayonnaise is quicker than the usual method of chopping herbs fine by hand, and it has an extra dividend: an emerald liquid that you can drink straight for its vitamins, add to soup, or use to cook vegetables.

Gather enough herbs and greens to about half fill your blender container: lots of parsley, some dill, chervil, basil, summer savory, thyme, watercress, dandelion greens—whatever you like in whatever combination. You might use fennel and parsley for mayonnaise to serve with cold fish; lamb's-quarters to go with hard-boiled eggs; nasturtiums, purslane, and horseradish to make a spread for cold cuts; and dill for poached salmon, of course.

Discard any tough stems, chop greens roughly, and place in blender container. Add garlic, onion, or shallots according to your taste. Barely cover herbs and greens with water, and blend until they are finely chopped. Drain through a fine sieve, reserving green liquid. Press with a spoon until most of the moisture and foam are gone, then place herbs in a bowl and add mayonnaise until you have the greenness and consistency you like. Chill for at least an hour for flavors to blend.

Add the reserved herb liquid to tomato juice for a healthful beverage. Add it to soup for flavor, and freeze it if you like. I often use it as a cooking liquid for new potatoes, small whole green beans, and little leeks and carrots. Arrange them on a tray, chill, then serve with a bowl of green mayonnaise.

I get satisfaction out of recycling things. Here is a special variation on this mayonnaise method that is practical and delicious: boil chicken breasts, then use the cooled cooking liquid to blend tarragon, chervil, and parsley. Strain the herbs to add to mayonnaise and use the herb liquid to boil asparagus. Bone the chicken, arrange it on a tray with the asparagus, chill, and serve with the green mayonnaise.

Quick Homemade Green Mayonnaise

As in the preceding recipe, you can use any combination of herbs and greens that you like. This blender mayonnaise is a creamy, smooth, pale-green sauce, unlike the texture of the other green mayonnaise. You can give it green flecks by chopping some chives into it when it's finished. Vary by adding anchovy paste, chopped hard-boiled eggs, or minced green peppers. Thin with more vinegar and oil for a good salad dressing. MAKES ABOUT 1½ CUPS

½ cup roughly chopped herbs
   and/or greens
 1 clove garlic, chopped
½ teaspoon dry mustard
½ teaspoon sugar

1 large egg
1 tablespoon lemon juice
1 cup olive oil
2 teaspoons vinegar
Salt

Pat herbs and/or greens dry if necessary, and put them in blender container. Add garlic, mustard, sugar, egg, and lemon juice. Blend at high speed for about 10 seconds. Reduce to lowest speed, and slowly pour in half the oil. Stop blender, add vinegar, and blend again at high speed as you slowly pour in remaining oil. The mayonnaise will quickly thicken. Add salt to taste, but not too much, since the flavors in the mayonnaise will become stronger after it has chilled for a while.

Herbed Stuffed Hard-Boiled Eggs

So-called deviled eggs can be much more interesting and flavorful than the often bland mixture of egg yolks mashed with mayonnaise and specked with paprika. Herbs add variations of flavor to the yolks and colorful garnish to sprinkle on top. Here are some suggestions on ways to make stuffed eggs the feature of your buffet or cocktail hors d'oeuvres.

Basil. Mash yolks of hard-boiled eggs with finely chopped basil, minced scallions, and mayonnaise. Mix in a little finely chopped ripe tomato, season, and fill hard-boiled egg-white halves. Top with a small tomato wedge. If you want to sprinkle basil on top, serve immediately, before it discolors.

Chervil. Chop cooked shrimp fine, mash with egg yolks, and mix in chopped chervil, a little dried mustard, mayonnaise, and seasoning. Decorate stuffed eggs with shrimps halved lengthwise and a sprinkle of chopped chervil.

Chives. Simply add thinly chopped chives and a dash of Tabasco to mashed yolks and mayonnaise. Or make a variation of eggs à la russe: combine chives, chopped green olives, chili sauce, Tabasco, and mayonnaise with mashed yolks. Decorate with sliced olives and chopped chives.

Cress. Wild cress, curly cress, and watercress add piquancy to eggs. Chop greens fine, and mix them with mashed yolks, soft cream cheese, and mashed smoked salmon, sardines, or capers.

Dill. Chopped dill, perhaps with a bit of grated horseradish, is a delicious flavoring for egg yolks mashed with mayonnaise. Try adding some crumbled Roquefort cheese, or mix in finely chopped pimiento.

. . . And that gets us, skipping across borage, celery, and coriander, all the way up to *D* in the alphabet. You take it from there, and enjoy inventing. Pair robust herbs and garlic with crumbled strong cheeses, and mix them into yolks with a binder of soft butter or mayonnaise.

Use delicate herbs and cream, soft cream cheese, or mayonnaise blended into yolks. Add asparagus or artichoke hearts squeezed according to the Julia Child Grande Cuisine Towel Method: purée cooked vegetables in food mill, place purée in a soft towel, gather up, and squeeze as you would a jelly bag to extract all liquid possible. Scrape purée off towel and add to egg-yolk mixture.

Stuffed eggs are often oversalted. Herbs may provide most of the seasoning needed, but if you think the stuffing needs an extra jolt, add a little cayenne pepper, Tabasco, garlic juice, dried mustard, horseradish, or puréed sorrel.

For extravagant stuffed eggs, mix good pâté de foie gras or caviar with mashed yolks and bind with soft butter, adding mixed minced herbs to taste.

Arrange a variety of stuffed-egg combinations on a bed of greens or lettuce for a party. The eggs, decorated with chopped herbs that suggest their flavoring, are attractive in themselves, but you can surround them with olives, cheese, cherry tomatoes, and other colorful finger foods.

Homemade Herb-Garlic Cheese

Velvety rich, this simple homemade cheese resembles Boursin *ail et fines herbes* but is better because its garlic and herbs are sprightly fresh. For mild flavor, use parsley, tarragon, chervil, and/or chives and only a few cloves of garlic. A more assertive cheese might combine sage, thyme, and rosemary and up to 6 cloves of garlic. MAKES 2 CUPS

3 cups heavy cream	2 tablespoons finely chopped herbs
2 tablespoons buttermilk	(see above)
2 to 6 cloves garlic	Salt and white pepper

Heat cream slowly to lukewarm (80° to 100° F.). Stir in buttermilk. Peel and halve garlic cloves, tie them in cheesecloth, and add to liquid. Let stand at room temperature until the texture resembles curdy yogurt. This may take up to 48 hours; coagulation occurs faster in hot temperatures.

Remove garlic bag, squeezing it to release all liquid possible. Line a colander with a piece of cloth—old sheet, soft towel, or several layers of cheese-cloth—large enough to tie up the curds. Pour curds into cloth, tie up tightly, and drain in colander over sink for about 1 hour, squeezing occasionally to release all liquid possible. Place in refrigerator over a large bowl, cover, and chill for about 12 hours.

Remove curds from bag, stir in herbs, and season to taste. Divide curds into three smaller bags, tying them up as you did the larger bag. Return to colander, place over bowl, cover tightly with plastic wrap, and drain in refrigerator for 12 hours or until cheese is firm. Unwrap and eat immediately, or store refrigerated, wrapped in plastic, up to a week.

Wayne's High-Protein Herb Bread

Most cookbooks tell you that only a small portion of soy flour—one-seventh to one-fifth of the total amount of flour—will work when making bread, because soy flour supposedly lacks adequate gluten. This recipe uses half soy flour, half whole-wheat flour, and a whole pound of cottage cheese. The resulting two loaves of bread may be a bit heavy, but the recipe works and tastes good. It is moist and flavorful with all its fresh herbs.

Just for this recipe, the protein content of ingredients is listed, since it is so significant. Each loaf contains more than 150 grams of protein, nearly three times the amount the human body is considered to need daily and four times the amount in most loaves of el cheapo soft white grocery-store bread.

Add any combination of herbs you like to this dough. We just go out to the garden and gather a mixed handful. The bread is hearty enough to stand up to such robust herbs as sage, thyme, and oregano. MAKES TWO 2-POUND LOAVES

	PROTEIN (GRAMS)
1 pound whole-curd cottage cheese	56.0
¼ cup honey	negligible
¼ cup butter	.3
3 packages active dry yeast	8.0
3 cups soy flour	155.0
3 cups whole-wheat flour	60.0
2 level tablespoons soy protein powder	28.0
1 cup finely chopped herbs	variable
	307.3

Blend cottage cheese in the blender with ⅔ cup water until smooth. Mix with honey and butter in a saucepan. Heat to a boil, remove, and let cool to lukewarm—100° to 105° F. (Bringing the mixture to a boil will cause the cottage cheese and water to separate and look curdled—don't worry; it doesn't affect the final product.)

Dissolve the yeast in ¼ cup lukewarm water (100° to 105° F.). Caution: if the liquid temperatures are much above 110° F. the yeast will not work.

Thoroughly mix together the flours (don't bother to sift them; you'll only have to add more flour later if you do) and soy powder. Add the herbs and mix well. Add lukewarm liquid mixture to dry ingredients. Stir with a wooden spoon until the spoon won't work any more, then empty bowl onto a floured surface and knead firmly until all the ingredients are thoroughly mixed and the dough is smooth—5 to 10 minutes.

Place dough in a greased bowl and cover. Put it in a warm spot to rise until double in bulk.

Punch dough down, turn out on a floured surface, and knead lightly. Shape into loaves, place in greased loaf pans (about 9 by 5 inches), and let rise 1 hour or until pans are full. Preheat oven to 400° F. When dough has risen, place loaves in oven. After 15 minutes, reduce oven temperature to 350° F. Continue baking about 30 to 40 minutes longer or until the loaves sound slightly hollow when tapped with a knuckle. Let cool about 10 minutes, then remove from pans. Eat warm for best flavor. This bread is good toasted, and it freezes well.

Bread with an Herb Spiral

Cutting into these loaves is a pleasure for the eyes and the nose: the green spiral is beautiful, and the smell of the fresh herbs makes your mouth water. We do many variations on this recipe, using strong herbs such as sage, oregano, garlic, and crushed hot red peppers with crumbled cooked sausage in the filling; milder herbs (chervil, parsley, scallions) with grated cheese; simply lots of dill; or a combination of all the herbs and greens that flourish in the garden at the moment. These loaves freeze well. MAKES 2 LOAVES

1 cup milk	*4 cups finely chopped herbs*
2 tablespoons butter	*4 cloves shallots, minced*
2 tablespoons sugar	*2 tablespoons butter*
1 teaspoon salt	*2 eggs*
2 packages active dry yeast	*Salt and pepper*
About 7 cups flour	*Cayenne pepper (optional)*

Scald milk, and stir in butter, sugar, and salt. Cool to lukewarm (105° to 110° F.). Add yeast to 1 cup lukewarm water, and stir to dissolve. Stir into milk mixture. Gradually stir in flour, mixing with a wooden spoon and adding flour until dough is stiff enough to leave the sides of the bowl.

Turn out onto a floured surface and knead about 10 minutes. Place dough in an oiled bowl, and turn to cover all surfaces with oil. Cover and let rise in a warm place until doubled in bulk, about 45 minutes. Punch dough down, and let it rest 10 minutes.

Cook herbs and shallots in butter just until they wilt. Let cool at least 5 minutes. Beat eggs lightly, reserve 2 tablespoons, and combine the rest with herbs and shallots. Season to taste.

Divide dough in half, and roll each half into a rectangle about 9 inches wide and ¼ inch thick. Brush dough tops with reserved egg. Spread herb filling smoothly over tops, leaving an inch uncovered all around the edges. Roll up tightly lengthwise, and seal edges by pinching them with your fingers. Place loaves, seam sides down, in greased 9-by-5-by-3-inch bread pans. Brush tops with oil, cover, and let rise about 1 hour. Bake in preheated 400° oven for about 1 hour, until loaves are brown and sound hollow when tapped.

Although slices of this bread will hold together better when it's cooled, spiral herb bread tastes best falling-apart hot from the oven.

Corn

Herb Frittata *lima beaned*

Morning, noon, or night, a frittata is good hot, cold, or at room temperature. A frittata is not quite omelet, not quite quiche, but it combines qualities of both in simple form. We usually make it with fresh vegetables, although it is an excellent way to use up leftovers, be they bits of overripe cheese, dabs of vegetables, or scraps of meat.

This recipe is extremely flexible regarding herbs and everything else except the eggs and butter—and even those depend on the appetite of your guests. Make frittata a few times, and you'll never run out of ideas for quick and nutritious meals.

If you like, omit meat from the recipe and serve the frittata with crisp bacon, ham, or chicken. Use herbs and greens that go well with the vegetables and meat and cheese you choose: tarragon with seafood, asparagus, and Gräddost is one of our favorites. SERVES 4

6 tablespoons butter
1 onion or 4 shallot cloves, finely chopped
1 cup cooked vegetables (corn, limas, fava beans, squash, spinach, lamb's-quarters, asparagus, leeks, and/or violet leaves)

½ cup chopped cooked meat (ham, chicken, sausage, or shrimp)
½ cup finely chopped herbs
8 eggs
Salt and pepper
1 cup grated cheese

Melt the butter in a 9-inch ovenproof skillet. Sauté onion or shallots until limp. Stir in vegetables and meat, and heat until they are warm. Add herbs. Beat eggs, adding salt and pepper to taste as you would for scrambled eggs. Stir eggs into skillet mixture. Cover and cook over low heat until eggs are solid around the edges, about 10 minutes. Sprinkle cheese over top. Place skillet under broiler, and cook until eggs are firm throughout (test with a fork in the middle if you're unsure) and top of frittata is lightly browned.

Green Herb Rice

Make it in a ring, use it for stuffing fowl, tomatoes, or peppers, or simply pile it in a dish to serve with meat. Use herbs that go with whatever you're serving, and add marigold petals for color, grated horseradish for piquancy. The addition of cooked vegetables, meat, or cheese can make this a whole meal. SERVES 4

1 onion, chopped
4 tablespoons butter
2 cups long-grain rice
½ cup roughly chopped herbs and
  greens (such as chervil, parsley,
  Swiss chard, savory, spinach,
  lamb's-quarters, kale, dill)

4 cups chicken or vegetable broth
Salt and pepper

Sauté onion in butter for 5 minutes, add rice, and cook, stirring, until rice is slightly golden. Place herbs or greens in blender container, add broth, and blend until herbs are finely chopped. Pour over rice mixture, bring to a boil, cover tightly, turn down heat, and cook until rice is fluffy and moisture has evaporated—up to 30 minutes, depending on rice and moisture in herbs. Add seasoning to taste, toss rice, cover, and let sit 5 minutes before serving.

Herb Marinades for Grilled Foods

We cook on the outdoor charcoal grill as frequently as possible in summer, and herbs are essential in the marinade or basting sauces for grilled foods. While a few foods, such as a perfect steak, need no seasoning, most grilled foods benefit from oil and herbs as they cook. The oil keeps them from drying out over the high heat, and the herbs provide flavors quite different from those that herbs add to dishes cooked in the oven or on the stove. Herbs on the grill can be as aromatic as well-roasted coffee beans.

I usually make marinades in the blender, using about 6 parts oil or butter to 1 part lemon juice or vinegar, and blending with herbs and garlic until they are finely chopped. Then I add other ingredients, depending on the food to be grilled. If possible, food should be marinated at least several hours in the mixture before grilling. Drain it before cooking and use the marinade for basting the food as it grills.

The suggested grilling times for the following foods are very approximate. The heat of your coals and the distance of the food from the heat make a big difference. But outside eating is casual: if something isn't quite cooked, nobody minds if you put it back to get done. Your guests are enjoying the fragrance of the outdoors and the grilling food so much that they relax to savor it, especially if they have a big platter of fresh vegetables to munch while waiting.

Here are some of the combinations we like. Maybe they'll give you ideas for your own:

CORN ON THE COB. Blend butter, lemon juice, and dill, coriander leaves, parsley, or basil. Gently pull back corn husks, remove silks, and brush herb mixture across kernels. Fold husks back, and grill, turning frequently, until husks are browned and grains look opaque. Test for doneness by biting into an ear. For moister corn, soak unhusked ears in water for 15 minutes, grill, and brush herb mixture on cooked, husked corn just before eating.

SQUASH. Blend oregano, marjoram, sweet green peppers, onion, and/or savory with oil and lemon juice. Cut squash (zucchini, yellow squash, young Hubbards, or patty pans) into 1-inch slices, sprinkle with salt, and drain for 15 minutes. Marinate in herb mixture, drain, and place on grill. Cook for about 10 minutes, brushing with marinade and turning to brown both sides. Or place squash with marinade in a baking pan, cover with foil, sprinkle with grated cheese, and cook just until tender, perhaps 20 minutes.

POTATOES. Chop dill and add it to soft butter. Or blend a mixture of herbs with melted butter. Add a bit of Tabasco or horseradish if you like. Scrub potatoes and cut off any spots, but leave them as unpeeled as possible. Slice about ½ inch thick, and parboil for 10 minutes. Drain, and toss gently with herb butter. Grill, turning and basting with any leftover butter, until potatoes are well browned and can be easily pierced with a fork. For small new potatoes, parboil, skewer, baste, and grill until tender.

MUSHROOMS. Almost every herb, green, and aromatic complements mushrooms, and you can use lemon juice or vinegar, olive oil or butter, in their marinade. It's your chance to create a mushroom masterpiece. If you have huge mushrooms, try marinating them in a mixture of oil, a little vinegar, and chopped sorrel, garlic, and thyme or oregano. Grill them about 15 minutes, turning frequently. Button mushrooms should be parboiled or sautéed for 5 minutes, skewered, brushed with a gentle herb butter—say, melted butter blended with shallots and tarragon—and grilled just until tender.

ONIONS. You can grill separated quarters of large onions or whole peeled tiny onions. Parboil about 5 minutes, and let cool. Combine oil or butter with marjoram, marigold leaves, thyme, or fennel leaves. Add a dash of cognac if you like. Skewer onions, and grill, turning and basting, for about 10 minutes.

SEAFOOD. Delicate seafoods that can be cooked on the grill—sole fillets, bay scallops, shrimp—should be marinated in a gentle mixture of oil, lemon juice, and herbs such as basil, parsley, tarragon, and chervil. Seafoods with stronger flavor and oilier texture can be seasoned with oil, lemon or lime juice, garlic, sage, thyme, or fennel and a dash of soy sauce. Marinate seafood in the herb mixture for a few hours, drain, and baste during grilling.

CHICKEN. We cook chicken on the outdoor grill so often and use such different marinades that it is hard to generalize about what's best. Chicken parts vary in tenderness and flavor, and your appetites and what's available in the herb garden vary as well. For chicken breasts, try a marinade of oil or butter, lemon juice, and tarragon, parsley, and shallots. For chickens grilled whole on the spit, halved, or separated into serving pieces, use a heavier marinade if you like: add tomato sauce, sugar, thyme, oregano, marjoram, garlic, and perhaps a dash of soy sauce to your basic marinade of oil and lemon juice. Skin chicken if you wish, cover it with marinade, and let sit for up to 12 hours. Prick with a fork every few hours to let marinade penetrate. Grill, turning and basting frequently, until chicken is brown and very tender.

LAMB. I generally use cubed lamb and skewer it for shish kebabs along with vegetables. Marinate the lamb for 24 hours in a blended mixture of oil, lemon juice, garlic, parsley, mint, perhaps coriander leaves and oregano. Sometimes I add yogurt. Lamb chunks should be loosely skewered, cooked over white-hot coals, and turned until all sides are brown.

BEEF. The cut and tenderness determine the marinade and length of cooking time. If you have a somewhat tough cut, marinate it for a day in oil, red wine, garlic, pepper, and robust herbs such as rosemary, thyme, and sage. Grill meat, basting with marinade, until cooked to doneness you like. Baste hamburgers with melted butter or oil, a dash of Tabasco, and rosemary or thyme.

PORK. A roast grilled on the spit is best. Marinate it at least 12 hours in oil, a dash of vinegar, and lots of chopped sage. Add garlic to marinade or make slits in the meat and insert garlic slivers. Baste with marinade as roast cooks.

End-of-the-Herb-Garden Tomato Sauce

When the frost is beginning to lower, it's that time at the end of summer that is known as the tomato-sauce hour. I fill my big pot with all the Italian plum tomatoes it will hold, pile herbs on top, and let it simmer into a very herby sauce to freeze for winter dishes, especially pasta. Herbs to include if you have them: oregano, marjoram, savory, thyme, sage, parsley, and chives. Add even more than I've suggested; then, if you like, thin down the heavy herb flavor with plain tomato sauce before you use it. MAKES ABOUT 2 QUARTS

10 pounds very ripe tomatoes
1 pound Bermuda onions, scallions,
*   Egyptian onion tops, or wild*
*   onions*
½ pound sweet green or red
*   peppers*
2 cups roughly chopped celery
*   with leaves*
About 1 quart mixed herb sprigs or
*   leaves (see above)*

¼ cup vinegar
½ cup sugar
Salt and pepper

Quarter tomatoes and put them in a large nonaluminum pot. Roughly chop onions and peppers and add to pot. Add 2 cups water, place celery and herbs on top, cover, and simmer for about 3 hours, stirring occasionally. Put vegetables through food mill, using medium blade. Return purée to heat, add vinegar and sugar, and simmer, uncovered, for 1 hour. Stir frequently with a wooden spoon. The sauce should become fairly thick. Reduce it further if you want a thicker sauce. Season to taste.

PART II

ASPARAGUS

Asparagus officinalis
 *perennial*

An odd first entry for this section on herbs and greens and aromatics? Perhaps, but asparagus is green and herbaceous, and I simply must include the most lovely vegetable in the world.

When I was a child in Virginia, we ate only wild asparagus. (It's the same species as the cultivated, but the wild stalks are generally thinner.) In early spring we would start peering along the fencerows for the slender verdant spears. Rarely did we find enough to serve all by itself; our little fistfuls were chopped up and cooked with potatoes in a cream sauce.

Then the city folk discovered the treasure in our special fencerows: they would jump out of cars and snatch asparagus shamelessly. It didn't matter much by then—we were about to move to the city ourselves, and our Denbigh fencerows would soon turn into lawns. Sometimes I think no asparagus tastes as good as it did back then; but when I pick the first asparagus shoots from my cultivated beds I feel the same thrill.

Asparagus is the best garden investment you can make. After some initial labor, you can practically sit back and watch the returns pile up. An asparagus bed, given even minimal care, should reward you for a lifetime.

The ideal method for preparing an asparagus bed involves some planning. Start in the fall. For fifty asparagus plants (considered by most as adequate for a family of four but barely sufficient for two real asparagus lovers), mark off a sunny, well-drained area about 20 by 10 feet. Remove the sod if necessary. Till the plot thoroughly, working in lime, manure, compost, bonemeal, and whatever other organic matter you have handy—asparagus can't get too much fertilizer.

It's a good idea to sink or lay a barrier around the bed; use metal lawn edging, old boards, or anything else that will keep weeds from creeping into the rich soil. Cover the bed with a mulch, such as spoiled hay.

Order one-year-old asparagus plants from your local nursery if possible, since a greenhouse can store them properly until just the right time to set them out. Many mail-order companies will also send roots at the proper planting time for your area. In spring, as soon as you can work the ground, mark off rows at least 3 feet apart in the asparagus bed. Pull the mulch back from the rows and dig trenches 1 foot deep and 1 foot wide, banking the soil along the edges. Spread composted manure or other fertilizer along the trench bottom, and work it into the soil.

As soon as you get your asparagus roots, cover them with damp papers or cloth, hurry to the asparagus bed, and set the plants, crown up, about 2 feet apart in the trenches. Spread the roots out in all directions, and immediately cover them with 2 inches of soil. It's important that the roots not dry out. Water the trenches well.

The fun, but frustrating, part soon begins. When small asparagus spears shoot up from the root crowns, it's tempting to pick a few, just for a foretaste. Resist for the good of the plants—they must develop into foliage if they are to produce strong roots. Start filling in soil around the growing plants until the trench is level, then mulch the bed heavily. Toward the end of summer apply more fertilizer and mulch. Cut off foliage when it turns brown, and cover the entire bed with a winter mulch. In spring pull back mulch from the rows to warm the ground. Work fertilizer into the topsoil along the rows.

Now you get your first treat. You can harvest the largest asparagus spears for about a month, but use restraint: the plants are still immature, so leave plenty to turn into foliage. Fertilize and mulch again in fall, and in spring follow the procedure you did the previous spring. This year you can begin harvesting all the asparagus you want. Your effort and patience are amply rewarded when almost daily you return from the garden with enough asparagus for a meal.

Every year we eagerly buy the first asparagus that appears in the grocery store. It tastes wonderful, we eat a lot, and we should be tired of asparagus by the time ours is ready to pick, but every year we marvel that ours is so much better, almost another vegetable. We snap it off as far down as it's tender, so there's no waste (commercial asparagus is apparently cut for weight—it's often mostly woody stems). And garden-fresh asparagus probably tastes so much better because it hasn't lost nutrients and moisture from storage.

For best growth, continue fertilizing asparagus every spring and fall, and keep piling on mulch to discourage weeds. Some people take shortcuts in growing asparagus, reasoning that because it goes wild it's so hardy that it needs little care. I must admit that I am surprised every spring at the healthy asparagus shoots I find in neglected areas of our property. You can, if you like, simply plunk the roots on the ground, mound soil over them, and let them fend for themselves. But having made three asparagus beds now, I urge you to do it right the first time. I put my first asparagus roots in a spot where floods wash off the topsoil every spring, and I failed to mulch it, so weeds soon took over. I put the next bed too close to the woods, where the asparagus roots must compete in partial shade with tree roots. The yield from our last asparagus bed is twice as good because we planned it properly and determined to give it the best care.

Growing your own asparagus from seeds takes even more patience. It's a cheap way to get a lot of plants, and I'm glad I started seeds as well as ordering roots when I began growing asparagus. The seeds that I sprouted in pots indoors, set out in the garden for the summer, then transplanted carefully to the permanent bed the following spring were ready to start harvesting two years later.

Female asparagus plants bear green berries that turn red toward fall. Cut them off when they appear. They weaken the plant, they may self-seed and crowd your asparagus bed, and they're poisonous. Because the green berries look like peas and the red ones look like candy, they're especially alluring to children (as I learned when my little boy gobbled some while I was weeding—we spent an unpleasant morning with emetics).

Loathsome as slugs are, they have good taste when asparagus is available. If you see stalks that have small peeled, slimy areas, rescue your asparagus fast. It is common knowledge that two slugs crawl in to replace every one killed (in damp weather whole armies of slugs lie in wait), so be persistent. I've used traps—saucers of stale beer and empty grapefruit halves—but for bad invasions I go out very early each morning with tweezers and a jar of kerosene and try to dunk them before they hide for the day. Sprinkling sharp sand around the plants or the asparagus bed helps; slugs don't like to drag their soft fat bodies over it.

Asparagus beetles are a nuisance in some areas. They gnaw out the tender asparagus tips, and the larvae excrete a black fluid that stains the plant. Look for small beetles with yellow or black spots and plump gray larvae. Chickens do a good job of eating up asparagus beetles. You can shake off beetles and larvae into a jar, or use rotenone if you're desperate. The beetles hibernate in the woody plant stems; be sure to cut foliage to the ground in the fall, and burn it if you've had beetle problems.

For mild Japanese beetle infestations try hand-picking beetles or dusting plants with lime. Milky spore disease, marketed as Doom, attacks the grubs and is an effective biological control if beetles are very troublesome. But, generally, asparagus is fairly pest-free. Your biggest concern will be keeping up with picking and using it—and that's no problem.

A platter heaped with unadorned steaming green asparagus spears is so perfectly beautiful and delicious that we have it daily the first week or so of harvest. I rush the asparagus from the garden, tie it into a bundle with two strings (or tie separate bundles if stem sizes vary widely), and stand it in about 4 inches of boiling water in the bottom of a glass double boiler. I invert the double-boiler top over the bottom and steam just until the asparagus tips start to get limp—as little as 5 minutes with thin spears. Then I quickly run cold water over the asparagus to retain its bright color, cut the strings, drain the asparagus on a towel, and reheat it briefly with melted butter.

You can also buy an asparagus steamer—nice if you cook a lot, and asparagus is special enough to deserve its own pot. To steam a few spears, not enough to tie up, place some crumpled foil in one side of a frying pan. Add an inch of water, bring to a boil, and lay asparagus spears in with the tips propped out of water by the foil. Cover pan and cook just until tender.

As the asparagus crop burgeons, we start preparing it in other ways, but we always make sure it will be the dominant flavor, and we keep the dishes simple: cool cream of asparagus soup, asparagus with hollandaise alongside eggs Benedict, asparagus vinaigrette, raw pencil-thin spears of asparagus dipped in mayonnaise, asparagus omelet and frittata. Asparagus has an affinity with butter, eggs, and lemon juice, and it combines well with salmon and ham.

It's a great pleasure to have so much homegrown asparagus that you can share big handfuls with friends as well as asparagorging yourself. And, if you still have some left, asparagus is easy to freeze: plunge spears into boiling water, blanch 3 minutes, run cold water over, drain, and pack in freezer containers.

I'd eat asparagus even if it were highly caloric and void of vitamins, so its nutrient content and low calories are lagniappe. Six large green spears contain only about 20 calories but generous amounts of vitamin A, calcium, phosphorus, iron, sodium, and potassium. Think, as you spread all that fertilizer on the asparagus bed, how it's going to return in delectable form to nourish your body. Plot your own asparagus bed now if you don't already have one.

Cream of Asparagus Soup with Tarragon

Spring-green, nutritious asparagus soup is easy to whip up and chill for lunch after you gather the stalks in the morning. Or stop by the market on your way home from work and serve asparagus soup hot as a dinner appetizer. You can use even the slightly tough stem bottoms of asparagus if you slice them thin; I save the toughest stems for soup (especially if they're the stringy ones from the store). I've also made this soup with asparagus that has started to bud out into foliage; it's flavorful even if too far gone to serve whole. Make up a big batch of this soup without the cream or milk and freeze it. Thaw and add milk, cream, or more chicken broth before serving. SERVES 4

2 pounds asparagus
1 small onion or several shallot
  cloves, minced
4 tablespoons butter
2 cups chicken broth

1 tablespoon lemon juice
1 cup milk or cream
1 teaspoon chopped tarragon
Salt and white pepper

Steam or boil asparagus until tender. Cut off and reserve asparagus tips. Chop stalks into 1-inch pieces and place them in blender container. Sauté onion or shallots in butter until soft. Add to blender, pour chicken broth over, add lemon juice, and blend until puréed. Add milk or cream and tarragon. Season to taste. Heat soup gently or chill it. Gently arrange reserved asparagus tips on top just before serving.

Asparagus Vinaigrette Mimosa

Cold crispy-tender asparagus is delicious with green mayonnaise or just mayonnaise, with herby vinaigrette or just lemon juice. It's also good—and different—as something to dip into sour cream at a party. Fixed as below, it deserves a separate course at dinner, and I like it for lunch with crusty hot bread. SERVES 4

2 pounds asparagus	1 teaspoon chopped chervil
1 tablespoon Dijon mustard	1 teaspoon chopped parsley
1/3 cup white vinegar (preferably rice-wine vinegar)	1 teaspoon chopped tarragon
	1 teaspoon finely sliced chives
2/3 cup olive oil	2 hard-boiled eggs

Tie the asparagus in a bundle and steam it until barely tender. Run cold water over it, drain, and chill in the refrigerator.

Place mustard, vinegar, oil, chervil, parsley, and tarragon in blender container. Blend a few seconds, just until everything is well mixed. Stir in chives.

Make mimosa by putting eggs through a sieve or finely chopping them. When ready to serve asparagus, pour dressing over it and sprinkle mimosa on top.

tomatoes

BASIL

Ocimum basilicum
❀ annual

Pesto, the most inspired invention
using large quantities of an herb,
is synonymous with fresh basil.
Basil is synonymous with tomatoes
too. I plant it around my tomatoes,
where it is supposed to deter various pests
with its strong aroma and where it is handy
to pick off sprigs to add to tomato salads,
spaghetti sauce, and pizza.
In addition to the common green sweet basil,
you can grow purplish-bronze basil (often
described as "ornamental," but it's as flavorful as the green kind); bush basil (*O. mimi-
mum*), less than a foot tall; Japanese or
lettuce-leaf basil (*O. crispum*); lemon basils;

and many others. All varieties of basil that I've tried have a similar flavor, clovelike, pleasantly oily—but distinctively basil, and you'll know what I mean after you've crushed a few leaves between your fingers.

Common sweet basil grows up to 3 feet tall, with light-green leaves (darker if the soil is rich) that are pinched along the central vein and curl under as they get larger. Green sweet basil has white flowers that form in whorls around the ends of the stems; purple sweet basil has pinkish flowers.

Basil seed germinates quickly outdoors when the soil is warm. Sow it thinly in rich, loose soil in a sunny spot, then thin seedlings to about 1 foot apart. The plants thrive when pinched back, so start using leaves as soon as you like. Keep blossoms trimmed off (add them to stock) to encourage foliage. Cutting flowers deprives bees of a favorite food, so spare a few blossoms for them, and if you live in very warm climates the flowers may self-seed after ripening.

Basil usually flourishes so madly that you'll have plenty to add to fragrant bouquets. The purple branches are especially striking arranged with baby's breath and lavender spikes. Add a recipe for pesto, and give a bouquet to a special person.

Harvest basil quickly when frost is predicted—it turns dead-black when it gets too cold. Strip the lower leaves off some of the sprigs and put them in water to root for indoor plants. I was discouraged with the failure of the basil plants I potted up to bring indoors. Then I discovered rooting. The stems sprout surprisingly quickly in water. Plant them in potting soil to which you've added some limestone or eggshells (see page 23), and put them in the sunniest place possible or under plant lights. If you pot up plants to bring indoors, give them a good bath first to wash off any whiteflies, and pinch off buds and flowers. Keep pinching them off as more form; because basil is an annual, it will die after it has gone to seed. You can start seeds in pots toward the end of summer, and compact bush basil is good for indoors. Purple basil makes a nice contrast with houseplants. Give indoor basil some liquid fertilizer occasionally. I've found garlic spray (see page 12) fairly effective for discouraging the pests that attack basil indoors or out.

If you really like dried basil, I probably shouldn't try to talk you out of preserving your crop that way. No dried herb is the same as fresh, of course, but basil, because of its potent oils (you can see the dark cells if you hold a leaf against the light), becomes especially emasculated when it's dried. It must be dried as fast as possible; it turns black if it takes too long.

Many forms of preservation retain more of basil's fresh flavor than drying does. Angelo Pellegrini, in *The Food-Lover's Garden*, tells of one method that is as marvelous as his book. Mince basil leaves until they are almost a pulp (or put them through the food processor), then mix with freshly grated Parmesan cheese. The cheese absorbs the basil oil; keep mixing in cheese until everything is crumbly dry. Pack the mixture in glass jars, starting with a thin layer of pepper and salt on the bottom, adding a half-inch layer of basil-cheese, more salt and pepper, and so on until the jar is nearly full. Pour a quarter-inch layer of olive oil on top, seal, and refrigerate. Pellegrini suggests using this mixture with butter, garlic, and parsley to make a sauce for pasta, and it's delicious for many other purposes: to top baked potatoes or soup, to sprinkle on pizza, spaghetti, or eggs.

I also like to preserve basil in olive oil or butter: whirl clean dry leaves in the blender with oil or melted butter until the basil is finely blended. Pesto (see following recipe) freezes well and tastes wonderfully like summer along about January. Tomato sauce redolent of basil and other herbs can be frozen or canned. Basil vinegar is good for salads, and if you make it with purple basil it turns a lovely pink. Just put several basil sprigs in a jar, pour warm vinegar over them, and start using after a few weeks.

I tried drying basil with silica gel, and it was one herb that didn't work well; the flavor was better than that of ordinary dried basil, but the leaves shriveled and lost color. If you have pesto in the freezer and a few basil plants on the windowsill to tide you over until summer returns, who needs the dried stuff anyway?

Year-Round Pesto

We love pesto—basil, garlic, and oil—combined with cheese and pasta: a deliciously filling vegetarian meal. Even in the summer we like to have some basil mixture handy in the freezer so we can scrape out curls to top baked potatoes or grilled seafood or hot soup. But pesto tastes best of all in midwinter.

When we add the summery-tasting basil sauce to lots of Parmesan and toss it with linguine, we can actually believe that the Vermont winter won't last forever.

These directions may sound complicated, but pesto is simple, and once you've made it, you probably won't need a recipe the next time—you'll know how to vary proportions to your taste and the amount of basil you have. (Maybe you'll even want to try substituting parsley or dill for the basil—the method is wonderful for preserving their fresh flavor too.)

Following are the proportions Wayne used to make about a pint of pesto base, starting with 12 ounces by weight of basil sprigs before the leaves were stripped off (use the stems to flavor stock). He points out that one should be flexible: your basil may be more or less juicy; you may need more oil, depending on the temperature; blender sizes vary (he packs our 5-cup one nearly full of basil for this amount). Have two 1-cup or several smaller freezer containers ready if you plan to freeze this, and you probably will, since this base, when completed, makes enough to serve eight people generously. If the blended basil sits around uncovered, it will darken, and you want to preserve its beautiful bright green color. It will keep a few days in the refrigerator if you pour a layer of olive oil on top.

4 packed cups basil leaves　　　*¾ cup olive oil*
4 small cloves garlic

Put basil and garlic in blender, pour oil over, and blend, scraping basil down from sides of jar, until mixture is smooth. Or use food processor. If you like, freeze immediately at this point.

To serve pesto with pasta for four people, you'll need:

1 cup pesto base　　　　　　*Pine nuts or walnuts (optional)*
½ to 1 cup freshly grated Parmesan　　*Salt and pepper (optional)*
　cheese　　　　　　　　　*1 pound pasta*
Olive oil

If you are using frozen pesto base, thaw it, still covered, in a bowl of warm water. You want it to be at room temperature, but if it's heated or exposed to air for long it will blacken.

Stir pesto into Parmesan. Add enough oil to thin the mixture to the consistency you like in spaghetti sauce. If you want to add nuts (we find pesto rich and tasty enough without them, but they add protein), finely chop or pound about a tablespoon per person, and stir them into the pesto. Season to taste, but be careful—Parmesan is salty.

Cook pasta to the tenderness you like, drain, and quickly toss with a little olive oil, then the pesto. Serve immediately, with a bowl of extra Parmesan for sprinkling on top.

Gazpacho with Basil

As much salad as soup, gazpacho is a refreshing summer lunch, especially good if its vegetables and herbs come fresh from the garden. It is sometimes thickened with bread crumbs or corn flour or rice in different parts of Spain, and is often served with ice cubes floating in it. We like it simple: the contrast of the smooth ripe-tomato mixture—in essence, highly aromatic fresh tomato juice—with the crisp vegetables and croutons for "thickening." SERVES 4 AS A MAIN COURSE

10 very ripe medium tomatoes	*2 sweet green or red peppers, diced*
2 cloves garlic, chopped	
4 tablespoons olive oil	*4 celery ribs, diced*
3 tablespoons vinegar	*1 cucumber, diced*
1 dash Tabasco	*2 medium onions or 1 bunch scallions, chopped*
2 tablespoons finely chopped basil leaves	
Salt and pepper	*2 hard-boiled eggs, chopped*
	3 cups croutons

Chop tomatoes roughly, and put them through a food processor or food mill, using medium blade. (You can also purée them in the blender if you don't mind the seeds.) Place garlic in blender or food processor container, add oil, vinegar, and Tabasco, and blend until smooth. Add to tomatoes, and chill thoroughly, preferably 24 hours, so the flavors blend. Before serving, stir in basil and season to taste. Arrange remaining ingredients in separate bowls. Ladle soup into bowls (chilled glass ones are nice). Pass garnishes separately and let each person stir what he likes into his gazpacho.

Seafood Grilled on a Bed of Basil

Basil grows so profusely and is so quickly killed by freezing temperatures that when the weatherman says, "Frost in the lower valleys tonight," we hurry to gather the remaining basil. We pile some of it on the outdoor grill with seafood that cooks quickly. The heat diffusing through the basil gives the seafood a flavor that requires no adornment, but you can use any mild sauce you like, including pesto (see recipe) if you want to carry out the theme. SERVES 4

4 big handfuls basil branches   *Melted butter*
2 pounds bay scallops, cleaned and
*   deveined shrimp, sole fillets, or a*
*   combination*

Prepare a charcoal fire in your usual way. When the coals are covered with white ash, rinse the basil to wet it thoroughly, and arrange it on the grill in a reasonably neat pile about 2 inches thick without pressing down on the leaves. Place seafood on top of the basil, brush with butter, cover with a large lid or aluminum foil, and put the grill about 6 inches above the coals. Delicate seafood usually cooks in less than 5 minutes, but this method requires 15 to 20 minutes (sneak a peek at it occasionally after 12 minutes). When the scallops have lost all their translucency, when the shrimp are completely pink, when the fish is easily flaked with a fork, the seafood is ready to serve with melted butter.

Sort of Mullein velvety

BORAGE

Borago officinalis ✿ *hardy annual*

Amid the insignificant flowers of many
herbs, borage shines as brilliantly as a
bluejay among a flock of sparrows.
Bluejays aren't useful to sparrows, and borage
isn't really very useful in the kitchen compared
to less flashy but more flavorful herbs. I plant it
(or let it replant itself) mostly for its vivid blossoms
and velvety green-gray foliage, but I also use it in salads and for tea.

When I first planted borage, I checked reference works for horticultural
information, because when I try anything new I like to get the experienced
advice of experts. I got generous advice. Some authorities said borage grows 12
inches tall; others said 3 feet. Most said borage likes moist soil; a couple said use
dry soil. Use rich dirt and plenty of manure, said one adviser, while another
maintained that borage thrives in poor soil. My conclusion as a novice: borage
apparently doesn't care, so why should I?

I plunked my plants into rather rocky dirt and let the rain take care of
moisture. The plants produced gorgeous flowers nodding with bees—a nice
visual break between the lovage and the horehound. The next year my neglected
borage had seeded itself into all adjacent territory, where it got so crowded

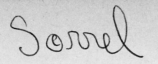

(horehound and lovage also self-seed) that the plants remained small and the leaves were tender for salads.

If you want to grow borage, perhaps you should decide how you want to use it. For eating? Then encourage the foliage with rich, moist soil. For decoration or the bees? Hold back on fertilizer and provide plenty of sun for the flowers.

Borage seeds planted outdoors when the soil is warm germinate within two weeks. The stalks sprawl, so thin them to at least a foot apart. Borage leaves are 4 to 6 inches long, and my plants grow to about 2 feet tall. They shoot up rapidly and soon produce pinkish buds that open into blue stars with black cone-shaped centers.

Borage isn't often grown indoors, but why not? The leaves became softer, less rough, and were good for salads on the plants I tried. Provide soil, moisture, and light as you would for African violets, whose leaves are similar in texture and appearance.

Grow borage outdoors against a stone wall or among less flamboyantly flowered herbs. Gather the flowers (but leave plenty for the bees), and arrange them in a blue bouquet. Scatter the edible flowerets over the top of a salad, or candy them: brush them with lightly beaten egg white, dip them in superfine granulated sugar, and spread them out to dry. They're pretty on top of vanilla ice cream.

Tea made from fresh borage is bland, mildly spicy, and I like it brewed with mint leaves. Tea made from dried borage often tastes musty, since borage doesn't dry well. If you want to dry it, be sure that the leaves are really crumbly. It's better to make up a borage concentrate for winter by covering mashed leaves with hot water, steeping them for a day or so, then straining off the liquid and freezing it in cubes. You can thaw out one cube at a time to make a cup of hot tea or add to lemonade or white wine. Both leaves and flowers retain their color well when dried in silica gel (see page 41).

The flavor of fresh young borage leaves reminds me of cucumbers, and I think they're the best part of the plant to consume. You can add handfuls to salads, cook them like spinach, or add sprigs to vegetables, stews, or roasts.

Borage is high in potassium and calcium. It emits sparks and pops when burned because it contains nitrate of potash, so throw some leaves on the barbecue for a small firecracker show.

CARROTS

Daucus carota sativa annual

Mirepoix, a cooked aromatic mixture of vegetables, simply must have the sweet accent of carrots. Court bouillon usually requires carrots for flavor. Soups and stews and sauces rely on the color and aroma of carrots. So I'm including carrots in this book mainly because of their value as an aromatic, a flavoring as essential as celery and onions are to many dishes. Like celery and onions, carrots are fairly easy to grow, they store well, and they are basic to good cooking.

Carrots come in various sizes and shapes, from the stubby fat to the medium short to the long slender. All of them need loose, sandy soil: their roots must penetrate the dirt freely if they are to grow to their proper size.

Prepare outdoor soil for carrots as soon as possible in spring. Spade deeply into the dirt and work in some lime and compost (but not manure, which causes carrot roots to fork or sprout "whiskers"). Sow carrot seeds thinly. I mix the fine, slow-germinating seeds with radish seeds, which sprout quickly; radishes are ready to pull before the carrots need the space, and they identify the row so I can weed easily.

Carrots should be thinned whenever their roots touch one another. If you don't give them adequate space, they will be crooked and thin, or their roots will twist around those of their neighbors. If roots split, the soil may have too much nitrogen. Deter carrot fly larvae, which eat the roots, by covering seedlings with cheesecloth, and rotate the crop from year to year if you have problems.

I plant enough carrots of several varieties so that I can start pulling them to use when they are small, have enough to feed the deer, and still have some left when frost comes. You can preserve carrots in the ground until heavy snow falls by covering them with baskets or boxes and leaves.

Several times in this book I've compared other foods to carrots in vitamin A content, since carrots contain such large quantities of this vitamin: 11,000 International Units per 3½ ounces of raw carrots; 10,500 when cooked. Avoid peeling them if you want to save all their nutrients.

Carrots are good raw, of course, dipped in herb mayonnaise or simply pulled from the soil, brushed off, and munched on the spot. Braising them preserves their flavor and vitamins better than boiling does. You can pickle carrots with other vegetables, or make them into a lovely orange cream soup. Your small garden-fresh carrots are best for such recipes.

For aromatic purposes, however, mature—even somewhat woody—carrots are fine. Their flavor is stronger, and when they're chopped or puréed it doesn't matter if they're a bit tough. The simplest court bouillon can be made with a large chopped carrot, a chopped onion, a sliced stalk of celery, a bay leaf, and a few peppercorns. Simmer them in a quart of water and a cup or so of white wine for about half an hour. Strain the liquid and use it to poach vegetables. Fish scraps or shrimp shells may be added with the raw ingredients for a court bouillon to poach seafood. The sweetness of carrots balances the acidity of the wine and subtly seasons the food they are cooked with.

Mirepoix, which enhances the flavor of sauces and meat and shellfish dishes, is most easily made with equal parts finely diced carrots, onions, and celery. Simmer them in butter about 10 minutes. This mixture can be cooked further with herbs, bacon or other meats, and stock, then strained to make sauce. We usually use mirepoix with chopped herbs as a bed for braising meats and baking fish or chicken. After the food is cooked, we blend the drippings and mirepoix to make a sauce that is filled with flavor and low in calories.

Carrots cooked until soft and spun in the blender with parsley make nourishing baby food. Carrots store well in a cool place if they are packed in sand, and they last a long time in the refrigerator. To freeze them, slice them thin, steam them for 2 minutes, plunge them in icy water, drain, and package. I save even the peels and trimmings, including the foliage, to add to soup stock. From top to bottom, carrots are useful, and I'd be bereft without them.

CATNIP

Nepeta cataria 🐾 *perennial*

Rule number one: don't plant catnip in your herb bed. My cats, and their neighborhood friends and enemies, enjoy rolling around in the perennial **herb** garden anyway—I hate to think of the destruction they'd cause if I provided additional attraction.

Domesticated catnip plants grow up to 3 feet tall. They are rather coarse-looking, grayish, and not ornamental, another reason to put them off in a corner where the cats can enjoy them and you don't have to look at them. A member of the mint family, catnip has square, erect, branched stems with roughly triangular, toothed leaves that are downy, especially on the undersides. The spiked flowers are inconspicuous but rather pretty up close: pale pink with red spots and anthers.

Wild catnip grows over my head in a marshy spot at the bottom of our banks, but I've never seen the cats gambol in it—maybe because it has less fragrance than domesticated catnip, maybe it's too tall, or maybe the cats don't like to get their feet wet. But I think they are unconcerned about it because of a curious thing about cats and catnip plants: only when the leaves are bruised or cut do the cats pick up the odor and become interested. I had a plant growing healthily big in the catnip bed, untouched by pets Grimalkin and G. K. Chesterton, until I pinched off a big leaf and tore it up for them. In two days the plant was bare branches; the cats kept going back and tearing off leaves. They even settled their differences with neighbor cats as they all sprawled in ecstasy together.

Remember this if you set out catnip seedlings, and protect them with some sort of cover until they've become well established. Several plantings I made were nibbled to extinction because I didn't realize that merely handling the plants bruised the leaves enough to attract the cats. You can sow seeds directly in the ground when the soil warms up in spring. Plant them fairly thickly, since germination is often poor, cover them lightly with soil, and keep them moist until they sprout. Or divide roots from established plants in spring. Plants should be set about 2 feet apart. Most mints prefer rich, moist soil, but catnip does well in the poor, sandy soil under our old apple tree. It is a hardy plant once it gets going, and its vigorous roots can be a problem—another reason for keeping it out of herb and flower beds.

One catnip species, *N. mussinii*, makes a good houseplant because it is smaller than ordinary sprawly catnip. It has a minty fragrance and pink flowers. Grow it and the various other *Nepeta* varieties and hybrids in lean soil, and keep them well watered.

Catnip is sometimes used in cooking, as one would use mint, and it has high vitamin A and C content. It is reputed to be an effective rat repellent (logical, if there are cats in the area).

Catnip tea is slightly minty, slightly bitter. I find it pleasant enough if I brew it with other mints or add lots of lemon. However, I grow catnip mostly for the cats. The dried catnip I've bought is usually so dead and gone that my cats nose at it and doze off, whereas they freak out on what I've dried myself.

Dry your own by cutting catnip branches and hanging them in a bundle until the leaves can be crumbled off. Then pack the leaves and broken stems (which also have good aroma) in jars. Use them to make tea or cat treats, as primitive or fancy as you like. I simply tie up a tablespoon of catnip in a piece of old sheet, but you can make catnip-stuffed silk mice for a special feline.

CELERY

Apium graveolens  annual

Poor dear celery—used routinely, taken for granted, too seldom appreciated for its many virtues. Not until I grew my own did I realize how good it can be and how many ways it can be used.

Because celery is available everywhere year round, most people don't bother to grow it. Perhaps they have also heard the rumor that it's a fussy plant. It's not. If you have a few extra feet of space in your garden, try a few celery

plants, if only for the pleasure of breaking off a crisp dark-green stalk to munch as you wander among your vegetables. It's amazing how much flavor celery has before being blanched, wrapped in plastic, and stored for months (as much commercial celery is).

I set out celery seedlings. You can buy them at nurseries or start your own indoors, but they should be transplanted to the garden when they're only about 3 inches tall. If they stay in crowded flats too long they tend to go to seed early. Make a furrow about a foot deep, or dig holes about 6 inches apart, and place a layer of manure, then several inches of rich, fine, loose soil, in the bottom. Set the seedlings in carefully—they are fragile—and pull soil around them. Continue filling in the furrow or holes as the plants grow until the soil is level. I plant radishes or lettuce around the celery plants. They are ready to harvest before the celery needs the space. If you have a long growing season and want a large crop, you can sow seed directly in the furrow.

Celery withstands cold well. It can be grown in winter in the far South and protected with coverings for some time after frost in the North. Its greatest demand besides fertile soil is plenty of water. I encourage it to grow as dark green and vitamin filled as possible by watering it with fish emulsion or liquid manure, and I don't understand why people want to blanch out its nutrients and flavor. Blanching produces tenderer stems, however, and if that's the way you like celery, you can keep banking the soil around the stems, tie newspapers around them, or slide drain tiles over them.

Celery takes up to five months to mature, but I grow the plants mainly to use young stems and leaves, crackling fresh, as I need them throughout the summer, rather than harvesting the mature heads. Before frost, plants can be dug up with their root balls and placed in a cool spot to use over winter. When plants bolt, you can collect the aromatic seeds for flavoring. Frozen celery is watery when thawed, but see page 38 for how to freeze stuffing seasoning containing celery. My grandmother canned celery; it had a pleasantly soft texture and mild flavor. Some people also dry the leaves as they do herbs to flavor soup.

Check seed catalogs for the many varieties of celery and for disease-resistant types. While you're at it, look for seed for celtuce, a member of the lettuce family whose leaves and heart can be eaten raw or cooked, and celeriac, with an edible root like a turnip. As their names suggest, both resemble celery in flavor and texture, and they are prepared in the same ways.

If aphids attack young celery plants, hose them off and apply a garlic spray (see page 12). Plant marigolds near celery to discourage nematodes. Keep plants well watered and properly spaced to avoid fungus and other diseases.

When you buy celery look for dark-green bunches with crisp bright leaves. Pascal, as this beautiful celery is often labeled, has more flavor and food value than pale, blanched celery with its emaciated leaves.

Celery often has grit in its base and between the stalks. Cut off about an inch of the root end, wash it carefully, and use it to flavor broth. Separate the stalks, wash them and the leaves under running water, shake them dry, and store them in a plastic bag in the refrigerator.

Using celery is no problem unless you forget, as I often do, that it's always there in the refrigerator, waiting to be appreciated in many ways. Add leaves and thinly sliced ribs to all sorts of salads and sandwich fillings. Cut stalks along with leaf tops into strips and serve them with an herb dip. Fill hollows of stalks with cheese spread.

Celery stalks and leaves are called for in many basic stocks. I keep a separate plastic bag in the refrigerator for stem bottoms, tough leaves, and leftover bits—just what's needed to flavor homemade soup.

Cooking brings out a delicate sweetness in celery. It's valuable as an aromatic because you can stew it to pieces and the good taste will remain in the broth. Try cooking celery also in ways that retain some of its fresh texture and vitamins. Slice it diagonally and stir-fry it until bity-tender. Or boil it until you can barely pierce it with a fork, 10 minutes or less, run cold water over it to retain color, reheat, and serve hot with herb butter, or chill in vinaigrette to serve cold.

CHERVIL

Anthriscus cerefolium
🌿 annual

The dainty foliage of the little chervil plant gives an indication of the delicate aroma and flavor of its sweetish, subtly peppery, very special leaves. My chervil usually grows less than a foot tall, and be- cause it is both compact and attractive I use it as a border plant in the herb and flower beds. Both flat-leafed and curly varieties of chervil are available. All that I've tried have that distinctive chervil flavor, but the double-curled variety is prettiest.

Since chervil matures about six weeks after it germinates, make successive sowings if you want a continuing crop. When the plants are several inches tall, it is time to sow some more, because chervil takes up to two weeks to germinate. I often let a few plants go to seed and reseed themselves.

Plant chervil seeds in fairly rich, light soil, preferably in a semishaded spot, where the ground will remain moist. Chervil will not thrive in dry clay, but it will do well in the shade of other plants, so you can even stick it in between vegetable rows. You can plant chervil almost any time the ground can be worked. If you sow it in late fall in cold areas, you'll get an early spring crop. Thin seedlings to at least 6 inches apart. Mulching close to the plants keeps them weed-free, retains moisture, and prevents mud splatter. The seedlings look like parsley, but they become more ferny and are lighter green, almost gold-green. The flowers are small, white, and umbrella-shaped. My plants have never been bothered by pests.

If you grow chervil outdoors you can collect dry seeds to sow indoors in rich soil for a winter crop. Chervil is a good houseplant; it is small and doesn't require as much sunlight as many other herbs. If you buy seeds, be sure they are fresh; chervil seeds lose their viability rather quickly, so it's risky to try to plant leftovers from the year before. You're not likely to find chervil seed on most racks, but many mail-order seed companies carry several varieties.

Dried chervil is sweeter than the fresh leaves, with much less of their licorice flavor, but it's more trouble to dry than those herbs you can just hang up by the branches, and it loses color. When I do dry chervil, I make a project of it by drying the other ingredients for *fines herbes* at the same time. I spread out on a screen approximately equal amounts of chervil, chives, tarragon, parsley, sometimes basil, perhaps thyme, and let them dry in a shady, airy spot until they are crumbly. Then I tie them in little packets of cheesecloth to add to stock and sauces.

Silica gel drying (see page 41) is effective for chervil, especially the curly leafed kind. The leaves stay green and taste much like fresh chervil when reconstituted in liquid. Young chervil sprigs freeze well; pack them loosely in small plastic bags. Chervil butter, made by whirling the leaves in the blender with melted butter or chopping them fine into soft butter, is good on almost all vegetables and seafood. You can make chervil vinegar even when the plants are blossoming: cut off sprigs and put them in a jar. Pour white vinegar over them, and let them steep in a warm place for at least a week. Strain, and use in vinaigrette for delicate greens and lettuces.

Fresh chervil loses its sprightly flavor if heated for long, so add it to cooked foods only at the last minute. Use it as a chopped garnish instead of parsley, or try substituting it in any recipe that calls for a small amount of minced parsley. Chervil adds an accent that is distinctive but not overpowering. It heightens the flavor of new peas and potatoes, asparagus tips, small carrots, or anything else young and fresh from the garden. It goes well with fish and oysters, fowl, pale-colored meats, and egg dishes. In bouillon or vichyssoise a little chopped chervil adds a big difference in flavor.

though revered in many

Cold Mussels with Chervil Mayonnaise

Mussels, with their orange-pink flesh against blue-black shells, are a still life in color. They have a seductively delicate but sharply salty flavor. And they are inexpensive because they are abundant and because they are neglected in this country, even though revered in many others. This recipe is based on moules marinière, in which hot mussels are eaten with their broth. Reducing that cooking liquid and combining it with mayonnaise and chervil makes a piquant sauce for the mussels and whatever cold vegetables you like. Served this way, it's a lovely lunch for two or an appetizer for four or a party platter.
SERVES 2 TO 4

2 pounds fresh mussels
2 tablespoons chopped shallots
5 sprigs parsley
1 cup white wine
2 cups mayonnaise
1 tablespoon chopped chervil

Garnishes of your choice, such as
radishes, small leeks, cold
parboiled Brussels sprouts,
asparagus, fiddleheads, milkweed
flowers

Pickled   chutney   Bread and Butter

Scrub mussels under cold running water with a stiff brush. Remove any vegetation on the shells, and pull out the beards. Discard open mussels that don't close under the cold water. Place shallots and parsley in a large saucepan, put the mussels on top, and pour the wine over them. Bring slowly to a boil, cover pan, turn down heat, and steam just until mussels open. Let mussels cool until you can handle them, then open them over the pan to catch all their liquid. Discard the empty half of the shell (and discard any mussels that haven't opened), and arrange on the half shell on a large platter. Refrigerate under plastic wrap.

While the mussels are chilling, strain the mussel broth through several layers of cheesecloth arranged in a strainer. Rinse cheesecloth and put it back in the strainer. Boil the strained liquid until it is reduced to about a tablespoon, cool, then strain it again through the cheesecloth into the mayonnaise. Add the chervil, and fold in until well blended. Refrigerate.

When the mussels and mayonnaise are cool, put a small dollop of mayonnaise on each mussel and arrange vegetables of your choice around the platter. Use remaining mayonnaise as a dip for vegetables.

Chopped Chicken Livers with Chervil

Herbs give chopped liver a special flavor and pleasing bits of green color. Watercress, parsley, and tarragon are good substitutes if you can't get fresh chervil. If you're as fond of chopped liver as I am, you'll have a big sandwich while it's still warm, so maybe you'd better figure the recipe won't serve quite as many as I've suggested. SERVES 8 AS APPETIZER

1 pound chicken livers
3 small onions, thinly sliced
½ cup butter, oil, or rendered
   chicken fat
2 hard-boiled eggs-

2 tablespoons chopped chervil
Salt and pepper
Thinly sliced rye or pumpernickel
   bread

Rinse and drain chicken livers. Sauté onions in butter, oil, or fat for about 10 minutes, stirring to cook them evenly. Remove onions with slotted spoon. Cook livers in same skillet for about 10 minutes, stirring frequently. Place livers with their cooking liquid, onions, eggs, and chervil in food mill, and grind, using medium blade (or use food processor). Season to taste. Serve at room temperature with bread.

CHIVES

Allium schoenoprasum 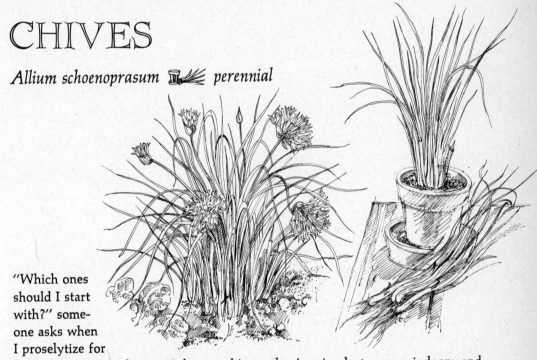 *perennial*

"Which ones should I start with?" someone asks when I proselytize for herb growing. I unhesitatingly say chives: they're simple to grow indoors and out, cooperative in the way they spread, useful and pretty—and thus they encourage people to go on to other herbaceous adventures.

The packet of chive seeds I started years ago has returned a harvest almost too bountiful. I've divided clumps and shared with so many people that it's getting hard to find any more takers. I've transplanted chives into so many places that they're taking over flower beds. But when all the pinkish lavender chive heads flower like little pompoms in June, I lose my nerve to "weed" them and start pondering where I can put some more root divisions. They usually end up in the vegetable garden. As a member of the onion family, they probably help repel unwanted insects. Even when they're plowed under, they come back in odd places the next year, but they don't intrude on the vegetables the way many perennial herbs will.

Common chives, the kind you can often buy in little pots in the grocery store, have slender, tubular, bright-green leaves that grow up to a foot long. Garlic or Chinese chives (*A. tuberosum*) have grayish leaves that are flat like grass blades and grow up to 2 feet long. They taste stronger than common chives and have white, starlike, fragrant flowers.

To grow chives outdoors, sow seeds thinly as soon as the ground is workable. One seed packet will yield far more plants than you probably need, and you'll have to wait a while for harvest, so maybe you would prefer to buy or beg some plant divisions that you can start clipping right away. Chives seem to thrive in almost any kind of soil; rich soil makes them luxuriant. When the blossoms appear, you have to make a decision: cutting the flower stalks back to the ground encourages the foliage; letting them go to seed is likely to produce many new chive plants in the spring. I let most of the plants bloom until the flowers start turning brown, then trim them off close to the ground and add the armloads of stalks to the compost heap. I keep several clumps near the kitchen clipped all the time so they continually produce tender shoots for eating. The plants die down after heavy frost, but new shoots appear very early in spring. Remove the old brown mass of foliage (it pulls off easily) to give the new leaves a good start.

Garlic chives, because they germinate and reach eating size fast, can be started indoors. Don't try to start common chives from seeds in the house—it simply takes too long to produce good-sized leaves. Pot up a small clump from outdoors and trim it down to about an inch tall. Allow the shorn plant to freeze overnight a few times to encourage new growth and kill insects that may be hanging on.

When you buy a pot of chives, you'll get best results if you trim the chives to an inch tall and use the foliage right away. Now put the pot in the refrigerator for about two weeks. This gives it the rest it needs before starting new growth. If it is packed into a small pot, replant it in a larger container that has good drainage and allows room for growth. Add soil around it, water well, and set it in a sunny spot. It will soon send up fresh leaves, which you can start trimming when a few inches tall. Chives must be trimmed regularly—they shoot up and topple over quickly—and some liquid fertilizer will give them greener growth. If the plants look as if they're giving out, they may need another rest: let them dry out a bit, trim them, then put them in the refrigerator for a few weeks.

When I see great clumps of chive flowers blooming outdoors, I want to enjoy their beauty while I work in the house. I combine them in a big vase with other purples and blues that bloom at the same time: columbines, irises, delphiniums, lupines. Since I'm going to cut the chives down anyway, it's a good time to make and give away herb bouquets. Chive flowers are quite edible, if a bit crunchy, and they make an unusual garnish for salads.

Drying chives is a waste of time when they're so easy to have fresh year round. If you like to have some chopped ones handy or you want to preserve part of a big crop when the shoots are only a few inches tall, try freezing chives: line up a pile of clean dry stalks on the cutting board, slice them thin, place them in small containers or cellophane packets, and freeze immediately. Or make chive butter to top soup, spread on bread or grilled meat, and stir into vegetables. Cream thinly sliced chives with soft butter. Add some white or cayenne pepper or a bit of dry mustard if you like.

Surely nobody has trouble thinking of ways to add chives to food—their attractive color and mild onion flavor complement most salads, breads, vegetables, soups, and meats—but I've never found a way to eat up all the chives that proliferate around here. Although they contain many vitamins and minerals (especially vitamins A and C, sulfur, calcium, and phosphorus), their nutritive value is negligible in the small amounts one usually uses. Chive soup is about the only recipe I know that requires great handfuls of the herb, and you can add a lot of finely chopped chives to mixed green salads. Maybe chives are best enjoyed in small quantities in food and in glorious sprawling expanses outdoors.

Chive Soup

The chives are sprouting lavender flower heads and you're about ready to cut them down to encourage new growth. Now is the time to make this tasty green soup with a garnish of chive flowers. You can make up a large quantity of the potato-stock-chive mixture to freeze, adding the milk and cream to this base when you're ready to serve. When you pick chives at flowering stage, use only the leaves, not the tough flower stems. MAKES ABOUT 2 QUARTS

3 medium potatoes
1½ cups chicken stock
½ pound chives, chopped into
½-inch pieces

About 3 cups milk
1 cup cream
Chive flowers (optional)

Peel and slice potatoes. Cook them in chicken stock until soft. Place chives, potatoes with stock, and 1 cup of the milk in blender container or food processor, and blend until smooth. Pour mixture into saucepan, and add cream. Stir in remaining milk until the consistency is about that of thin pancake batter—or however thick you like it. Heat just to boiling, but do not boil. Serve hot or chilled. If you like, sprinkle several chive flowers on each bowl of soup before serving.

Low-Calorie "Sour Cream" with Chives

People who like sour cream on baked potatoes often succumb to the temptation to really pile it on—a reckless act at more than 25 calories per tablespoon. This topping has five times more protein than sour cream but half the calories. It tastes enough like sour cream to fool almost everybody, especially when you add lots of chives. MAKES ABOUT 1½ CUPS

½ cup buttermilk
1 cup uncreamed (whole-curd)
cottage cheese

½ teaspoon lemon juice
3 tablespoons finely chopped
chives

Shake the buttermilk, place it in the blender with the cottage cheese and lemon juice, and blend at highest speed until very smooth. Or you can use a food processor. Fold in chives, and refrigerate at least 3 hours before serving; it thickens as it chills. It will keep for about a week under refrigeration.

Chive Scalloped Potatoes and Broccoli

This is a good way to use up bits of leftover or dried-out or overripe cheese. Every combination of cheese and potatoes I've ever tasted was good, and there are few potato dishes that aren't enhanced by chives. Try chopping them generously into mashed potatoes, hash browns, and potato soufflés to add color, flavor, and vitamins. You can substitute other vegetables for broccoli in this recipe: green beans, dandelion greens, snow peas, peppers, or a combination of what's handy. A few cups of diced ham or chicken make this a one-dish meal. SERVES 4

3 large potatoes
1 cup small broccoli flowerets
3 tablespoons butter
2 tablespoons flour
2 cups milk

½ cup sour cream
1 cup shredded cheese
4 tablespoons chopped chives
Salt and white pepper

Slice potatoes thin and boil them along with broccoli for about 3 minutes (this keeps the vegetables from releasing their liquid into the sauce when baked). Quickly run cold water over vegetables, and drain well.

Grease a 1½-quart casserole with a bit of the butter, then melt the rest in a saucepan. Stir in the flour, and cook, stirring, for a few minutes. Heat the milk, and pour it into the flour mixture. Stir over heat for a few minutes, turn heat down, and add sour cream and cheese. Cook gently, continuing to stir, until sauce thickens and cheese is melted. Stir in 3 tablespoons of the chives, and season to taste.

Place half the drained vegetables in the casserole, pour half the sauce over, then add remaining vegetables and remaining sauce on top. Bake at 350° F. for about 1 hour. Place casserole under broiler until top is browned, and sprinkle remaining chives on top before serving.

CORIANDER

Coriandrum sativum  *annual*

Although many Americans have traditionally thought of coriander as a powdered, dried seed to use in cookies or curry, fresh coriander leaves are becoming increasingly popular in this country, as people experiment with foreign cuisines. It is known variously as Chinese parsley, cilantro, and dhania. Coriander grows easily from seeds, makes a nice border plant, and its high-vitamin leaves can be used to flavor all those Chinese and Indian recipes you'd like to try. You can harvest the seeds, too, if you don't eat all the leaves.

Coriander seedlings look a bit like Italian parsley, with oval, toothed leaves on the main stem. As the plant grows to about a foot tall, the leaves on the side branches start to resemble dill, lacy and delicate. The pretty flowers, similar to small dill heads, are very pale mauve and loved by bees.

A few years ago, expecting to have a baby any minute, I hurriedly dumped some coriander seeds into the dill bed, where the soil is rich and well aerated by moles. Coriander germinates slowly, but the next time I had a chance to check it, the unthinned, unwatered, unweeded seedlings were doing as fine as the new son. Ideally you should sow seeds thinly; you can soak them overnight to speed germination, but ignore advice to crack them—it's too hard to do it properly. Thin plants to about 6 inches apart and keep them moist and weeded. They don't transplant well because of their long taproots. We started harvesting leaves and experimenting with recipes when the plants were just a few inches tall, thinning them in the process.

Some old herbals describe coriander as having a fetid odor. It's not quite that, but it has a heavy licorice smell. Our outdoor grill, used almost constantly in summer, is near the coriander-dill bed. It's pleasant as night falls to smell the fresh herbs as we eat green chicken tandoori and dilled cucumber salad by firefly light, with mosquito choral music in the background. When coriander leaves are cooked, as in tandoori (see recipe), their strong flavor is somewhat tamed; many people prefer their raw pungency.

Coriander grows quite well indoors from seed started in rich soil in deep pots, but don't expect it to produce seeds unless you keep it under plant lights. Pests aren't usually a problem, indoors or out (coriander is even considered an aphid repellent), but if insects appear, keep washing the foliage with tepid water or apply a garlic spray (see page 12).

The leaves of coriander are about as satisfactorily dried as parsley, which is to say not very. If you like the fresh flavor, preserve it by whirling coriander leaves in the blender with oil or melted butter. Coriander seeds are easily harvested when they become light brown and dry; hold a bag under the seed heads and pop them off. Let a few drop on the ground, and cover them lightly for next year's crop. Coriander self-seeds so readily that it sometimes goes wild.

Recipes using dried coriander seeds abound, and since this book is mainly about fresh herbs, I'm skipping them here. Try stuffing coriander leaves inside a chicken before you roast it, chop them onto fish, add some to cream cheese, and use them in much the same way you do parsley, but less generously—unless you like a dominant licorice flavor. See Indian, Spanish, and Chinese cookbooks for other ideas on using coriander, but do try the ones that follow.

Lentil and Rice Salad with Coriander

Kusherie, an Egyptian spiced lentil and rice dish, gave me the inspiration for this nutritious salad. Fresh green coriander is the perfect color and flavor accent to the pale lentils and rice. As a variation, try cooking the lentils until mushy, mashing them to a purée, and mixing them thoroughly with the other ingredients to serve as a dip. SERVES 4

1 cup lentils
3 tablespoons olive oil
1 tablespoon lemon juice
½ cup chopped scallions
1 cup cooked rice

2 tablespoons chopped coriander
  leaves
½ cup plain yogurt
Salt and pepper

Check lentil package directions, and soak overnight if necessary. Drain, cover with water in a pot, bring to a boil, and simmer just until tender—as little as 30 minutes for processed lentils, up to 1½ hours for unprocessed ones. Drain, and toss immediately with oil, lemon juice, and scallions. Let cool at room temperature, stir in rice, and chill in refrigerator. Before serving, stir in coriander and yogurt and season to taste.

Green Chicken Tandoori Grilled with Potatoes

Real chicken tandoori uses many dried spices—coriander seeds, turmeric, nutmeg, cloves, and cumin—and is delicious. (See Madhur Jaffrey's *An Invitation to Indian Cooking* for an authentic tandoori recipe, plus many using dhania, as fresh coriander is called in India.) I set out to make a radical variation of tandoori, substituting fresh herbs for spices and stressing green coriander leaves. Servings for the following recipe are quite generous—it is so good that people eat a lot. You can stretch it to serve four if you buy a larger chicken, add some extra potatoes, and serve plenty of salad. SERVES 2

1 small frying chicken
2 large potatoes
1 cup roughly chopped coriander
leaves
½ cup roughly chopped parsley
1 small onion, chopped

2 cloves garlic
3 tablespoons olive oil
½ teaspoon crushed hot red pepper
2 tablespoons lemon juice
8 ounces plain yogurt

Split the chicken in half, skin it if you like, and prick it all over with a fork. Peel the potatoes, or simply scrub them, and slice them about 1 inch thick. Place potatoes in a large bowl, and put chicken on top.

Combine remaining ingredients in blender container, and blend at high speed until herbs are finely chopped. Pour mixture over chicken and potatoes. Marinate at least a day in the refrigerator, turning chicken occasionally and pricking it again with a fork.

Heat charcoal in grill until white hot, then remove chicken and potatoes from marinade and place them on the rack as far away from the heat as possible. Keep turning and basting them with marinade every 10 minutes or so. The marinade will slide off at first, but eventually it forms a crispy green-brown coating. Add more charcoal to the fire if necessary. After about an hour everything should be ready—when a chicken leg separates easily from the thigh and the potatoes feel tender when pierced with a fork.

Stir-Fried Snow Peas with Coriander

Coriander leaves, often called Chinese parsley, are used to effect in China to flavor many dishes, especially stir-fried foods. Coriander gives a zing to crisp snow peas, and you can stir-fry other vegetables—such as thinly sliced carrots, celery, broccoli, and zucchini—and shredded meat along with the peas. SERVES 4

2 tablespoons cooking oil
1 cup thinly sliced scallions
4 cups snow peas
½ cup chicken broth
2 teaspoons cornstarch

½ cup finely chopped coriander
leaves
Soy sauce (optional)
Sugar (optional)

Heat oil in a wok or large skillet until it is almost smoking hot. Add the scallions and snow peas, and toss them quickly, just until they are coated with oil. Add chicken broth, cover skillet, and cook for 3 minutes while you mix cornstarch with 2 tablespoons water and the coriander leaves. Stir mixture quickly into peas, and cook, stirring, until sauce thickens. Taste, and add a little soy sauce and/or sugar if you like.

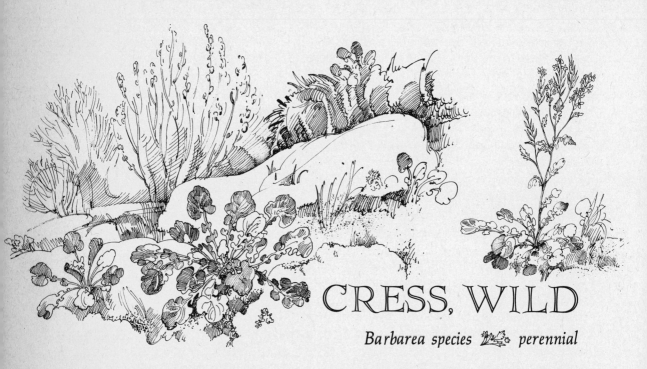

CRESS, WILD

Barbarea species perennial

My brother and I earned our first nickels from wild field cress. Armed with dull knives, a bushel basket held between us, we slogged through the muddy spring fields, looking for cress heads among last year's dried corn stalks. It took a long time to fill that basket heaping full, but when we did, some greens off the top went to Mama to cook for supper. We went with Grandpa to the market in Williamsburg to sell the rest.

When I go out now to look for the first cress in the melting snow I remember our chilly, eager fingers in those Virginia mornings, the exciting sounds at the farmers' market, and how we came home, pockets jingling, to the smell of cress greens cooking on the stove. Today those memories mingle with other pleasures associated with cress: its bity flavor in salads and its extraordinarily high vitamin C content (three times an equal weight of orange juice).

Wild cress was often called "creesy greens" in Virginia. It is also known as mustard greens, yellow rocket, rocket cress, scurvy grass, and has who knows how many other local names, since it grows in many areas. Cress is one of the first edible plants to appear in spring. It has a flat head of glossy, dark-green leaves. They resemble watercress, with up to eight pairs of lobes and a larger lobe at the tip. The plant spreads out to about a foot across and a foot upward before it sends up spikes of bright-yellow flowers.

Cress is best when you tear the lobes off the young leaves and add them to lettuces in salad. Its flavor is similar to that of watercress but much more piquant, so you probably won't want to use it alone in salads. Wash cress carefully, since it grows close to the ground during mud season. Cress leaves often have holes created by a minute aphid that attacks other crucifers (cress is a member of the same mustard family, *Cruciferae,* as cabbage and kale). Don't worry—holes won't hurt you, and a good washing will probably get rid of something you can't see anyway.

Once in a while I long for a good old mess of southern boiled cress, in which there is no attempt to preserve nutrition or eliminate calories. You cook out the vitamins while you cook in the salty ham flavor, an indulgence I wouldn't condone if it didn't taste so good. The simplest method of cooking creesy greens is to pile a pot full of clean leaves, throw in a ham hock and some water, cover, and boil slowly for at least 2 hours, until the meat is falling off the bone and the greens are a dark glazed mass. Serve with cornbread to mop up the pot liquor. If such down-home cooking doesn't appeal to you, you can steam cress greens until tender and serve them with butter and a dash of vinegar.

When cress sends up a flower stalk, its leaves become almost too bitter to enjoy, but you can eat the bud clusters, which taste much like the young leaves. Break the buds apart and add them raw to salads, or cook them by pouring boiling water over them, then boiling for about 5 minutes. Taste a bud, and if you find it too crunchy or bitter, repeat the process. Serve the buds hot with butter or marinate them in vinaigrette to serve cold.

DANDELION

Taraxacum officinale  *perennial*

"A mother of ten, when the food was scant, set out with a basket and gathered the plant," writes my mother of her mother. I am grateful to both of them for passing on an affection for the dandelion, that so-called weed that people actually use chemicals to destroy.

Whenever I see an expanse of golden dandelion heads buzzing with bees in the sun, I wonder how frequently the plant would be grown in flower beds if it were scarce and considered exotic. Children whose souls have not yet been benighted by such pejorative terms as "weed" immediately appreciate the beauty of dandelions; they gather bouquets and blow fluffy seed heads with charmed absorption. You can expand their interest by making them whistles from dandelion stems. Then take them home and expand their taste buds by sharing a dish of dandelion greens with them.

The benefits of dandelion as food may surpass even its aesthetic qualities. Old-timers considered dandelion greens a spring tonic for a good reason: after a winter with few fresh greens, they got a potent shot of several nutrients that prevent vitamin-deficiency diseases. One cup of cooked dandelion greens, only 60 calories, provides an incredible 21,000 International Units of vitamin A, several times the recommended daily allowance. But that's not all. A cup of dandelion greens also has 252 milligrams of calcium, 3.2 milligrams of iron, .24 milligrams of thiamine, .29 milligrams of riboflavin, and 32 milligrams of vitamin C. Compare these figures with your one-a-day vitamin jar listing and you'll see how impressive it all is.

Fine, you may say, but it's also irrelevant, because dandelions taste bitter and tough; further, it's a bother to gather and clean them. Dandelions, however, can be pleasantly bity and quite tender. You're getting exercise in the fresh air when you pick them—and they're free food.

So start—or restart, if you've been disappointed by dandelions in the past—by adding some small tender leaves to a mixed green salad. Even tasteless store-bought iceberg lettuce becomes edible when the tang and texture of dandelion leaves are added to it.

If you gather dandelion greens in dubious spots, such as empty lots in the city or around manure piles or along the highway, do wash them carefully. They may have been sprayed by weed-killers, and they're probably gritty. When you acquire a taste for dandelions and are ready to eat them in greater quantities, you can use practically the whole plant, all of which is edible. With a sharp knife, dig around the long root a few inches deep and pull up the stalk. You can use as much of the root as you like, all the little buds, and the unblemished leaves. Older, dark-green leaves are tough—though they can be good cooked if they are finely chopped—and it's best to use the plant before it flowers.

By now, perhaps, you look forward to the almost ritualistic gathering of the first spring dandelion greens. In the slush, you pick them along with wild cress for a salad to celebrate the end of winter. As the ground dries out and days get longer, dandelion greens go into green mayonnaise, they're blended and strained to add to tomato juice, they contribute vitamins and color to meatloaf and white beans, and they're frozen for a treat during snowy winter months. When the flowers bloom, you collect them for dandelion wine. As the growing season ends, you may dig up the roots to grate into salads or dry them to make dandelion "coffee."

No wonder you can now order dandelion seed from several nurseries.

Dandelion, Bean, and Tuna Salad

Raw dandelion greens are often too bitter to serve alone, and when dandelions are at their best, in early spring, few other fresh greens are available to combine with them in a mixed green salad. When they're added to bean, potato, rice, or macaroni salads, however, they provide bright color, texture, and vitamins. SERVES 4

1 cup dried white beans
1 large onion, chopped
Several sprigs parsley
3 tablespoons olive oil
2 tablespoons lemon juice

1 clove garlic, minced
1 big handful dandelion greens
7 ounces canned or freshly cooked
   tuna
Salt and pepper

Soak the beans in water for about 8 hours. Drain, place in a saucepan, and add onion and parsley. Cover with water, bring to a boil, and simmer just until beans are tender. The time will depend on what kind of beans you're using, but after about 2 hours start tasting to test doneness; you want them to be soft throughout but not mushy. When they're done, drain them, remove any parsley stems, and place beans in a mixing bowl. While they're still hot, toss them with the olive oil, lemon juice, and garlic. Cover bowl and refrigerate until beans are chilled.

Wash dandelion greens well, pat dry, and tear into small bits. Roughly flake tuna. Toss it with beans and dandelion greens, and season to taste.

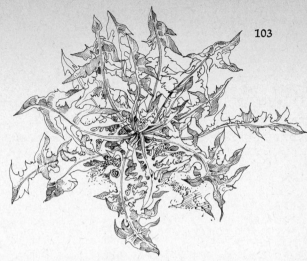

Dandelion Green Noodles

It started as a whimsical experiment when I'd weeded a pile of dandelions and wanted to do something with them. I substituted them for spinach in our usual recipe for green noodles, and the dandelions made the noodles both tastier and a brighter, darker green. This basic recipe also works with other greens: lamb's-quarters, kale, cress, Swiss chard, and, of course, spinach. Just adjust the amount of flour to the moisture of the greens until you have a stiff dough. Cook homemade noodles in boiling water for about 8 minutes, and serve them as you would the ones you buy. These are so flavorful that they're good simply tossed with butter and grated cheese. Makes about 1 pound

4 ounces (about 2 packed cups)   1 teaspoon salt
  finely chopped dandelion greens   1 to 1½ cups flour
2 eggs

Put dandelion greens and eggs in blender container, and blend until smooth. Place in a bowl, add salt, and start beating in flour, continuing until dough is very stiff. Turn dough out onto a floured surface and knead about 5 minutes. Roll dough with a floured rolling pin until it is a noodle-thin sheet. Let it stand to dry for about 1 hour, then cut it into strips of whatever width you like. It's best to use fresh noodles the day you make them, but you can refrigerate them for a few days between layers of paper towels.

Grandma Hertzler's Dandelion Greens

My grandmother cooked for ten children plus many guests and farmhands in southern Virginia. She's now past ninety and has more energy than I have. Could it be all those dandelion greens she ate? Her recipe for preparing them is so abbreviated that I tried to revise it for specific quantities, but I finally decided it works fine as it is:

"Cook dandelion greens until tender. Fry bacon. Brown flour (as for gravy). Add water, vinegar, sugar (or other sweetening), and chopped hard-boiled eggs. Stir into dandelions."

Grandma adds that if you don't fry things (she fries food for company only), you can "add dressing without bacon—suit to taste."

However she does it, it tastes good. Remember that the dandelion greens must be washed clean before cooking, and the bacon (or ham, if you like) should be chopped. When you've eaten dandelions this way a few times, you'll know how to vary ingredients to taste. You might start with about a gallon of greens, a couple of strips of bacon, a tablespoon or so of flour, and enough water and vinegar to make a thick sauce. Add sugar to taste, depending on how sweet or sour you like your greens, and one or two hard-boiled eggs.

DILL

Anethum graveolens 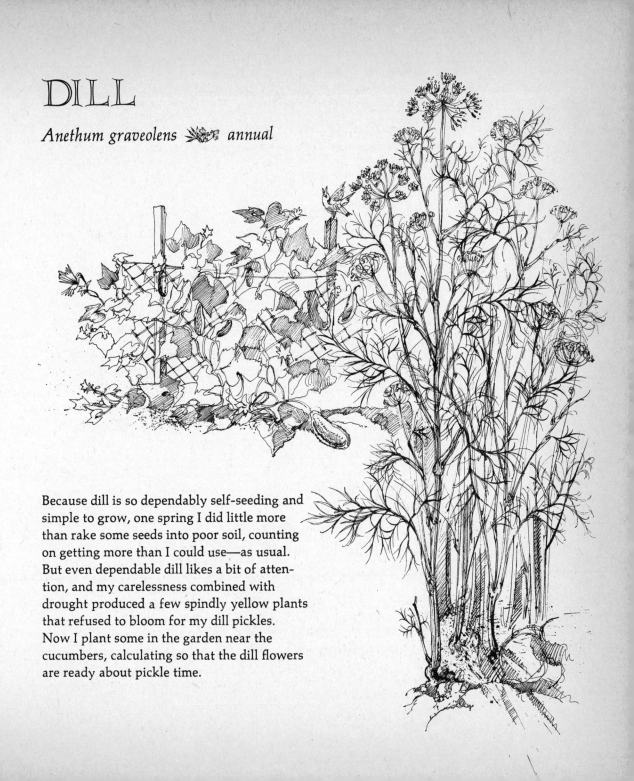 annual

Because dill is so dependably self-seeding and
simple to grow, one spring I did little more
than rake some seeds into poor soil, counting
on getting more than I could use—as usual.
But even dependable dill likes a bit of attention, and my carelessness combined with
drought produced a few spindly yellow plants
that refused to bloom for my dill pickles.
Now I plant some in the garden near the
cucumbers, calculating so that the dill flowers
are ready about pickle time.

Grow dill somewhere—summer doesn't smell or look or taste right without it. Plant it around cabbage or kale; dill is supposed to improve the growth of brassica vegetables. Plant it around tomatoes as a trap plant for the tomato worm. Or scatter it around in a bed of warm-colored flowers; its yellow-green blossoms blend well with calendulas, nasturtiums, and marigolds.

Since dill is supported by somewhat fragile stems, it's best to plant it in clumps rather than rows, so the stronger plants prevent the weaker ones from falling over. As soon as the ground is workable, dill should be sowed directly in rich, well-drained but moist soil—its slender taproot resents transplanting—and thinned to about 10 inches apart. It takes about two months to bloom, but meanwhile you can use thinnings and the feathery leaves to add to salads, blend into cream cheese, or flavor vegetables, especially your first tiny carrots and beets. The plants grow from 2 to 4 feet, depending on the variety. The brand most commonly sold has gray-green stems and large lacy seed heads.

Dill freezes well. Chop it into ice-cube trays and put them in the freezer. When they are solid, break out cubes and put them in plastic bags so you can reach in and get one to thaw whenever you need it. Or you can freeze smaller amounts of chopped dill or sprigs in small squares of plastic wrap.

If you like dried dill, tie branches of the plant together and hang them in an airy, shady place until you can crumble the leaves into jars. Dried dill is much heavier in flavor than fresh leaves, and even a small amount can dominate mild-flavored foods. Generally you figure you can substitute one-third to one-half the amount of dried herbs for fresh ones; with dried dill it's better to start with maybe one-sixth, then taste to see if you want more. For some special dishes—perfect fish and delicate sauces—dried dill doesn't taste quite right in any amount after you've gotten used to their flavor with fresh chopped dill.

Start dill seeds indoors at your own risk. I've never grown dill quite satisfactorily over winter; its tendency to scraggle increases, its fragrance weakens, and it is difficult to grow enough to get a generous crop. Give it plenty of sun or put it under plant lights, and feed occasionally with liquid fertilizer. I keep trying to keep dill going indoors, even though I like it best with garden-fresh vegetables (hard to come by in Vermont in the winter), because every once in a while a friend will rush fresh salmon from Boston or New York. Then fresh dill is essential in the green mayonnaise and cucumbers that, by immutable law, must accompany cold poached salmon.

Dill seeds have a strong fragrance, and many people use them more than the leaves. They are good in breads and pickles. If you haven't used all your dill flowers for pickles, watch the flower heads and note when the seeds are dry enough to drop. Hold a paper bag under the heads, and shake them to remove seeds. I rake the ground around the dill plants, shake the seeds onto the ground, and cover them lightly to ensure an early crop the next year. Then I go out and buy a jar of dill seeds when Wayne makes dilly bread. I combine dill flowers with other delicate herb flowers in an airy bouquet, and add dried dill flower heads to dried herb bouquets.

But fresh dill leaves are best. They're rich in minerals and aroma. Used generously, they make a good substitute for salt: try a hot dish of tiny new potatoes and freshly shelled peas with no additive but finely chopped dill. For decoration, chopped dill is as good as parsley. A fresh trout, quickly sautéed and sprinkled with dill, is exquisite. Dill is good in deviled or any other kind of eggs, and it makes rice special. The flavor is distinctive, but it is nevertheless a delicate herb that seems inappropriate for most beef dishes, although it is delicious with veal and liver. Whenever you add dill to cooked food, put it in only near the end of preparation to retain its fresh flavor—it's a wonderful thing to savor.

Crisp Dilled Cucumbers

Cucumbers with dill must accompany cold poached salmon. Of course, they're also delicious all by themselves too. A Japanese friend of mine chills the cucumbers three times, each time draining them and adding fresh water and salt. Hers are beautifully crisp, but I usually make this good shortcut. SERVES 6

4 medium cucumbers or equivalent amount of small ones	⅓ cup vinegar
	1 teaspoon soy sauce (optional)
1 tablespoon salt	1 tablespoon chopped dill leaves
⅓ cup sugar	

If cucumbers are waxed, peel them. Otherwise, just scrub them and score them with a fork. Cut them in very thin slices, using a potato peeler or the slicing blade on a grater. Add salt, cover with very cold water, and refrigerate for several hours. Meanwhile combine sugar and vinegar in a small saucepan, add soy sauce if you like, and heat, stirring, until sugar dissolves. Add dill and set aside to cool. Drain and rinse cold cucumbers, then squeeze them to remove as much liquid as possible. Place them in a glass bowl or jar, pour the vinegar mixture over, and chill.

They will keep for several days.

Potato and Cucumber Salad with Dill

Most people have a favorite potato-salad recipe, and you can use a variation of your own, adding chopped cucumbers and fresh dill. Depending on what's in the garden, you might add peas, chopped greens, or tomatoes. Little new potatoes and tiny cucumbers naturally make the best salad of all. SERVES 6

1 pound potatoes
3 tablespoons olive oil
1 tablespoon lemon juice or dill
  vinegar
1 tablespoon minced shallots
2 hard-boiled eggs, finely chopped

½ cup finely chopped celery
1 cup chopped cucumbers
2 tablespoons mayonnaise
2 tablespoons sour cream
4 tablespoons chopped dill leaves
Salt and white pepper to taste

Cook potatoes until tender. Cool them only until you can handle them without getting burned, then peel and slice or dice them into a bowl. Immediately stir in oil, lemon juice or vinegar, and shallots. Toss lightly, and refrigerate until chilled. When you are ready to serve, add remaining ingredients and stir until mixed.

Shrimp with Dill Sauce

Almost all seafood goes well with dill, and scallops can be substituted in this recipe. The dish tastes best if you use fresh shrimp, cooked in a court bouillon for about 7 minutes, then peeled, but frozen ones will do. This is good served with rice and new peas. SERVES 4

2 tablespoons butter
2 tablespoons finely chopped
*   shallots*
¼ cup dry white wine
1 cup heavy cream

1 pound cleaned cooked shrimp
1 generous tablespoon chopped dill
*   leaves*
Salt and white pepper

Heat the butter in a skillet and add the shallots. Cook gently for about 1 minute. Add the wine and cook over high heat, stirring, for 1 minute. Stir in the cream and continue to cook and stir for 2 minutes. Add the shrimp and almost all the dill, and season to taste. Heat gently until shrimp are hot through. Serve with remaining dill sprinkled on top.

Liver in Dilled Sour Cream Sauce

Dill and sour cream turn liver into a special dish. You might make this with the first dill thinnings and serve it with your first spring dandelion green noodles (see recipe). SERVES 6

2 pounds calf's liver, sliced ½ inch
*   thick*
¼ cup flour, seasoned with salt and
*   pepper*
4 ounces butter (preferably
*   clarified)*

2 tablespoons minced shallots
¼ cup chicken or beef stock
1 cup sour cream, at room
*   temperature*
1 tablespoon chopped dill leaves
Salt and pepper

Dredge liver in seasoned flour. Heat butter in a large skillet, and add an uncrowded layer of liver slices. Sauté until liver reaches the degree of doneness you like: about 3 minutes per side for rare meat, 6 minutes per side for well done. Remove liver to a hot platter and keep it warm while you sauté remaining slices. Remove them to platter, and add shallots to skillet. Cook gently for a few minutes, then stir in stock and heat it. Add several tablespoons of hot stock to the sour cream. Keeping heat low, gently stir sour cream into the skillet a little at a time so it won't separate. Stir in dill, season to taste, and return liver to skillet. Heat gently until everything is warm enough to serve.

Dilled Veal Blanquette

Beautiful with its julienned carrots and leeks, creamy, and expensive if you use better cuts of veal, but cheaper stew meat is fine if it's baked longer. I must credit Craig Claiborne with the idea of slivering the vegetables, which elevates a classic veal stew into an elegant presentation. You can serve it over rice or noodles. SERVES 4

2 pounds boned veal	2 leeks
4 tablespoons butter	2 carrots
1 large onion, finely chopped	½ cup heavy cream
2 tablespoons flour	3 tablespoons chopped dill leaves
1½ cups chicken broth	Salt and white pepper

Cut veal into cubes about 1 inch square. Heat 2 tablespoons of the butter in a large flameproof casserole, add veal and chopped onion, and cook, stirring, until onion is translucent. Stir in flour, add chicken broth, and bring to a boil, stirring. Cover and bake in a 350° oven for 1 hour, or until veal is quite tender. Depending on the age and cut of the veal, you may have to bake some more.

Meanwhile, trim leek tops and roots, split leeks lengthwise, and wash them thoroughly. Slice them into thin julienne strips. Peel carrots and julienne them as small as possible. Sauté leeks and carrots in the remaining butter just until they are crisply tender—barely limp when you pick up a carrot sliver with a fork.

After you have removed the veal from the oven, stir into it the cream, about half the leeks and carrots, and most of the dill. Season to taste, then bring it slowly to a boil. Place in a hot serving dish, and garnish with remaining leeks, carrots, and dill.

Mama's Hot Semi-Kosher Dill Pickles

When little brother Gordie brought Bert, his fiancée, along to pick me up at the train station so I could attend their wedding, Mama had packed a lunch for us. I wondered about the dill-garlic fragrance in the car, and I discovered its source when Bert opened the package of pickles. We munched away, getting acquainted and reacquainted and stopping frequently for liquid refreshment. As Mama says, these pickles are "not exactly mild."

You'll need about 25 little cucumbers (3 to 4 inches long), or you can use bigger ones and slice them lengthwise. They must be fresh and unwaxed.

MAKES 6 TO 8 QUARTS

5 to 6 pounds cucumbers

Scrub the cucumbers to remove any grit, and soak them in cold water for several hours or overnight. Drain them while you sterilize 6 to 8 wide-mouth quart jars. For each jar you'll need:

1 pinch powdered alum
2 cloves garlic or several wild garlic
*   bulbs*
1 small hot red pepper, fresh or dried

2 dill flower heads or several dill
*   sprigs*
1 grape leaf, fresh or canned

Pack cucumbers in jars, and add alum, garlic, and hot pepper. Push dill down among the cucumbers, and place the grape leaf on top.

Combine:

1 quart vinegar
1 cup salt (preferably coarse or kosher)

3 quarts water

Bring to a boil, stirring to dissolve salt, and pour over cucumbers. If you don't have enough liquid to cover all of them add a little more boiling water. Seal jars. You can start eating pickles after a few weeks.

Dill Pickled Green Beans

The following ingredients may look vague, and the directions complicated, but once you've tried the recipe you'll understand why: size of beans and jars vary, and these pickles should be packed for attractiveness as well as flavor. Seeing them lined up on the shelf usually makes my mouth water so much I have to break a jar open immediately. You can also use yellow snap beans, and yellow and green ones mixed are pretty enough to present as a gift. Everybody who likes dill pickles seems to love these crunchy beans.

Choose your jar size according to the beans you have available (or vice versa). Thin, small beans (the best) fit well in pint jars; larger ones can go in 12-ounce jars. Since the beans should be packed standing, wide-mouth jars are the easiest to fit them into.

For each jar you'll need:

Fresh green beans
Sugar
Water
Vinegar
Salt
1 hot red pepper, fresh or dried
2 cloves garlic or several wild garlic bulbs
1 dill flower with stem

Take a jar of the right height for general bean length and pack it full of upright beans. (A big fat handful is about right for a 12-ounce jar.) Pour water over beans to fill jar, then dump it into a measuring cup. Note the amount, empty the measuring cup, then do a little arithmetic to figure the amount of pickling liquid to replace the water. The proportions should be approximately 2 parts sugar to 2 parts water to 4 parts vinegar, so if you measured a cup of water poured off, put about ¼ cup sugar, ¼ cup water, and ½ cup vinegar in the measuring cup. You needn't be too fussy about exact measurements; if you like pickles more sweet or vinegary or mild, juggle the proportions to your taste.

Figure out how many jars and tops you'll need for the amount of beans you have, and prepare them according to directions on canning labels. Multiply the number of jars by the amount of pickling liquid you've calculated per jar.

Measure out sugar, water, and vinegar into a nonaluminum pot, and add about a teaspoon of salt per jar. Add the peppers and the stems from the dill flowers, and place over low heat to simmer while you prepare the beans.

Put a big pot of water on to boil. Wash beans and snap off ends. When water is boiling, drop beans in and cook at high boil only until they are barely tender (5 minutes for small beans, only 10 for large ones). As soon as they are crunchily cooked, put them in a colander under cold running water.

If you've prepared everything, your jars and lids should be sterilized and hot. Turn the simmering pickling liquid up to a gentle boil. Take a jar, hold it on its side, and pack beans into it as tightly as possible. When the jar is crammed full, add garlic and push the dill flower head in wherever you can. Spoon a red pepper out of the pickling liquid and press it down among the beans. Pour boiling liquid over beans up to ⅛ inch from top of jar, seal, and turn jar upside down for a few minutes. Proceed with remaining jars.

Canned beans take at least a month to develop full flavor. If any jars don't seal, or if you want to skip the canning process, store beans in refrigerator to eat after about three weeks.

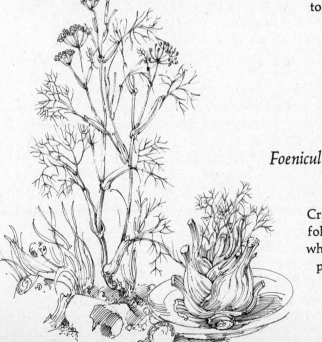

FENNEL

Foeniculum species 🌿 *perennial*

Crisp edible bulbs, ferny edible foliage, aromatic edible seeds— what more could one ask from a plant? Fennel is both herb and vegetable, savory both raw and cooked.

Florence fennel (*F. dulce*) is the finocchio prized by Italians for its globelike clustered white base. It grows a foot or more tall on stalks that resemble celery but has a thicker base that branches into foliage like coarse dill. All parts of fennel have a sweetish anise-celery flavor.

Wild or common fennel (*F. vulgare*) is grown largely for its foliage and seeds. It's a much bigger plant—up to 6 feet tall—with fleshy hollow stems and thin, very finely cut leaves that look and taste like those of Florence fennel. The yellow flower heads, flat and lacy-looking, bear seeds which are dried for flavoring. They often self-seed, and fennel has gone wild in many areas.

Both varieties of fennel are perennial, but Florence fennel is usually harvested as an annual. Both prefer rich soil. Florence fennel especially needs loose, moist ground for good root development. Some people plant it in trenches as they do asparagus. Unless you want to blanch the stems, trenching isn't necessary. I plant seeds in early spring in a row in the garden and thin seedlings to about 8 inches apart. Wild fennel can be similarly planted, but it's more appropriately grown in the perennial herb bed. It's pretty enough to use as a background in the flower bed.

Fennel can be grown indoors for foliage, although you won't get large bulbs or seeds. Give it average soil and keep it pruned. Use fragrant sprigs as you would dill.

Start harvesting fennel foliage as soon as you like, to flavor salads, vegetables, and fish. Use outer ribs of Florence fennel as you would celery. Harvest bulbs before the plants flower. Seeds should be collected when they're dry enough to rub loose. Hold a bag under the seed heads, break them off, and rub out the seeds as you blow away the chaff. Use fennel seeds in breads, sausage and other spicy meat mixtures, and cabbage dishes.

The simplest way to serve Florence fennel is also the best to my taste. Slice raw fennel ribs or roots, place them on a tray with other crunchy fresh vegetables—radishes, carrots, scallions—and serve with an herb dip. Thinly sliced fennel can be marinated in vinaigrette. Cooked fennel is also good: braise it, bake it au gratin, and make it into a cream soup. Slice fennel bulbs about 1 inch thick, boil them until just barely tender, and serve them with meat sauce or garlic butter or grated cheese.

In many cuisines fennel is associated with fish. Its flavor, while distinct, complements rather than dominates delicate seafoods. Serve fennel bulbs as a side dish with broiled fish steaks or add chopped leaves to seafood dishes. The following recipe bathes the fish inside and out with ferny fennel flavor.

Sea Bass Roasted with Fennel

Loup flambé au fenouil—European sea bass flamed with fennel—is a famous treat along the French coast. I've varied the recipe by using fresh instead of dried fennel, and I've adapted it to roasting, although the fish is also delicious grilled outdoors on a bed of damp fennel sprigs. If you have a fish-flaming basket or hinged outdoor broiler you're all set; we make do with splitting the fish and covering it with foil, so it steams over the fennel rather than broils. You can pour warm cognac over the fish and flame it before serving.

Vary this basic recipe further by trying other fish. Use dried fennel, thinly sliced fennel bulbs, or even fennel seeds if you can't get fresh leaves—the anise scent and flavor will bring out the best in the fish. SERVES 4

4-pound whole sea bass, cleaned
Salt and pepper
About 10 fennel sprigs

Olive oil
1 tablespoon chopped fennel leaves
½ cup melted butter

Dry fish inside and out, sprinkle it with salt and pepper, and stuff its cavity with fennel sprigs. Brush oil over outside of entire fish. Place on a large baking sheet and roast it in a preheated 400° oven. Check after 30 minutes to see if it is done: the cavity should no longer be reddish, a bit of juice should be collecting under the fish, and the flesh should feel springy when you press it. It may need a few more minutes of roasting, but it's better undercooked than overdone—you want flaky but juicy flesh. Place fish on a platter and sprinkle a little of the chopped fennel on it. Stir the rest into the butter and serve along with fish.

FIDDLEHEAD FERNS

🌿 *perennial*

Ferns have visually delighted human beings for a long time. Certain ferns have also provided nutritious food to many cultures. Today, people are discovering that fiddleheads, the little scrolls of new fern growth, are delicious food. Fiddleheads are even considered exotic, although they grow prolifically, free for the picking, all over the United States.

We were eager to try them when we moved to the country. Without wasting time on research, we hastened to fill bags with every furled fernlike sprout in sight. I'm no longer sure what varieties we dumped into water and boiled, but they tasted like soggy wood. Since then I've learned what to look for and what to do with fiddleheads.

Although few ferns have poisonous young shoots, many are unpalatable.

Two species are particularly good for eating. If you're able to identify them, you won't have to compost fiddleheads, as we did that first batch. If you can find an experienced person to take you fiddleheading the first time, it's the best way to learn what to pick, but here are some tips for finding them on your own.

The ostrich fern has a confusing scientific nomenclature. It is variously known as *Matteucia struthiopteris*, *Matteucia pennsylvanica*, *Onoclea struthiopteris*, and *Pteretis nodulosa*. It grows in rich, moist soil, often along streams in wooded areas. Identify it by its plumelike dark-brown spore stalks, which stand stiffly through winter. In early spring dense clumps of young fronds push through the leaf mold around the plumes.

Ostrich fern fiddleheads look like small green snails covered with onion-skin. They grow as quickly as asparagus, and, like asparagus, they keep producing when cut. Don't worry that you're destroying wild plants by harvesting them; the initial leaves are sterile. The ostrich fern is easy to transplant, since it has long runners that send up new growth. I've pulled up pieces of root to put in shady spots around the house, and they've invariably flourished. You can also dig up fern crowns (the mounded cluster at the base of the stalk) after frost, put them in boxes of dirt in the cellar, and harvest fiddleheads during winter.

Brake or bracken ferns (*Pteridium aquilinum*) grow in dry open woods or pastures. The mature fronds are tall and roughly triangular, separated into three branches. They become pale yellow or brown with a purplish tinge, and at this stage they are toxic. The fiddleheads are rusty-looking, with a felt coating. They appear in early spring among the tangled, mashed-down dead leaves of the previous year's bracken.

Gather both kinds of fiddleheads while they are still tightly curled, only a few inches high. Break them off as far down as the stem snaps easily. Use them as soon as possible or refrigerate them up to a few days, but don't let them dry out.

There are at least two schools of thought about cooking fiddleheads (and some fiddlehead lovers eat them raw). Some people maintain that fiddleheads should be steamed for only a few minutes; others think they taste best if they're boiled for half an hour, or boiled in several changes of water. I prefer steaming them until they taste tender but are still a bit crunchy.

First, hold the fiddleheads between your fingers or palms and rub off the woolly or papery membranes. Steep the fiddleheads for about an hour in white wine and herbs if you want to remove some of the woodsy odor. Place them in a large skillet, cover them with water, and bring to a boil. Cover skillet and simmer about 4 minutes. Quickly run cold water over them to retain their bright-green color, then drain. Taste one. If it's too crunchy, put them back to boil some more, continuing to sample until they taste right to you. Add some sugar or salt if you think they need flavoring. Or, as friend-scientist Frank Malinosky suggests, sauté lots of diced onion in butter, add parboiled fiddleheads, cover, and cook until tender.

Brake fiddleheads are mucilaginous, often compared to okra in texture and flavor (they also taste a bit like wild rice and almonds). You can serve them as a vegetable with lemon juice and butter or add them to stew. Ostrich fern fiddle-heads are dry and need lots of butter, cream, or sauce. One fiddlehead fancier compares their flavor to mild asparagus married to avocado. Cooked fiddleheads can be deep-fried as tempura or served cold in vinaigrette. You can chop them and add them to salad or soup. Freeze them by dropping them in boiling water, boiling 1 minute, plunging them in cold water, and placing in freezer containers.

When I go out in the greening spring to hunt for tiny fiddlehead "eggs," I feel as if I'm reliving childhood Easter-egg hunts, and the drawings should help you identify which "eggs" to find.

Fiddleheads with Brook Trout Meunière

My Most Memorable Breakfast: when Wayne disappeared with fly rod at dawn while I was still in bed, then presented me with a sizzling sautéed brook trout. If you gather fiddleheads and watercress on your way to the fishing hole, you'll have a meal whose perfection no beef Wellington can rival. SERVES 2

4 cups fiddlehead ferns
4 small (8- to 12-inch) trout
Milk

Flour
8 tablespoons butter
Chopped watercress or parsley

Rub the membranes off the fiddleheads, then drop them in boiling water. Boil for 5 minutes, place in a colander under running cold water, and drain.

Clean trout, dip them in milk, and roll lightly in flour. Sauté in 4 tablespoons of the butter until fish are browned on both sides. Remove to a hot platter. Add 2 tablespoons butter to skillet, and briefly sauté fiddleheads. Place them on platter surrounding fish.

Melt remaining butter in skillet, stir in watercress or parsley, and heat until bubbling. Pour over fiddleheads and fish, and serve immediately.

GARLIC

Allium sativum  *perennial*

I buy sugar and salt only a few times a year, but garlic seems to turn up on every other grocery list. Because the season is so short here in Vermont, I've found I can grow garlic only for its foliage. Big bulbs take at least seven warm months to mature.

"Polite" society has sometimes frowned on garlic as a vulgar aromatic because of the odor it can create on the breath, but all the great lusty cuisines use it to advantage. Nowadays, even in our somewhat rural community, I can find firm, fresh garlic heads in many stores, indicating good turnover in sales (old garlic heads feel spongy or dry when you press them). I hope it means lots of people are switching to the real thing instead of using dehydrated garlic in all its dreadful forms. Putting garlic salt on fine food is inexcusable when fresh garlic is so easily available to enhance dishes. And fresh garlic is considered to have medicinal benefits for good reasons: it's high in phosphorus, potassium, iron, and thiamine. An ounce of garlic contains more than a gram of protein—a lot for a vegetable—and, as you'll see, garlic can be used in enough quantity to make its protein content significant.

In addition to the common white-skinned garlic, which has small white flowers, you can plant the kind with red flowers and skins. Elephant garlic has lavender flowers and bulbs up to eight times larger than regular garlic; they are much milder. Artichoke garlic, a sport variety, resembles the vegetable it's named for. And there are many other varieties and hybrids. See the section on onions for a discussion of wild garlic.

If you are so fortunate as to have a long growing season, do grow your own garlic. It takes little space, and you may save quite a bit of money, since garlic is expensive in stores. Separate the cloves or sections on a garlic head (most onions can be grown from seeds, but garlic very rarely is), and place them, points up, about 6 inches apart in loose, preferably rich, and somewhat sandy soil. Barely cover the tops with soil. You can plant early in spring or in fall, or try both to see which works better in your area. Clip a few mild young shoots to use like chives if you like. Keep the plants well weeded, and put a mulch around them, but keep it several inches away from the stem so the plant can push out of the ground when it's ready. When the tops start to yellow and dry, mash them over gently with your foot to stop leaf growth. About three weeks later, when the tops are brown, take up the bulbs. Let them dry in the sun for a few days, then store them in a cool, dry place.

People do grow garlic indoors. It's not a very practical way to produce a crop, but it provides greens with a mild garlic flavor. Don't throw out garlic bulbs that are starting to get soft. Stick them in some soil, indoors or out, and they may sprout and grow.

Scientific studies indicate that the oil in garlic is noxious to many "lower"

organisms (for instance, mosquito larvae and cabbageworms) and at the same time nontoxic or even beneficial to such "higher" creatures as people, birds, and pets. One way to use garlic's strong smell to advantage is in a homemade insect-repellent spray (see page 12).

Garlic is also often used in companion planting (see page 11) for a similar purpose. When you use it in the garden to repel insects, be sure to start it well before you set out whatever vegetables you plant it alongside. The garlic must be a few inches high before it can start to be offensive to pests above the ground, and it can be planted as early as you can work the soil.

Garlic heads store well, but a good way to preserve garlic flavor in convenient form is to make garlic oil. Separate cloves on a head of garlic, and put them, peels and all, in the blender. Fill container about halfway up with oil. Blend until garlic is well chopped, then strain the oil into a jar and cap it tightly. Keep garlic oil in the refrigerator, and remove a few tablespoons at a time to stir-fry vegetables or add to marinades or salad dressings.

Make garlic vinegar by adding a few peeled cloves to a small bottle of cider or wine vinegar. Let it steep in a sunny window for a few weeks, then remove the garlic (mince it into salads) and use the vinegar in marinades or vinaigrette for hearty greens.

Ways to use just a bit of raw garlic are manifold. Your taste will tell you how far to go in your generosity when you add it to foods in its raw pungent state. For green salads, rub the bowl with a cut garlic clove, or squeeze the juice to add more generously to such strong salad greens as dandelion and chicory. Make seasoned croutons by rubbing half a garlic clove over toasted bread—good in soup, salad, or as is for munching. Make aïoli (see recipe below), a sauce heavily laden with raw garlic, when you're ready for a good dose.

Cooking with garlic is a complex subject that garlic lovers never tire of exploring and discussing. The only fact admitted is that heat changes the raunchy flavor and odor of raw garlic. How it's prepared before heating, how long it's cooked, and what it's combined with make the difference.

When garlic is squeezed through a press or finely minced and added to oil to sauté vegetables, it retains a potent flavor and odor. Slivered and pushed into incisions in a roast, it saturates the meat with pungency. Bruised or sliced and added to an herby mirepoix, it blends with the other vegetables. When whole peeled garlic cloves are cooked so as to retain their oil (as in the recipe for roast chicken on page 125), their flavor becomes chestnutlike—subtly sweet, slightly bitter, and buttery.

Italian cuisine uses garlic to particularly good effect with such complements as parsley, olive oil, and pasta, and garlic has become practically synonymous with Provençal cooking. Spaniards and Greeks and Chinese love it, and it's hard to find any cookbook in which garlic doesn't turn up somewhere. The following recipes use garlic generously, as a predominant flavoring, raw or cooked.

Guacamole

When our forest of potted avocado trees becomes too thick (or our waistlines become too thick), we forswear guacamole for a while. Rich guacamole tastes so good and avocado trees started from seeds are so pretty that abstinence is difficult, so I give away some of the avocado seedlings, and we're ready to start again.

Selecting the properly ripe avocados for guacamole can be difficult, since there are dozens of varieties. In general, pick ones that feel slightly soft and have dark stem ends. Or ask the manager of your grocery produce section or market to select dead-ripe avocados for you.

Save the pits to grow trees. I follow the traditional method: push toothpicks into them about three-quarters of the way up from the flat end, and use the toothpicks for support in a glass with water that covers the pit halfway. Put them in a dark place until they sprout, then pot them in soil. But many people have good results simply putting the pits directly into the soil, watering frequently, and waiting patiently until they sprout and a shoot pokes up through the earth.

Guacamole, a Mexican dip or salad, blends the soft blandness of avocados with the bite of garlic and other herbs. I'm giving the simplest method of making it to serve with tortillas or taco chips as an appetizer. Vary it as you like by adding ground hot peppers, diced tomatoes and cucumbers, or chopped onions. SERVES 4

2 large avocados
4 cloves garlic
Juice of 2 lemons

1 tablespoon chopped coriander leaves
½ cup mayonnaise

or Blender Quick

124

pound in a mortar if possible

lemon and olive oil

garlic cloves

Peel avocados and mash them with a fork until smooth. If you can't mash them to a purée, they're not ripe enough: put them in the blender or food processor with garlic and lemon juice, and blend until smooth. Otherwise, mince garlic into mashed avocados, add lemon juice and coriander leaves, and mix well. Place in a small serving bowl, and spread mayonnaise over top to keep guacamole from darkening.

Just before serving, stir mayonnaise into guacamole until well mixed.

Aïoli (Garlic Sauce)

Garlic aficionados can eat this fresh garlic sauce spread generously on thick bread. Those more timid love a little of it on top of hot vegetables, as a dip for crudités, or as an addition to soup. The following recipe is blender-quick. If you want to make it by hand, mash the garlic cloves in a mortar, pound in the egg yolks, then beat in oil gradually and add lemon juice. You can add dry mustard or a few drops of Tabasco if you like it even spicier. MAKES ABOUT 2 CUPS

5 large peeled cloves garlic
1 cup olive oil

3 egg yolks
3 tablespoons lemon juice

Place garlic cloves, ¼ cup of the oil, egg yolks, and lemon juice in blender container, and blend at low speed until garlic is smooth (or use food processor).

as a dip for crudities

Add remaining oil gradually to prevent splattering. When oil is all used, the sauce should be creamy. Serve it at room temperature, or refrigerate or freeze it for later use.

Roast Chicken Stuffed with Garlic

rosemary, thyme, tarragon & Lemmon

3 large Garlic Heads

You'd think that three whole heads of garlic in a dish would drive all but the most fervent garlic devotees out of the house. When garlic is cooked this way, however, its fragrance and flavor are surprisingly gentle, almost sweet, and its texture is like mealy lima beans. SERVES 4

3 large garlic heads (about 1½ cups unpeeled cloves garlic)
8 tablespoons (1 stick) butter, at room temperature

1 tablespoon finely chopped rosemary, thyme, or tarragon
1 tablespoon lemon juice
4-pound roasting chicken

place butter in a Mixing Bowl

How you prepare the garlic affects its eventual taste in this recipe. If you peel the cloves by hand, the chicken will be quite garlic-flavored. For a subtler flavor, drop the separated cloves into a big pot of boiling water, boil for 5 minutes, run cold water over garlic, then carefully peel off skins, trying not to bruise the cloves.

Place butter in a mixing bowl, add herbs and lemon juice, and beat with a spoon until fluffy. Reserve about half the herb butter, and mix the rest with the garlic cloves.

Stuff chicken with garlic mixture and truss it with string. Place it on its side in a roasting pan, and brush it with some of the reserved herb butter. Roast in a preheated 400° oven for 20 minutes. Turn it to the other side, baste again with butter, and roast 20 minutes. Turn chicken on its back, baste with remaining herb butter, and roast for 20 to 30 minutes or until cooked to your taste.

Place chicken on a platter, cut string, and remove garlic cloves from the cavity with a spoon. You can serve them as a separate vegetable for each diner to mash with butter or spread on bread, or you can make a sauce by puréeing them with some of the roasting-pan juices.

table spoons lemmon juice

Snails with Garlic Butter

People can form expensive attachments to snails. They begin to frequent restaurants where the air is heavy with garlic butter, and they sneak out and buy costly snails by the case. They lose their heads, as my husband did when he ordered a dozen snails as an appetizer, greedily consumed a delicious dinner, then ordered another dozen snails for dessert. Know your guests—the following recipe may serve only one person.

12 cooked snails (3-ounce can)
2 cloves garlic, minced
2 cloves shallots, minced
8 tablespoons (1 stick) butter, at
    room temperature

2 tablespoons finely chopped
    parsley
French or sourdough bread

Drain snails in a strainer. If you want a creamy snail butter, pound the garlic and shallots to a paste, using a mortar and pestle, then mix with butter. For crunchier texture, simply add minced garlic and shallots to butter and mix well. Stir in parsley. If you have snail shells, put a bit of garlic butter in each one, insert the snails, and use remaining butter to cover the shell entrance. Place in an ovenproof pan. Or put snails in a snail platter or shallow ovenproof bowl and spread snail butter on top. For best flavor, let stand several hours before cooking.

Place snails in 450° oven and heat until butter is bubbling, about 10 minutes. Serve immediately with crusty bread to dip in the butter that runs over into the platter.

ice box lettuce

GREENS

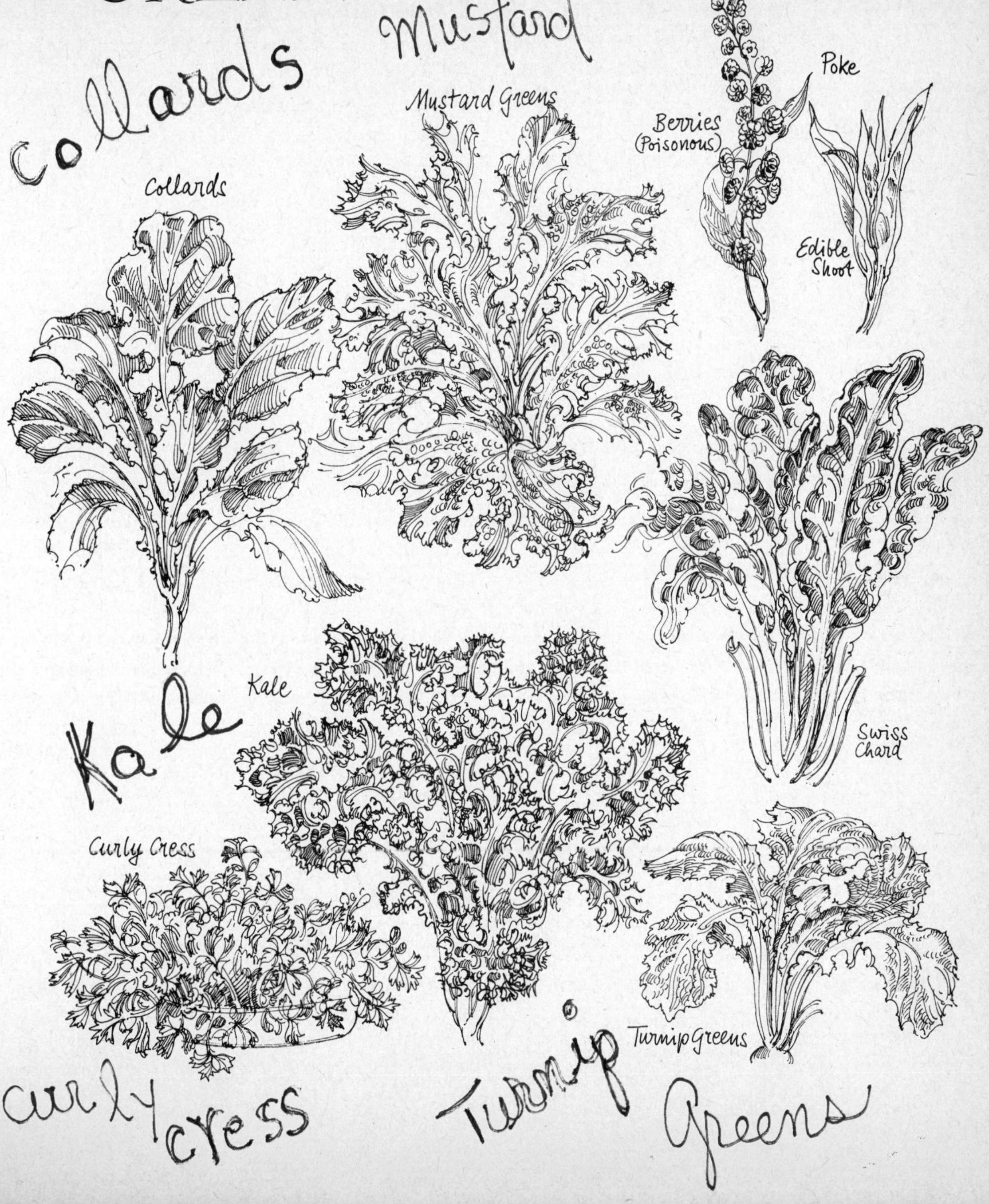

collards

Mustard

Collards

Mustard Greens

Poke

Berries
(Poisonous)

Edible
Shoot

Swiss
Chard

Kale

Kale

Curly Cress

Turnip Greens

curly cress

Turnip

Greens

Christmas Wreath

Every good southerner knows what greens are. You'll get different answers if you ask them, but few people born and reared in the South will tell you that greens are a Christmas wreath. Most will start naming collards, kale, turnip tops, mustard greens, poke—and go on to give you vague recipes, passed down through generations, on *the* best way to cook them.

My Mennonite family was by no means "traditional southern," but some of Daddy's parishioners were, and after church we'd often eat Sunday dinner with a family whose house was always fragrant with collards and Virginia ham hock simmering on the stove. We children would run for the player piano to insert a roll of yellowing paper with little holes. It was exotic: the heady smell of greens and the music we never heard at home, where pianos and ragtime were *verboten.*

Greens are more than the salty mass of collards whose pot liquor we mopped up with cornbread. The term covers lettuces, spinach, cresses, dandelions, violets, rocket (I discuss these elsewhere), and many other leafy vegetables —even cabbage. But the following greens are what I, a lapsed southerner, consider *greens.* Most are members of the mustard family. All are hardy and easy to grow, and all are so rich in vitamins and minerals that every gardener should grow at least a few. They take little space or effort.

COLLARDS. Cooked collard greens are for the stout-hearted. They taste cabbagy but much richer, more bitter, and slightly nutlike. A big dish of collard greens makes you feel like going out and chopping wood. That's probably because they're so full of vitamins. The standard variety, Georgia collards, grows more than 2 feet tall in rich, moist soil. The leaves are large and smooth. Plants mature in 40 days, but you can start picking small side leaves before then to add to salads. Collards survive both heat and cold, and seed can be sown whenever you can work the soil. You can start seedlings indoors to set out as you would cabbage. If you pick the outer, lower leaves of collards first, the plant will continue to produce leaves at the top until it flowers. My mother breaks off the top when the plant is about a foot tall to encourage tender side shoots. These can be cooked, stems and all, with a little butter until tender.

KALE. Closely related to collards, kale is even hardier—its flavor seems heightened by light frost. Curly kale, with blue-green tightly ruffled leaves, is attractive enough to plant in the flower bed; the dwarf variety, about a foot tall, makes a good border plant. Other varieties, including semicurled and smooth-leafed, grow as tall as 2 feet. Kale is one of the richest greens in vitamins A, B, and C. Grow and harvest it just as you do collards. Young leaves can be torn into salads, mature ones boiled or steamed, sprigs chopped for a garnish instead of parsley. It tastes much like collards, only milder. It's a good choice of greens to grow indoors. Seed the dwarf variety in rich soil and give it plenty of light.

TURNIP GREENS. Some of us, given a choice, would rather eat the tops of turnips than the roots. If you grow your own you can enjoy the treat of eating small new turnips and their tender tops together. The foliage of all the many varieties of turnips is edible, but if you value the nutritious greens more than the roots, look in seed catalogs for ones that specify especially good tops. Turnips prefer loose, good soil, but they'll grow almost anywhere. The leaves should be used for cooking before they're tough—up to 8 inches long—and are good cooked with stronger-flavored greens. They contain enormous amounts of calcium, phosphorus, potassium, and vitamins A and C. Bud clusters can be cooked like broccoli. Turnips grow best in cool weather—it's about the only thing they're fussy about—so plant them early in spring or for a fall crop in the North; they'll survive over winter where temperatures don't go below 20° F.

MUSTARD GREENS. The numerous plants called "mustard" are confusing. You can buy seeds for both broad-leafed and curly-leafed mustard greens, and you can forage for wild mustards of various species, so it's hard to describe the appearance of mustard greens. They can be fringed or lobed, mild as spinach or pungent as Dijon. The kind of mustard I've grown outdoors looks much like turnip greens, and it's as mild as French's mustard. The greens grow quickly; a month after seeding they're mature. They're good indoor plants because they sprout and grow readily, and you can pick leaves to add to salads, sandwiches, or boiled greens. Check seed catalogs for the many varieties of mustard greens, and check Gibbons, *Stalking the Wild Asparagus,* for identifying wild mustards and making your own prepared mustard from their seeds.

CURLY CRESS. Quite different in appearance from wild cress and watercress (discussed elsewhere), it has leaves that resemble parsley and taste as peppery as nasturtiums. It grows extraordinarily rapidly—it's ready to eat within two weeks after seeding—so make successive sowings for a continuing crop. Curly cress is a dark-green, small, attractive plant, fine for a border outdoors or for growing indoors. Use it raw in sandwiches (it's good with small mustard-green leaves), in salads, or chopped into cream cheese.

POKE GREENS. I've never found poke in Vermont, but I wish I could. I remember popping its purple berries (they're considered poisonous) into my mouth out behind the corn crib where no one could see. I made ink from them (it faded more quickly than the stains on my hands). Our family started eating the succulent young shoots and leaves only after we learned from southern neighbors that weedy poke and poke pickers were no more peculiar than we were.

Poke is a potentially dangerous plant, and it should never be eaten raw. I recommend it for food only because it's so good, plentiful in many areas, and free. Just take some precautions. First, identify pokeweed, which is easiest to do when it's mature. It grows up to 8 feet tall, with large oblong leaves on a green-purple stem. Its white flowers, borne in long clusters, turn into purple-black berries. Don't eat poke at this point, and never eat the roots, but mark the spot, since poke is a perennial. In the spring look for the fleshy, tender sprouts. Prepare them as you would mature asparagus: peel off any tough skins, but leave the cluster of leaves at the top. Boil shoots for about 10 minutes, drain off water, and boil in fresh water for about 20 more minutes. (Unfortunately, all this cooking is necessary to remove the bitter taste.) Cook young leaves at the top of the stalk the same way. Their flavor is delicate but distinctive.

SWISS CHARD. This is related to beets, and its leaves look and taste somewhat like a combination of beet greens and Savoy cabbage. It has no edible root like beets, but it is a versatile vegetable: its large leaves are crunchy and mild, delicious in salads; the thick, fleshy midribs are tender and can be cooked like asparagus or creamed like mashed potatoes; both leaves and stalks are wonderful sliced into stir-fried dishes or cooked with other greens. Swiss chard is available in varieties with light-green, dark-green, and crimson leaf stalks. All varieties are high in vitamins and easy to grow, even in hot weather. Most varieties also withstand cold and drought, so you can sow seeds in early spring. The plants take about 2 months to mature. Chard is an excellent vegetable for a small garden, since a few plants produce abundant growth and you can keep harvesting the outer leaves and stalks for months. If you cut off the whole plant, several inches above the ground, new leaves will spring up until severe frost.

It's hard to know where to stop when discussing greens. I could also mention beet greens, radish tops, Chinese cabbage, and numerous wild greens. They are too little appreciated in the North, even by southerners transplanted as

I was, although most greens that I've listed here grow well in cool climates. Is it because they're considered peasant food, unsophisticated? Is it because they've often been cooked into such an unaesthetic mass that they don't appear appetizing? Is it because they're a bit of trouble to clean and prepare? Maybe you've reacted to an overdose in childhood, as my husband has. Maybe, like some native Vermonters I've talked to, you've never heard of collards and kale.

But every cuisine uses some form of greens; they can be prepared in imaginative ways to accent their distinctive flavors. What my family called a "mess of greens" was a combination of whatever was plentiful at the moment—wild and cultivated, sharp-tasting and bland—cooked with some salty flavorful pork (ham hock, salt pork, bacon), often with potatoes to soak up the fat. It's delicious, but the excessive salt and long cooking make such boiled greens less healthful than many other ways of preparing them. Try simply steaming them until they are tender, then serve with butter and lemon juice. Chop them and stir-fry them with other vegetables. Use them to make green noodles (see page 103). Purée cooked greens with milk to make a cream soup. Combine them with forcemeat for pâtés, meatloaves, and stuffings. Blanch and freeze greens.

Green up your environment. Grow greens; sample and experiment with greens; forage for greens. You'll get the satisfaction of good flavor and good health.

HOREHOUND

Marrubium vulgare

perennial

Nostalgia is surely a respectable reason for growing an herb. I first grew horehound because I was curious about the source of that cough syrup I remembered from childhood. I also think horehound is an attractive plant in the herb bed or among indoor herbs because of its crinkly gray-green leaves. Add a plant to your herb collection and you can make your own horehound drops, tea, or syrup.

You can be pretty sure an herb is hardy and easy to grow if it tends to self-seed and go wild. Horehound is good at this, and every spring I find horehound seedlings in odd places. They thrive in poor soil, and my first plants probably died out because I was too generous with manure and water. I figured, since horehound looks much like a woolly mint and is a member of the mint family, that it would like similar conditions. The mint family is large, and it is best not to generalize about the relatives except that they all have square stems. Horehound does, and its leaves are "mintlike," oval and notched like spearmint. They have a woolly down, especially on the undersides, that gives the plant a white cast.

Start horehound from seeds, root divisions, or cuttings. You aren't likely to need many plants unless you want to use them as a hedge or go into the coughdrop business, so you might want to order a single plant from one of the several nurseries that now stock horehound. The plants grow up to 2 feet tall, and you should allow that much space between them. They quickly sprawl; clip them as soon as they get weedy-looking. In early summer small cream-colored flowers appear in whorls around the axils all along the whitish feltlike stems. This is a good time to trim the tops for use.

Now I must admit that I don't find the flavor of horehound appealing, nor can I adequately describe it. The raw leaves taste unpleasantly bitter to me and are not very aromatic on my plants, and I have to add a great deal of honey to horehound tea to make it palatable. But some people like horehound immensely and believe that it has medicinal properties (no doubt they're right—after all, it got me through childhood croup). They describe its flavor as bitter-sweet and musky rather than acrid. If you like the taste of horehound candy, test fresh horehound for yourself.

To make tea, cough syrup, or candy, first prepare an infusion: strip off horehound leaves and chop them into a measuring cup. Measure twice as much water, bring it to a boil, and drop in the horehound. Boil for 5 minutes, let cool, strain into a jar, and refrigerate until ready to use.

For tea, add twice as much boiling water as horehound infusion and sweeten to taste. For syrup, add twice as much honey as infusion and a little lemon juice to taste. To make candy, add twice as much sugar and about ⅛ teaspoon cream of tartar per cup of infusion. Stir to dissolve, and cook over low heat until a drop forms a hard ball in cold water (290° F. on a candy thermometer). Pour into a buttered plate and break apart when cool.

Dried horehound leaves are better used for tea than for candy. The ones I've tasted have lost flavor, unlike most other herbs, which gain in potency when dried. To dry horehound, hang branches in a shaded place until you can easily crumble the leaves off.

Horehound makes a fine houseplant if you have room for nonessential herbs. It's easy to care for, isn't bothered by pests, and provides a nice contrast to greener plants. Pot it in sandy soil, trim it back to keep the leaves small and the plant tidy, and water sparingly. It's a good conversation starter if nothing else: "Remember that stuff you swallowed at night when you had a cough? Well, here's what it came from."

HORSERADISH

Armoracia rusticana
perennial

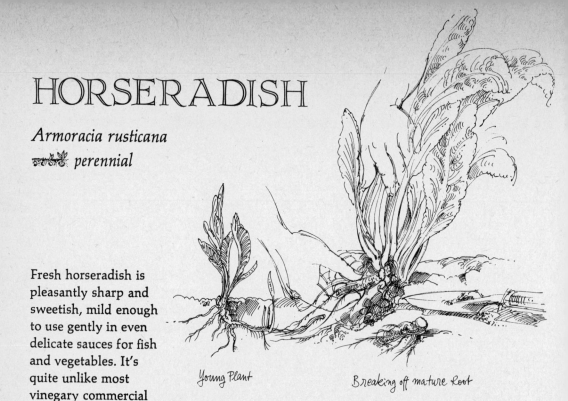

Young Plant

Breaking off mature Root

Fresh horseradish is pleasantly sharp and sweetish, mild enough to use gently in even delicate sauces for fish and vegetables. It's quite unlike most vinegary commercial canned horseradish. It contains large quantities of vitamins A and C—amazing, since it's a white root—and is rich in minerals, especially calcium and potassium. And it's an excellent salt substitute.

Horseradish is very hardy and easy to grow. The only problem you'll have is preventing it from spreading where it shouldn't, so consider carefully before you plant it. I mistakenly put mine at the edge of my perennial herb bed. Its huge leaves shade herbs that need the sun, its roots have gone far and wide, and I'm afraid it's there to stay. It's a large and coarse but not unattractive herb, so you might put it in a separate bed with flowers around it (horseradish flowers are inconspicuous) or plant it at one end of your asparagus bed.

Many nurseries now sell horseradish roots, or you can pull up a piece of root from a friend's plant in early spring. Dig a hole about a foot deep in loose, rich soil, stick the root in, water it, and cover it with dirt. It will soon send up a rosette of leaves that become broad and wavy, more than a foot long. The leaves are good to eat when they're small. They have a tang much like watercress and add dash to a salad. You can also boil them, preferably with milder greens to temper their strong flavor.

Various pests bother horseradish leaves, including the familiar ones that attack the cabbage family, but they don't hurt the roots, so their only real nuisance is the unsightliness of the plants. Cabbageworms (see page 14) can riddle horseradish leaves. Sometimes I pick them off, but usually I let them eat away, grateful that they're leaving the broccoli and greens alone.

You can dig horseradish roots anytime that the ground isn't frozen. I just feel around in the soil around the plant and break off a piece of root whenever I need it. Some people harvest the whole crop before the ground freezes by pulling up the plant, breaking up the larger cylindrical root sections, and packing them in wet sand in a cool place. The roots can then be used as needed during winter, and any left over can be replanted in spring.

Horseradish has been widely naturalized in this country and can often be found growing along ditches. The roots of wild plants tend to be stringier and more bitter than those grown in cultivated soil, but they're basically the same, so if you have limited gardening space, go foraging. (Or, if fresh horseradish is unavailable but you have some big old radishes in the garden that are too hot to eat straight, grate them for a good horseradish substitute.)

Horseradish roots must be finely grated to release their flavor. Hand grating is tedious—the roots are very hard—and the shredding disk on a food processor is ideal for preparing horseradish. Or you can use a blender: dice the roots and put them in the blender container with enough water to barely cover them. Blend until finely grated, then place horseradish in a sieve and press it to extract all the liquid possible. A pound of roots will yield about 2 cups of grated horseradish. You can add it to taste to mayonnaise or cream cheese or sauces. If horseradish seems too strong for you, tame it by blending in some raw turnip. Or add color by throwing in diced beets or a handful of parsley.

Whenever possible, I prefer to grind the horseradish along with whatever liquid I'm using it in. Lemon juice is especially good for accenting horseradish flavor. Vinegar is fine if you want to make up a big batch of horseradish sauce; it will keep indefinitely in the refrigerator. Blend catsup with horseradish to make cocktail sauce. For a potent pick-me-up, blend horseradish and herbs with tomato juice (use it as a base for an unusual Bloody Mary). Horseradish loses flavor when it is cooked, but if you blend it into soft butter you can add it to hot vegetables just before serving.

Obviously horseradish is not an all-purpose herb to be lavishly dumped into everything. Used fresh and with care, however, it can complement more foods than most people suspect. Serve it with boiled meats and pot roast. Mixed with mustard, it is good with cold cuts or on meat sandwiches.
Experiment with substituting a little freshly grated horse-
radish for salt in recipes—you may be pleasantly surprised,
and you'll certainly be better nourished.

LAMB'S-QUARTERS

Chenopodium album
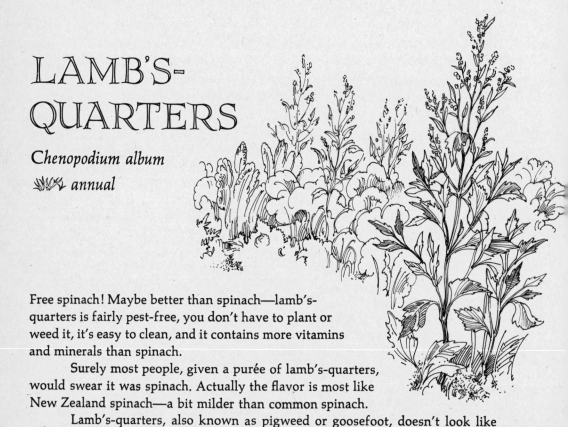 *annual*

Free spinach! Maybe better than spinach—lamb's-
quarters is fairly pest-free, you don't have to plant or
weed it, it's easy to clean, and it contains more vitamins
and minerals than spinach.

Surely most people, given a purée of lamb's-quarters,
would swear it was spinach. Actually the flavor is most like
New Zealand spinach—a bit milder than common spinach.

Lamb's-quarters, also known as pigweed or goosefoot, doesn't look like spinach, however. The variety encountered in most people's gardens has a silvery gray sheen to its green leaves. The undersides of the leaves are dusted with a mealy substance that comes off on your fingers when you rub it. Young lamb's-quarters leaves are oval or somewhat wedge-shaped, with wavy teeth. Leaves near the seed head are more lance-shaped. The small greenish flowers grow on many little spikes. Lamb's-quarters plants can become enormous in rich soil—I've seen them top the corn in my garden.

Other varieties of *Chenopodium* resemble lamb's-quarters and are also edible. The one known as Good King Henry (*C. bonus henricus*) is perennial. It is usually smaller than common lamb's-quarters and has a fleshier stem that can be eaten like asparagus.

The best time to eat lamb's-quarters is before the plants are a foot tall, when the leaves are small and tender. The larger plants are quite edible when cooked, but there's usually no need to bother with them, since young plants continue to shoot up all summer. Further, mature plants are particularly attacked by aphids—you'll often see the tips of the stalks covered with ants, which follow aphids around—so let big plants go to seed.

Use little leaves of lamb's-quarters for a spinach flavor in salads. Many other wild things need to be boiled to death to remove the bitter taste. Not so lamb's-quarters, although it does require more cooking than spinach. You can cook the small plants, stem and all, by steaming or boiling them 15 to 20 minutes. When cooked, they turn a bright dark green. You can substitute lamb's-quarters in any recipe that calls for spinach, but remember to use equal amounts by weight when raw or by cups when cooked. A big bag of lamb's-quarters looks as if it would feed a crowd; however, its leaves are flat and thin, and it cooks down to a small, if dense, amount.

If you want to get your calcium, eat lamb's-quarters—it has more than twice as much calcium as an equal weight of milk. Lamb's-quarters pulls a lot of other good minerals and vitamins out of the soil. A 3½-ounce serving has 4.2 grams of protein (high for a vegetable), 72 milligrams of phosphorus, 11,600 International Units of vitamin A, and 80 milligrams of vitamin C. It loses some of these nutrients when cooked, but it's still more nutritious than other greens on just about every count.

One reason lamb's-quarters is so prolific is that each plant bears thousands of tiny seeds. In the fall you may find a grayish carpet of them around the dead plant. Small birds love these seeds, and you can collect them for the bird feeder by holding a bag under the dried seed head and rubbing the seeds off. Some people grind the seeds to make flour, but that's a lot of work. After a summer of enjoying the plant's leaves, I'm ready to donate the fruit to the winter birds.

Lamb's-quarters freezes well, and weeding becomes worthwhile when you know you're going to get tasty, nutritious winter food in the process. Drop the leaves in a bag as you go along the rows. Rinse them, parboil them for a few minutes, and pack them in freezer containers. Or preserve lamb's-quarters in butter: cook the leaves for about 10 minutes, squeeze them in a dishtowel to remove as much water as possible, and place them in your blender container. Add enough melted butter to cover, and blend until smooth. Serve over poached eggs, baked potatoes, or pasta.

Eggs Baked on a Bed of Lamb's-quarters

An elegant brunch reward for weeding the garden early in the morning. Take a bag along, and pop all the lamb's-quarters tops into it. You can use even the leaves from full-grown plants for this, since they're going to be cooked and puréed. When you get back to the house, dump the lamb's-quarters into the sink, run water over them, then strip the leaves off into a 1-quart container. SERVES 4

1 tightly packed quart lamb's-quarters leaves (about 4 ounces by weight)
1 tightly packed cup grated Gruyère cheese

Soft butter
8 eggs, at room temperature

Bring about 1 cup of water to a boil in a 2-quart pot. Add lamb's-quarters, cover, and boil gently for about 15 minutes. Drain in colander until leaves are cool enough to squeeze with your hands to extract as much liquid as possible. Run the leaves through a food mill, using the coarsest blade, chop them fine, or shred them in a food processor. Reserve a small handful of the cheese and add the rest to the lamb's-quarters along with about a tablespoon of butter.

Generously butter eight small ramekins or ovenproof bowls and divide the lamb's-quarters mixture among them, spreading it in an even layer. Break an egg on top of each. Sprinkle with remaining cheese. Bake in a preheated 350° oven for 15 to 20 minutes, until eggs are set to the degree of doneness you like and cheese is lightly browned.

LAVENDER

Lavandula officinalis
perennial

The word "lavender" suggests many lovely things, but food is not usually among them. However, even if you think you have room for culinary herbs only, consider a little lavender somewhere, a few plants tucked in among perennial flowers, beside the steps, or in a corner—just about anywhere, since lavender will tolerate almost any conditions when it gets established. Once you've sniffed that fragrance on a hot day and walked amid the purplish spikes of flowers, you may be ready to tear down your barns and plant those stately English-style gardens so enhanced by expanses of lavender bushes.

The kind of lavender you'll get from most catalogs is English lavender, which grows 1 to 3 feet high and has slender gray-green leaves about 2 inches long. You can get more compact dwarf varieties, and there are tender lavenders with varying leaf shapes and shades of flowers.

Lavender seeds are slow to sprout (up to 3 weeks), and you should sow them as soon as you can work the ground. Lavender germinates best in cold soil. You can also plant it in the fall; the seedlings will come up early in the spring. I plant the seeds fairly thickly and save only the strongest plants, moving extras to any spot I can find to stick them in. Add some lime to your soil if it is acid, since lavender prefers alkalinity, though it's not fussy. Prune back scraggly bushes after they flower. It takes a couple of years for the plants to produce a lot of flowers if they're grown from seed; if you're in a hurry, some nurseries sell plants.

You can take cuttings from lavender plants, rooting 6-inch shoots in wet sand in the spring. Old plants can be divided: lift the whole clump in the spring, carefully separate sections of root, and replant them immediately.

In warm climates lavender is almost evergreen. My lavender froze the first year. Now I grow it against the foundation on the sunny south side of the house where it's too dry for most other herbs. If you're afraid plants won't winter over (they should be well covered with mulch if the temperature goes below zero in your area), you can bring some inside after the first few frosts. English lavenders lose their fragrance indoors; winter is their dormant period. Look for Mediterranean varieties that thrive on year-round warmth. Give them plenty of sun, a bit of lime in the potting soil, adequate air space, and not too much water.

Watch lavender plants for signs of infestation by lavender fungus and by various caterpillars. Remove damaged branches and burn them, and give the plants hard blasts of water to knock off worms.

Lavender makes beautiful bouquets, combining well with other purple flowers. To dry it, cut branches when the flowers are starting to open. Bunch them loosely and hang them upside down in an airy, shady place. You can crush the fragrant leaves to perfume your bath water or linen closet, to add to potpourris, to make tea, or to burn as incense.

LEEKS

Allium porrum

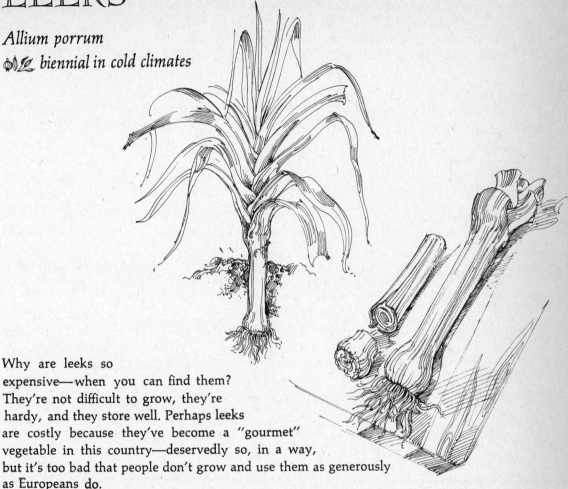

🌼🌿 *biennial in cold climates*

Why are leeks so
expensive—when you can find them?
They're not difficult to grow, they're
hardy, and they store well. Perhaps leeks
are costly because they've become a "gourmet"
vegetable in this country—deservedly so, in a way,
but it's too bad that people don't grow and use them as generously
as Europeans do.

Leeks rank with shallots as the aristocrats of the onion family, but leeks, combining mild onion flavor with green foliage, are more versatile. They can be used as flavoring, as a basic ingredient in soup, or as a dish in themselves. Small leeks are good raw, and even if leeks are cooked to a pulp in cock-a-leekie their flavor remains.

142

Although leeks resemble blown-up scallions, their leaves are quite different, flat and gently bent like wide ribbon. To ensure tender bottoms and flavorful tops, you must grow leeks in the environment they prefer.

The ideal method is to prepare a bed and trenches as you do for asparagus, since leeks like the same rich, loose, limy soil. At least prepare a bed for them ahead of time, preferably in the fall. Make trenches 6 inches deep in a well-drained, sunny spot. Add lime, compost, manure, and other organic matter to the trench. Cover it with a hay mulch.

You can start leeks from seeds indoors, sow seeds in the ground outdoors, or order seedlings from a nursery. Leeks need six months to mature from seeds, so if you have a short growing season you'll have to figure on a biennial crop, as I do, or plan to harvest them at a young age. Pull the mulch back from the trench, set in leek seedlings about 6 inches apart, and keep piling soil in around the growing seedlings until the trench is level. Mulch the plants heavily to smother weeds, let them grow through the summer, and cover them with hay for the winter. The following summer you can start harvesting them.

You'll have to adjust leek growing to conditions in your area, trying one thing and another until you find what works best. You can gently pull leek plants up with a ball of soil, put them in a box, and keep them over winter in your root cellar or another cool place. Use them as needed, and replant leftovers in spring. You can keep leeks going in a cold frame. Southerners can grow leeks year round if they give the plants lots of moisture. But leeks are definitely not an indoor plant.

Pests on leeks are the same ones that attack onions, but they're rarely a problem. To discourage onion thrips, scatter mothballs along the rows.

The bulb and lower leaf portions of leeks are high in potassium, thiamine, calcium, and phosphorus, but low in vitamins A and C. Upper green leaves have more of these vitamins, so include them whenever possible, especially in puréed soups.

Always wash leeks very carefully. Pockets of dirt invariably lurk between their leaves. If a recipe calls for whole leeks, gently open out the green leaves and run water through them in a fast stream. Otherwise, split leeks lengthwise and run water through each layer of leaves.

Braise leeks like celery or steam small ones in bundles as you would asparagus for a delicate hot vegetable. Chill cooked leeks and serve them with vinaigrette for a salad. Slice small raw ones into tossed salad. Add leeks generously to stocks and soups. Their subtle onion flavor is perfect with cream, as in the classic vichyssoise.

Green Vichyssoise

It's plain old potato soup—except. The leeks make a big difference in flavor, and your choice of greens and herbs makes it even more special. Vichyssoise is supposed to be best served icy cold. I think it's just as good at room temperature. SERVES 4

2 cups thinly sliced leeks
4 tablespoons butter
4 medium potatoes
4 cups chicken broth
1 cup chopped greens (spinach,
    lamb's-quarters, kale, sorrel,
    watercress, violet greens) or ½
    cup chopped herbs (parsley,
    chives, celery tops, tarragon)
1 cup heavy cream
Salt and pepper

Sauté leeks in butter in a 3-quart saucepan, stirring until they are limp. Peel potatoes, dice them fine, and add to pan. Pour in chicken broth, and cook until potatoes are tender. Place greens or herbs in blender container or food processor, pour leek-and-potato mixture over them, and blend just until potatoes are fairly smooth—you want to retain a bit of texture. Stir in cream, season to taste, and chill if you like before serving.

LEMON BALM

Melissa officinalis

perennial

The fragrance and flavor of
lemon balm are as lovely as
its soothing name. To make
a tea that reminds you of
lemon peel with a minty,
sweet accent, grow lemon
balm. Grow it also because
it smells good and tastes
good in many dishes.

Balm—or sweet balm, as it's often called—grows well in any fairly moist
soil, and it thrives in partial shade or full sun with rich soil. Like all mints, to
whose family it belongs, it's hardy, it spreads, and it can become invasive. The
leaves are mintlike: shield-shaped, crinkled, and serrated. Plants grow to 2 feet
or more outdoors.

My lemon balm germinated well, if slowly, from seeds sown in spring.
Seeds can be planted in late fall for early spring growth. Plants can also be
propagated by root divisions, cuttings, or layering. Lemon balm bears fragrant,
yellowish-white flowers. They are inconspicuous, but bees search them out, and
you can use them just as you do the leaves. If your winter temperatures go
below −20° F., cover lemon balm plants with a protective mulch.

Indoors, aphids and whiteflies may be a nuisance, especially if you
haven't cleaned plants well before bringing them in from outdoors. Wash foliage
well with soapy water if pests appear. Lemon balm is a good houseplant if it's
kept trimmed to a foot or less. Give it good light and plenty of moisture.

For a nightcap by the fireplace, place a few lemon balm leaves in a cup
and pour boiling water over them. Stir in honey and lemon juice to taste. This
is a variation on Grandma's lemon-and-honey cough syrup—truly a balm.

The simplest way to dry lemon balm is to cut branches just as they start to flower and hang them for about a week in an airy, shady place. Crumble the leaves into airtight jars, and use them for tea by steeping them in boiling water.

I like the citrus flavor of lemon balm in iced tea with other mints. Lemon and orange slices or juice can be added to the tea to make punch. Steep lemon balm leaves in Chablis, strain, and serve chilled with a balm sprig on top. Chopped leaves are good in fruit salads. Use lemon balm infusion for part of the liquid in jellies. Freeze whole leaves in water to make ice cakes for tea or punch.

Add a little chopped lemon balm to any dish that calls for lemon juice. The lemon balm adds subtly to the flavor, and the green leaves add immensely to the color of avgolemono, lemon butter, and lemon meringue pie.

Daffodil Avgolemono (Greek Lemon Soup)

Greek lemon soups and sauces are justly famous. When you add lemony green lemon balm leaves, the soup is the essence of spring. Present it with a centerpiece of daffodils. SERVES 4

4 cups chicken stock
¼ cup long-grain rice
3 eggs
3 tablespoons lemon juice

Salt and white pepper
2 tablespoons finely chopped
 lemon balm leaves

Bring the stock to a boil, add rice, cover, and simmer until rice is soft, 15 to 20 minutes. Meanwhile, beat the eggs until frothy, then slowly beat in lemon juice.

Just before serving, heat stock to a simmer. Add about a cup of stock very slowly to the egg mixture, beating constantly until well mixed. Slowly stir this mixture into the simmering stock and keep stirring while it simmers for a few minutes and thickens to a thin custard. Don't let it boil—it will curdle.

Taste soup, add salt and pepper if you think it needs seasoning, and stir in lemon balm. Serve immediately.

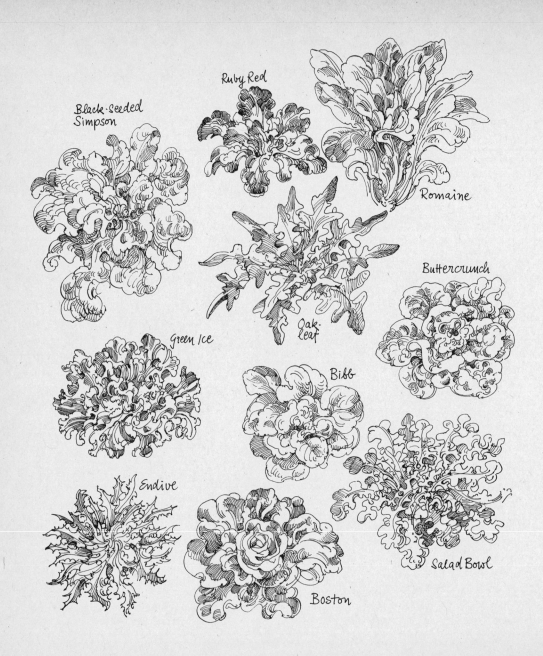

Black-seeded Simpson

Ruby Red

Romaine

Oak-leaf

Buttercrunch

Green Ice

Bibb

Endive

Boston

Salad Bowl

LETTUCES

Lactuca and other species 🥬 *annual*

In midwinter I miss many vegetables from the summer garden, but what I long for most is a salad bowl heaped with freshly picked lettuces and greens, dressed with herby vinaigrette. A good salad is not mere filler for a meal—it can be the pièce de résistance.

Grocery stores and markets carry a greater variety of lettuces than they once did, but their staple is predictable: pale, watery iceberg. If you share my feeling that most meals are incomplete without green salad, grow your own, outdoors or indoors, wherever you can and in as great a variety as possible.

There are so many kinds of lettuce, all of them good, that I'll list only my favorites:

🌿 *Green Ice* is the brand name of a loose-leaf lettuce that I consider the all-round best since it came on the market a few years ago. The curly leaves are glossy dark green, crisp but tender, and more flavorful than most loose-leaf lettuces. I sow it in early spring, and am still picking leaves off the same plants when frost comes, because it's slow to bolt and defies the heat that causes other lettuces to go to seed. It doesn't collapse under salad dressing. A salad of Green Ice, even if you add cucumbers and tomatoes, is still buoyant.

🌿 *Romaine (cos)* is special for its crunchiness and piquant flavor in all salads, especially Caesar salad (see recipe). It grows in an elongated V-shaped head up to a foot tall in rich soil. The outer leaves are darker green than the heart. It likes cool weather and goes to seed quickly in the heat, so plant as early as you can work the ground. Thin plants to at least 6 inches apart; crowded plants remain small and go to seed rapidly. Romaine is one of the best buys in lettuce in grocery stores in the winter, since it's greenly crisp and full of vitamins.

🌿 *Boston and Bibb* lettuces resemble small, gently opened cabbage heads with glossy dark-green leaves on the outside and inner ones blanched butter yellow. That may explain their name "butterhead," but the texture and flavor are also butterlike: smooth, soft, mild, sweet. Many varieties are available, including a miniature excellent to grow indoors. I use Boston and Bibb in all stages of growth, from thinnings to outer leaves to entire mature heads, which are beautiful served whole in a glass bowl, then halved or quartered at the table and dressed with a creamy herb mayonnaise. Butterhead lettuces make a fine border plant in the flower bed. They are the best greens to accompany salade Niçoise (see recipe).

Endive, known as "scratchy lettuce" to some little friends of mine, is a confusing name. It may refer to Belgian endive (witloof chicory), the plant grown for its pale, tight head of blanched small leaves. The scratchy-leafed plant I'm referring to is also called "chicory," which happens to be the name of the blue-flowered wild plant whose roots are used for coffee. Without going into scientific names, I'll say curly garden endive is a lettucelike plant (although not related to lettuce) with twisted, finely jagged, long, tapered leaves whose undersides may be slightly prickly. The texture of the outer leaves is coarse, the flavor mildly bitter. The inner leaves are soft and pale green, especially if you tie up the plant to blanch the heart. My garden plants are softer in texture than the endive I buy in the grocery store in winter, and when endive is grown indoors it's even more tender. Curly endive is a good source of vitamins and flavor. Salads of endive leaves only, with a mustardy dressing to complement their bite, can be delicious, but they're best, I think, mixed with milder lettuces. Endive greens can also be cooked until tender and served with butter and grated cheese.

Another type of endive is known as escarole or Batavian broad-leafed lettuce. It has broad, fleshy leaves curled along the edges and is milder in flavor than curly endive but still has a nice bitiness, especially in the outer leaves. The inner ones are soft, pale, and very mild. It's a good lettuce to buy in the grocery store because it combines quite different textures and flavors all in one head.

Ruby (red-leaf) lettuce tastes much milder than its intensely colored leaves would suggest. I plant it every year for the contrast it gives to the garden and to salads. A loose-leaf lettuce, it is slightly frilled, its leaves green at the base and shading into a rusty dark ruby color. They are somewhat fragile and tend to wilt, so unless they go into a salad fresh from the garden they should be crisped in a plastic bag in the refrigerator after a quick rinse under running water. Ruby is a good lettuce to grow indoors for variety in salads, and it makes a colorful border plant in the flower bed outdoors.

Black-seeded Simpson, an old-favorite loose-leaf lettuce, has a flavor that can be described as delicate or bland, depending on what you like. Sometimes etiolated greens are delicious in the right combination with other salad vegetables. Try the first Simpson lettuce thinnings with tiny sliced mushrooms and a light dressing, or add some of the pale leaves to a salad of mixed greens. Simpson grows quickly from seeds and is fine to grow indoors or in the cold frame.

"Head" lettuce is something else. Many people sow iceberg lettuce seeds or grow plants from the greenhouse because they're used to eating that sort of lettuce from the grocery store and think it's easier to make a big salad from one big tight head of lettuce. It is, indubitably, when you get iceberg shipped from areas where it's grown for weight and shelf life, not vitamins. When you grow it at home there are both benefits and problems. Home-grown iceberg lettuce is usually greener and thus contains more vitamins than the whitish commercial lettuce balls, and it tastes better. But it takes a long time for heads to form—up to 90 days—and meanwhile, if you want big heads, you can't pick off leaves generously as you can with loose-leaf lettuce. Once you've chopped off the head, that's it, end of crop. Iceberg lettuce is fussy about heat and lack of moisture. It needs twice as much space as loose-leaf lettuce if it is to grow properly—8 inches between plants rather than the 4 inches for loose-leaf. If you really want to grow it, harvest it when it's a small loose head; it's really good, like loose-leaf lettuce, at that stage.

Corn salad (*mâche or lamb's lettuce*) can be eaten in salad or cooked like spinach, which it resembles. It has a rosette of smooth dark-green leaves. Its flavor is mild, so use it alone in salad or mixed with stronger greens, such as dandelions and watercress. Corn salad grows best in cool weather; I've picked it long after heavy frost.

This list is subject to change, since each year I like to try something new in addition to the basics, and I urge you to do the same. You don't have to plant the whole package of lettuce seeds. Make short rows of many different kinds, or buy a packet of mixed lettuce seeds, which several companies now offer. Share leftover seeds with neighbors. Seeds also germinate well if you store them in a dry place from year to year. Your gardens will be attractive with all the different shades of green and red; bugs that attack one variety are likely to spare another.

Most lettuces require little space outdoors compared to sprawling plants such as squash. They can be grown as a border in flower beds, among herbs, in pots on the terrace, in flats in a cold frame, or in the vegetable garden, of course.

Soil for lettuce should be alkaline and contain enough nutrients, especially nitrogen, to produce rapid and leafy growth. Compost or manure and lime worked into the rows before planting will increase production.

Moisture to the roots is important, since lettuce is composed largely of water (that's why it's so low in calories). If the ground dries out, seeds won't germinate, and plants deprived of moisture will wilt and yellow. Mulching lettuce plants retains moisture to the roots while it keeps the leaves dry—important, since soggy leaves tend to rot into the dirt, inviting slugs and disease. Mulch also keeps lettuce free from mud splatter. Since we've started mulching close to the plants with newspapers covered with straw, I don't bother to wash lettuce leaves from the garden. I just check them for insects and tear them into the salad bowl—a great time saver. And you save water-soluble vitamins if you don't wash or soak lettuce.

Most lettuces like cool weather and are not harmed by light frost. In hot climates, plant lettuce in the shade of taller plants to help keep it cool. In cold areas you can prolong the lettuce crop by covering plants with bushel baskets on very cold nights.

Try intercropping lettuce with other vegetables that like rich, loose soil, such as onions, carrots, and radishes, or stick a few lettuce seeds or thinned plants into bare spots in the garden. Sow the seeds thinly, as always directed on the package (seed-packet directions are important with lettuce). If you sow it too thickly, you'll simply have to waste time thinning or it won't thrive. Try mixing small seeds like lettuce with dry, fine sand to help control your impulse to oversow; you can easily feed the seed-sand mixture out of your hand in a slow stream. Cover lettuce seeds lightly with fine soil; if you plant them too deep they will rot or fail to germinate.

Many pests and diseases attack lettuces, but if you plant several varieties and care for them properly you should be able, even in a small space, to enjoy plenty of lettuce and give a lot away to friends and predators. Keep plants healthy and strong against pests by spacing them properly and weeding them thoroughly. If necessary, use a garlic spray (see page 12) to discourage bugs. Rots, molds, and mildew are often caused by too much moisture on the leaves at the wrong time. When you water lettuce, do it in the morning and avoid wetting the leaves.

You can save lettuce seeds from plants that have gone to seed. Select flower stalks that are tall and heavy with dried blooms. Hang the whole plant upside down until it is quite dry, then pick out the seeds on a cold winter's night when your mind is wandering toward spring.

The major difficulty with growing lettuce indoors is that you need quite a bit to make a good-sized salad, and most people don't have the space and light to produce an adequate crop. Grow whatever you have space for, but concentrate on loose-leaf varieties that will add interest to the other lettuces and greens you may have to buy to supplement your special home-grown leaves. And consider using some of your space to grow more unusual salad ingredients, such as nasturtiums, curly cress, and kale.

Start lettuce seeds indoors in rich, moist soil. Since they like both coolness and light, pick the part of your house that best meets these conditions. A cool basement or closet with plant lights is ideal. Most loose-leaf lettuces mature from seeds indoors in about 45 days.

Is it possible to spoil a salad of mixed lettuces fresh from the garden? Yes. Fresh lettuces are good in themselves, and heavy dressings often overpower their delicate flavors. Use Russian dressing for vegetable salads, if you like. Use mustardy dressings for spinach salads or robust greens. Use herby, light, mayonnaise-based dressings for mixed salads of lettuces and greens. But those special home-grown lettuces that are buttery, soft, and mild deserve the best and the simplest: lemon juice, the finest oil you can buy, and fresh herbs that complement the flavor of your choice of lettuces.

A good green salad is always made from fresh, crisp, dry leaves. Moisture dilutes the dressing. Lettuce from a mulched garden usually needs no washing, but if leaves are gritty, rinse them quickly under running water, shake or pat them as dry as possible, or whirl them in a salad spinner. If you're not using them immediately, put them in the refrigerator in a plastic bag or roll them in a towel. Tear into salad bowl just before serving.

Some lettuce salad ideas follow, and you can vary them to your tastes and the availability of greens. Lettuce is also good braised or in soup. You can add leftover lettuce salad to gazpacho (see recipe), but big mixed salads of lettuces and greens are so good that people usually eat as much as you serve.

Caesar Salad

I celebrate the first romaine lettuce thinnings with a small Caesar salad. Actually, romaine at this tender stage is not crunchy enough to stand up to the rich dressing—it's simply a foretaste of the dark-green crisp romaine leaves that will be heaped into a capacious bowl and tossed flamboyantly at the table later in the summer. SERVES 4

1 clove garlic, peeled and halved
1 teaspoon salt
1 teaspoon dry mustard
1 tablespoon lemon juice
2 tablespoons olive oil
4 anchovy fillets, chopped, or 1
  teaspoon anchovy paste
1 egg
About 1 gallon torn crisp, dry
  romaine leaves (2 large bunches)
½ cup finely grated Parmesan
  cheese
1 cup croutons

Rub a large wooden salad bowl with half a garlic clove. Add salt, and use other garlic half to rub it into bowl. Add mustard and lemon juice, and beat with a wooden spoon until salt dissolves. Beat in olive oil and anchovy fillets or paste until well blended.

From here on, you must move quickly just before serving. Drop the egg in boiling water, cook for 1 minute, and run cold water over it. Place romaine leaves in salad bowl, sprinkle cheese over them, and break egg on top. Toss everything until romaine leaves are glistening. Add croutons, mix quickly, and serve.

Salade Niçoise

Boston or Bibb lettuce, while merely the foundation for this salad, is an important base that is needed to support and complement the substantial blend of other ingredients. Salade Niçoise is satisfyingly filling, a beautiful arrangement of contrasting colors and flavors, the perfect lunch for a summer's day. Vary it according to the vegetables and herbs available in your garden, but include the essential lettuce, anchovies, olives, hard-boiled eggs, and onions.

SERVES 4 AS A MAIN COURSE

1 large head Boston or Bibb lettuce
4 medium boiled potatoes, sliced
2 tablespoons vinegar
5 tablespoons olive oil
½ cup finely chopped herbs (basil, parsley, dill, and/or chervil) or greens (watercress, curly cress, and/or dandelions)
2 cups cooked green beans
1 green or red sweet pepper, sliced in rings
12 cherry tomatoes or 2 large tomatoes, peeled and quartered

10 or more anchovy fillets
7-ounce can tuna, drained
1 cup small black olives
1 cup stuffed green olives
1 cup diagonally sliced celery
2 hard-boiled eggs, peeled and quartered
1 large red or Bermuda onion, thinly sliced
Herb vinaigrette (see recipe)

Break lettuce head apart gently, rinse and dry it, and arrange it as a lining in a large salad bowl. Cover with plastic wrap and refrigerate.

Combine potatoes with vinegar, oil, and herbs or greens in a mixing bowl. Cover and chill.

Just before serving, place the potato salad in the bottom of the bowl of lettuce. Arrange the remaining ingredients, except vinaigrette, on top of the potatoes in a pleasing form, and carry the salad to the table for the diners to admire. Toss with vinaigrette, or let guests serve themselves with what they like and add vinaigrette to their tastes.

LOVAGE

Levisticum officinalis
 *perennial*

Lovage is so useful an aromatic that you should try to make space for it somewhere. Its distinctive flavor—like pungent celery—is an asset to soups, stews, and any other dish in which you would use celery. Further, lovage is attractive, it has a nice name, and birds like its seeds. Put at least one plant outdoors if you can: plant it in the background of a flower bed, or tuck it into a neglected corner. It can grow up to 6 feet tall in rich soil, and it doesn't mind partial shade. It doesn't seem to mind anything, and it's one of the first herbs to push through the still-frozen soil in spring. Weeds and crowding don't deter it, and insects don't bother it.

Lovage looks much like big unblanched celery; its flavor, however, is much stronger and its texture tougher than commercially grown celery. You can start it from seeds sown thinly in almost any season, but it's best to get a few plants or root divisions from a nursery or a friend. Plants about three years old can be dug up and divided (they should have little offsets). Lovage flowers rise above the foliage in pale yellowish umbels in midsummer. The seeds are quite aromatic, and if you or the birds don't eat them, they'll readily self-seed.

A number of other plants, several of which are also known as lovage, are similar in appearance to common lovage (also known as garden or Italian lovage), though not of the same family. Some of them are "escapes" or wild plants. Be cautious when you gather wild things that look like lovage or celery: they can be poisonous.

Small lovage plants can be grown indoors in rich potting soil. They will tolerate partial shade better than most herbs, though the foliage will be paler and the flavor milder than when plants are grown outdoors in the sun.

When drying lovage, hang loose bundles in a warm, dry place for several weeks, until leaves are crumbly. The stems are too wet and tough to dry satisfactorily, so discard them and crumble the leaves into containers. To dry the roots for tea or a potherb, wash them, slice, and spread on a screen in an airy place until completely dry.

If you've never eaten lovage, use it cautiously at first. Try a few chopped young sprigs in salads. Add chopped leaves and stalks to the soup pot, to mirepoix, or to stuffings. Braise larger stalks as you would celery. If you like the flavor, you can make lovage vinegar or tea by steeping the leaves in the appropriate liquid. Another wonderful thing about lovage is that you can use its large hollow stems to make drinking straws for children.

MARIGOLDS

Tagetes and Calendula species  *annual*

Once upon a time marigolds were orange or yellow. Their foliage had a strong scent, and their petals were used to color butter and flavor many cooked dishes. Then the botanists went to work hybridizing. We now have white marigolds and huge odorless marigolds. They are glamorous, but don't let them blind you to the value of ordinary marigolds.

Plain old smelly marigold flowers are a good and very inexpensive substitute for saffron. They make the vegetable garden colorful and repel nematodes and possibly other predators, such as rabbits. They can be used to make a yellow dye. They are beautiful in almost any setting, outdoors or in bouquets. They bloom in the hottest weather, in almost any soil, and are little bothered by pests.

Calendulas, or pot marigolds, are preferred by some people for use in cooking. They bloom in all shades of yellow and orange, have little scent in their leaves, and look more like flat asters than the *Tagetes* species.

Marsh marigolds (*Caltha palustris*), wild flowers, are quite different from common marigolds or calendulas. They flourish in wet spots and have buttercuplike flowers. Marsh marigold leaves are edible only when cooked. Their flower buds can be pickled as a substitute for capers.

Ordinary marigold seeds look like little rods with bristles on one end. They germinate quickly and grow fast. You can start them indoors several weeks before you plan to set them out. Don't start the large varieties too soon indoors, however, because they will get leggy and have a setback when transplanted.

If you have plant lights or a sunny window, petite marigolds are a fine plant for indoors. I once potted a 4-foot marigold and dragged it indoors just before frost. In the process, I also dragged in whiteflies that attacked my other plants while the marigold expired. It's better, I've found, to start seeds in pots in late summer for indoor winter flowers.

When fall nights get chill, pick big bouquets of your outdoor marigolds before the frost gets to the flowers. Strip off the stem leaves, since the foliage rots quickly under water. After frost has turned the plants black, add them to the compost heap or chop them and return them to the ground. Apparently even after they are dead and frozen they add nematode-repelling qualities to the soil.

Which kinds of marigolds to plant becomes a big decision for me every spring, since I'd like to have all of them. The Burpee seed company has specialized in marigolds, and their catalog has pages of enticing varieties, from midget to mammoth. Small French marigolds and orange calendulas are best for culinary purposes. Showy American (sometimes called African) ones are good background flowers or a border in the vegetable garden. All sizes and colors can be used to effect in the herb or vegetable garden and with other flowers. Just be sure to check the packet for their height when mature, and space them as directed for best growth.

Raw marigold flowers have little flavor, but when they're cooked they become subtly and pleasantly bitter. They are also good when dried. Pull the petals away from the center and spread them on a screen in a shaded airy place or put them in the oven at 200° F. until they are brittle. Or freeze a marigold liquid: put petals through the food processor or in the blender with enough water to make the blender spin, twirl them just for a few seconds, and freeze the mixture in ice-cube trays.

Fresh, dried, or frozen marigold flowers can be used in any way you would use saffron, but more generously, since they're milder and their color fades more than saffron does after cooking.

Make a colorful pilaf dotted with orange and green by adding a few tablespoons of chopped marigold petals and a few tablespoons of chopped herbs or greens to each 3 cups of cooked rice. Add marigold petals to pasta, hot soup, salad dressing, egg dishes, or biscuits.

And, in memory of the late Senator Everett Dirksen, who led the campaign, support the marigold for national flower. Maybe if marigolds are so honored, people will discover that they are not only lovely to behold but good to eat.

Marigold Arroz con Pollo

Traditional arroz con pollo (rice with chicken) is bright yellow-orange from saffron and paprika and is decorated with pimiento. This variation uses fresh herbs and vegetables. It is lightly fragrant rather than spicy, and is flecked with bright colors. Orange marigolds are best for this, but you can use yellow ones. SERVES 4

½ cup marigold petals
½ cup oregano leaves
1 large clove garlic, chopped
2½ cups chicken broth
2 whole chicken breasts, halved
    and skinned
¼ cup olive oil

½ pound mushrooms
1 cup rice
1 cup hot cooked peas
1 tomato, cut in wedges
Artichoke hearts, cooked (optional)
Asparagus tips, cooked (optional)

Place marigold petals, oregano, and garlic in blender container, and pour chicken broth over them. Blend until oregano is finely chopped. (Or you can use the food processor.)

Sauté chicken breasts in olive oil in a large Dutch oven until they are lightly browned. Remove chicken, and sauté mushrooms until they wilt. Stir in rice, and cook, stirring, for a minute. Stir in blender mixture and bring to a boil. Place chicken, meaty side up, on top of rice, cover, and bake in a 350° oven for about 30 minutes. Uncover and decorate with peas and tomato wedges. Top with artichoke hearts and/or asparagus, if you like.

MARJORAM *and oregano*

Majorana hortensis
🌿 tender perennial

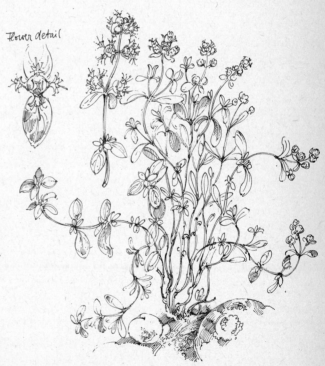

Flower detail

The first time I planted marjoram and oregano I couldn't remember which I'd planted where, so I checked herb books to find out the difference. The more I read, the more confused I got. Botanical names of these two related herbs have changed over the years, and references to them still differ, depending on which book you consult. Sweet marjoram is often listed as *Origanum majorana*, and oregano is sometimes known as wild marjoram. Further, both marjoram and oregano have many varieties, some quite unlike in appearance.

I didn't identify marjoram for sure until it started to bloom in July. Then I remembered it's sometimes called "knotted marjoram." The velvety knobs on the tips of the stems do look like little four-sided knots that would be difficult to untie. Each knot is made up of folded overlapping leaves out of which come very tiny cream-colored flowers.

If I'd planted my marjoram and oregano in a more congenial environment rather than scattering them thickly among some flowers and neglecting them, I might have been able to distinguish between them sooner. Marjoram has soft oval leaves that are light green on top and gray-green underneath—not as large or as dark as oregano leaves. Marjoram is a dainty-looking plant that grows about a foot tall on slightly woody stems—oregano gets shrubby and sprawly and grows twice as tall. Marjoram smells much like oregano but isn't as strong and seems sweeter (the difference is more pronounced when the herbs are dried). And although marjoram is a perennial in hot climates, it doesn't have oregano's extreme hardiness and must be treated as an annual in the North.

Plant marjoram seeds in a sunny, well-drained spot when the ground warms up in spring. They germinate slowly, so keep the area well weeded until the seedlings are established. Or you may want to start seeds indoors to set out, or get plants from someone else by root divisions or stem cuttings. Space them about a foot apart. Marjoram likes a slightly alkaline soil, which needn't be rich. Mulch close to the plants to keep the ground moist and prevent dirt splatter on the lower leaves. Pinching off the blossoms will encourage lateral leaf growth. I find the knots so interesting to look at that I leave most of them on, although I cut sprigs of them to add to bouquets of other herbs or flowers.

Marjoram is an erect plant outdoors. Indoors, unless it's grown under plant lights, it trails into a drooping mound, nice to grow in a hanging basket. Wash the leaves frequently to remove dust and insects, especially whiteflies. Marjoram is not pest-prone, but it is a member of the mint family and thus susceptible to the insects mints attract. The flavor and fragrance of marjoram will be milder indoors, and I'm not enthusiastic about growing it in winter. I prefer to use it generously in summer with fresh vegetables and switch to dried marjoram for heartier cold-weather fare.

Dried marjoram has a delicious perfume, sweeter and more aromatic than when fresh. Cut branches to dry when the knots start to appear. Hang them in a shaded spot until you can easily strip off the leaves and pack them into jars.

Knots and all, marjoram branches are attractive in a jar of vinegar and give it an "Italian" flavor that's good with olive oil on pungent greens. Or make marjoram oil by spinning leaves in the blender with oil, then straining them out. Near the end of summer I use up the remaining marjoram in tomato sauce to freeze.

Chicken Corn Soup Marjoram

As children we felt cheated at Sunday dinner when chicken was chopped up and stretched out to make soup—we wanted drumsticks. But we liked this soup anyway. Chicken corn soup, a legacy from the Pennsylvania Dutch, can start with an old hen or chicken breasts. Use homemade noodles (see page 103) instead of potatoes if you like. Add different herbs or greens; they make a big difference, since their color and flavor give this hearty soup character. SERVES 4

2 cups chicken stock
2 cups chopped potatoes
2 cups fresh corn kernels

2 cups chopped cooked chicken
½ cup finely chopped marjoram
Salt and pepper

Bring stock to a boil, add potatoes, cover, and cook until potatoes are barely tender. Add corn and cook for 5 minutes. Stir in chicken and marjoram, add salt and pepper to taste, and cook for about 10 minutes.

Audrey's Yum-Yum Button Breasts

Only my creative sister, Audrey Thompson, would invent a recipe that combines beef, pork, and chicken in this way. Substitute oregano, thyme, lemon balm, or an herb mixture for the marjoram if you like, and you can also adapt it well to crockery cooking. SERVES 6

2½-ounce can dried beef
3 whole chicken breasts, halved
4 tablespoons butter
6 strips bacon
½ pound button mushrooms

2 cups chicken broth
3 tablespoons finely chopped
  marjoram leaves
1 pint sour cream

Line a large Dutch oven or casserole dish with dried beef. Lightly brown the chicken breasts in butter, and wrap each one with a bacon strip. Arrange them on top of the dried beef. Sauté the mushrooms lightly in the same butter, then scatter them over the chicken. Mix chicken broth with marjoram, pour it over the chicken, cover, and bake at 250°F. for about 2 hours. Pour off the broth, mix it with sour cream, heat gently, and serve in a sauceboat alongside chicken.

Lamb Roasted with Marjoram

A leg of lamb is enhanced by marjoram, and some people think marjoram is essential to all dishes that use lamb or mutton. Dried marjoram is also good in this recipe; use half the amount specified below. (Rosemary goes well with lamb, too, and you can substitute it for marjoram, but use a bit less.) SERVES 6

3 tablespoons roughly chopped
  marjoram leaves
1 onion, chopped
2 cloves garlic

½ cup olive oil
1 lemon
Salt and pepper
6-pound leg of lamb

Place marjoram in blender container, add onion, garlic, and oil, and squeeze lemon juice on top. Add a generous sprinkle of salt and pepper, and blend just until marjoram is finely chopped. (Or you can use a food processor, or finely chop marjoram, onion, and garlic by hand.)

Cut slits in the lamb, and rub the herb mixture into the meat. Wrap lamb in foil or put it in a plastic bag, and marinate in refrigerator at least 12 hours.

Uncover lamb, place it in a roasting pan, and insert a meat thermometer. Roast at 350°F. for about 1 hour, basting with marinade and drippings occasionally. Check thermometer: when it registers 140°, the lamb is rare. If you like well-done meat, continue roasting until thermometer reads 170°. Let roast rest at room temperature for 20 minutes before carving.

MILKWEED

Asclepias syriaca 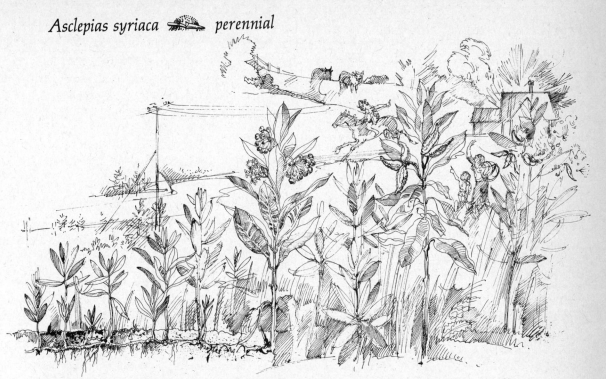 *perennial*

Poke may surpass it in tastiness, dandelions have far more vitamins, but milk-weed is my favorite wild plant for versatility. It grows rampantly just about everywhere, and picked at the right time, cooked properly, every bit can be eaten.

Milkweed comes in several varieties, but the kind you're most likely to see grows in fields and along fencerows, usually in patches, because of its long, creeping root stalks. (Don't confuse it with so-called butterfly milkweed, *A. tuberosa*. This cultivated ornamental is a more refined plant with woody stems and bright orange flowers, and its leaves may be poisonous.) Common milkweed stems are fat and sturdy; they exude a milky liquid when broken. The leaves are large, grayish green on top and pale and downy underneath. The sweet-smelling flowers resemble pink broccoli buds. Milkweed is one vegetable that most people

their splitting open and

won't mind your stealing off their property—even people who eat it, as I do, generally have plenty to spare. I've been so tolerant of my milkweed patches that they've become a perennial nuisance in the vegetable garden.

Most people recognize spiny milkweed pods, but by the time you see them splitting open and scattering their fluffy parachute seeds, it's much too late to eat the plant. Mark the spot, and start looking for young milkweed shoots in late May in the North. You'll know they're the right thing if you break one off and a white sap oozes out. These little pale-green shoots should be eaten before they're 6 inches high, and I think they're the best part of the plant. They look a bit like asparagus but don't taste much like asparagus; because they must be cooked thoroughly, their flavor is pleasantly bland.

All parts of milkweed must be cooked in several changes of water to remove the raw bitter taste. For milkweed shoots, strip off any side leaves, break off the white root part, wash stalks well, pour boiling water over them, and boil for 1 minute. Drain, then repeat the process, and return drained milkweed to pan. Now most of the nutrient value has been lost along with the bitterness, so I like to restore some vitamins and add flavor in the last boiling. I put a handful of fresh spring herbs and greens in the blender, cover them with chicken stock, whirl them until the herbs are finely chopped, then strain the liquid over the milkweed and boil for an additional 10 minutes. I drain the stalks (saving the cooking liquid for sauces or for boiling other vegetables) and serve the milkweed hot with lemon butter or cold with green mayonnaise. Or I return the milkweed to the blender along with the cooking broth to make a puréed milkweed soup.

After milkweed-shoot season has passed, you can start picking the young leaves to cook for greens. I don't fancy them—they come out a soggy, rather tasteless blob—but you might like them. Give them the same preparation as the shoots. Pep them up by adding vinegar and sugar, bacon, or sour cream. Or combine them with other cooked greens.

Young milkweed flower buds are pretty good, but don't expect them to have the texture or flavor of broccoli, which they resemble when cooked because they turn from pinkish to bright green. Pick buds while they are still tightly clustered, wash them thoroughly, and give them the same three boilings as the shoots, but boil only 5 minutes the last time. I like them cold with mustard vinaigrette, but they do have a watery texture after all that boiling. Use cooked flowerets in tempura to get the crunchy complement of the fried batter.

scattering their fluffy parachute seeds

Bee balm

Finally, if you've any milkweed plants left, you can eat the tender seed pods. You must get them when they're still hard and no more than 2 inches long or they'll be tough. Cook them in the same way as the shoots, but for 15 minutes in the last boiling. Their texture is much like that of okra, and you can add them to soups or serve them with a cheese sauce.

All milkweed parts can be frozen. Give them the first two boilings, cool them quickly under running water, drain, and pack in freezer containers. When you're ready to use them, drop them still frozen into boiling water, return to a boil, and cook for the final times recommended above.

How many other plants offer such a variety of edible parts and are free besides? Furthermore, milkweed flowers are pretty, and their fragrance adds to the pleasure of working in the garden on a warm summer day. You can use the brown pods in dried arrangements. If you don't have milkweed nearby, try barely covering some of the seeds or pieces of root in a spot not too near your garden. I bet they'll grow—milkweed is a most accommodating weed.

MINTS

Mentha species
perennial

It wasn't that I hadn't been warned about mint's bad habits. Those first few sprigs of mint roots my mother gave me simply looked so innocent and smelled so sweet that

apple mint

Spear mint

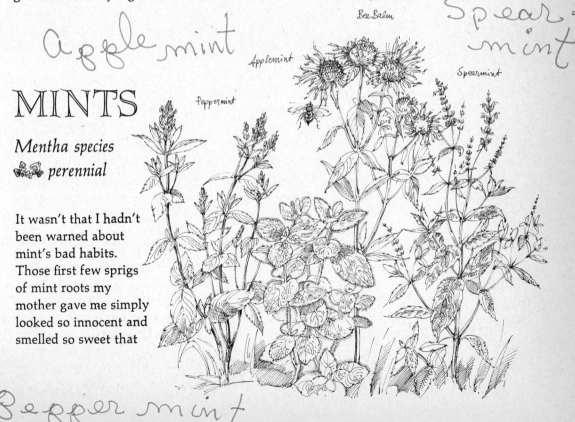

Peppermint

Bee Balm

Applemint

Spearmint

I figured it wouldn't hurt to stick them in behind the spring flowering bulbs. The mint would add greenery when the bulb foliage died down.

Sure enough, the mint was so obliging at providing foliage that the bulbs had to go elsewhere. I gave up trying to get the mint out and decided it was more useful than tulips anyway.

Mints spread through gardens and fields throughout the world. Spearmint, peppermint, and many others have a charming system of putting out tenacious stalk-producing roots that spread widely underground as well as runners that travel eagerly above the ground and root themselves. Over and under stone walkways, along the edges of the house, over the meadow and through the woods and, for all I know, back to Grandmother's house they go—a good reason for planting them if you want a delicious, reliable herb.

There are hundreds more than the dozen or so mints I've tried, since mints often hybridize. A small clump of spearmint and peppermint may be enough for most gardens, but you may want to add a few others of the following familiar varieties for contrast.

Spearmint (M. *spicata*) grows about 2 feet tall on square stems (like all mints), with oblong, unevenly toothed, green or sometimes purplish leaves about 2 inches long. Its small flowers grow in pale pink or purple spikes. I've found spearmint to be the worst trespasser in areas I want to reserve for other plants, but it's my favorite for tea and jelly.

Peppermint (M. *piperita*) has smoother, longer leaves than spearmint. They are darker green, with a purplish cast, and are very pungent—even weeding the plants will leave your hands smelling like peppermint the rest of the day and chewing a few leaves of peppermint will sweeten your breath. Too much of it is quickly too much: use peppermint gently in teas.

Apple mint (M. *rotundifolia*) is attractive planted with spearmint and peppermint because of the contrast of its larger, hairy, rounded, gray-green leaves. It grows up to 3 feet. Pineapple mint, an apple mint variety, has less woolly leaves, most of them beautifully variegated with white. My apple and pineapple mints don't much resemble their namesakes in fragrance or flavor; they're much like spearmint with a slightly fruity scent. Both have pinkish white flower spikes and are good mixed with other mints in teas.

Pennyroyal (M. *pulegium*) is, yes, a mint, sometimes known as true or European pennyroyal to distinguish it from wild or American pennyroyal

(*Hedeoma pulegioides*). It creeps along the ground and has downy oval leaves about half an inch long and small bluish or lilac flowers. Often used as a ground cover, pennyroyal is also loved in tea by many people, but I find its flavor bitter.

"Wild mint" may be a misnomer: many cultivated mints have gone wild, and so-called wild field mint (*M. arvensis*) is often grown in the herb garden. A 2-foot-tall, usually hairy plant, it has oblong leaves about 2 inches long and small lavender flowers that grow around the plant stem rather than in spikes like most mints. Water mint (*M. aquatica*) grows in little islands in our brook, where it's pleasant to trample and sniff it while wading. Its roundish leaves appear very pale gray-green because of the white down that covers them. Flower heads are lilac-colored. To me it tastes like mild spearmint, but apparently it's quite pungent in some places.

Mints do seem to vary in strength of fragrance and flavor in different locations. My brother transplanted our brook mint to rich soil in Lancaster County, Pennsylvania, and found its flavor there more like peppermint. A mint specialist, Don has provided me with information on orange mint and bergamot mint, which are confusingly listed as the same or different varieties in different reference books.

Bergamot, red-flowered bee balm (*Monarda didyma*), should be grown for the flowers and bees as much as for the flowers or smell. Don says, "I once made tea from *M. didyma* leaves—some call it Oswego tea—but was unable to finish a cup. It must be a sure cure for something or other."

Wild bergamot (*Monarda fistulosa*) is similar to *M. didyma*. Don transplanted a clump of it from high in the Blue Ridge Mountains of Virginia to Lancaster, where it survived many years. Its sparse lavender flowers contrast with the red of *M. didyma*. Its leaves make a tea even more bitter.

Orange mint (*Mentha citrata*) has oily, citrus-flavored leaves that blend well with a cup of spearmint tea. As an ornamental, orange mint stands out, with reddish stems and dark waxy leaves. It pushes up dense lavender flower spikes in midsummer.

Mints are rarely obtained from seeds. Get root divisions from a nursery or a friend (preferably a friend who is muttering while weeding long snakes of mint roots out of flower beds: you'll be doing each other a favor). Most mints root easily from a branch stuck in water or damp soil.

Almost all mints prefer moist, rich soil in partial shade—which is not to say they won't spread to arid clay in direct sunlight. It is most advisable to consider their invasive nature when you plant them. Make a separate bed away from the herb garden, plant them in a raised box, or sink barriers deep into the ground around their roots. Their advantage is that they'll thrive where many other herbs won't: in shady corners, along the brook, under an outdoor water faucet. Pinching back flowers when they appear in midsummer will make the plants bushier.

If your mint bed appears to be dying out, encourage new growth by cutting plants to the ground; then, using a sharp spade or long knife, cut through the soil and roots about a foot deep in several-foot squares. This encourages root sections to send up new foliage. Such measures are necessary only if your mint bed is confined. Mint will happily flourish for decades, maybe centuries, if unfettered. High on a hill near our house we found a foundation so old that a large tree had grown through the cellar. Fragrant mint grew waist deep all around. Its roots must be the offspring of a sprig planted by a pioneer who must have been hearty to survive at such a height in the Vermont winter.

Euell Gibbons had samples of mint analyzed for vitamin A and C content and found them excellent sources, equal to the same weight of oranges for vitamin C and richer in vitamin A than carrots. One rarely wants that much mint at one sitting, but you can snip quite a bit into salads, and a strong cup of mint tea is even more enjoyable when you know it contains so much nutrition. You can add vitamins, color, and flavor to baby food by puréeing some mint leaves into applesauce and pears.

Members of the mint family are often recommended as pest repellents; one even reads advice about planting peppermint in the vegetable garden to deter insects. My mints, however, seem extraordinarily attractive to pests, and I think it folly to introduce such a rampant perennial as mint among annual plants.

The latest enemies to attack my mints were some nasty creatures that ate the leaves and formed filmy specked curtains around the leaves they'd curled at the tops of the stalks. With magnifying glass and insect manuals, I identified them as a type of webworm, but that wasn't helpful in getting rid of them. They simply retreated into their webs when blasted with a hard spray of water, and I didn't want to use garlic spray on mint I was planning to eat. So I cut off the infested tops and burned them—the final solution for difficult pests.

Rust and wilt can also be serious problems with mints. One way to deal with them is to apply flame from a propane gas torch to the shoots when they first emerge in spring. This breaks the life cycle of the fungus that causes the disease, since it kills overwintering spores on the soil surface, and it won't hurt the mint.

The sad story is not ended. Aphids, whiteflies, and mites thrive on mint, and they're none too appetizing floating around in tea. A strong spray of hose water will chase some of them somewhere else anyway. Indoors, a wash of tepid water will send them down the drain.

I don't grow mint indoors anymore. My houseplant spearmint and peppermint lacked flavor and fragrance; their tiny-leafed runners just kept running. But if you're determined to have a mint julep in midwinter (and I must admit that when the January snow falls relentlessly outside, the idea of a julep on a sunny veranda is most appealing), you may have to support your habit by growing spearmint indoors. Don't despair: it's done successfully by people who give the plant rich soil, good light, frequent baths, fairly cool temperatures, and enough clipping of foliage and runners to keep the bush compact. One mint that does especially well indoors is Corsican mint (*M. requienii*). It has very small leaves, a peppermint scent, and a natural compactness that makes it more suitable to confinement than its sprawling cousins.

When using fresh mint pick only the larger leaves or pinch off the clean, juicy terminal leaf clusters—about six leaves at the top of the stems—to encourage lateral growth. For salads you'll want to use only the leaves, but stems and all can go into tea. To make tea, I usually pick a big handful of sprigs, drop them into a quart of boiling water, steep for 10 minutes, and strain.

Dried mint makes good tea, but it often tastes just a little musty to me—quite different from fresh mint tea, with its sprightly flavor. To dry mint, cut branches before they bloom and hang them in a shady place until you can strip the leaves off easily. Since I use mint mostly for teas, I make up a frozen concentrate which preserves much of the fresh mint flavor. To each pint of boiling water, add about 2 cups of roughly chopped mint leaves and stems, return water to a boil, remove from heat, cover, and let cool for about 1 hour.

Strain the liquid into ice-cube trays, freeze, break out cubes, and store them in plastic bags in the freezer. Heat a cube with enough water to make a cup of hot mint tea or add cubes to other mixtures, such as pekoe tea, punch, or soup.

Priscilla, my sister-in-law, recommends freezing clean, dry, fresh mint leaves in packets to save space in the freezer, and it's an equally good method. You can also freeze mint leaves in a block of ice to add to your punch bowl. Maybe it's just because *my* family and friends are so fond of mints, as the following recipes testify, but I've never met anybody who didn't like mint.

Don's Nose-Tingling Mint Cooler

This method, my brother notes, "traps the elusive essence of mint." It's a fairly strong mint essence, and I like to add a bit of soda water, lime juice, and/or Chablis to it. Float a mint sprig on top of each glass.
MAKES ABOUT 1 QUART

1 big tight handful mint sprigs   *½ cup sugar*

Wash mint sprigs if necessary, tear them into pieces (including stems), and pack into a nonaluminum quart container. Add sugar and mash it lightly into the leaves with a wooden spoon. Bring 3½ cups water to a boil, pour it over mint leaves, and cover container. When cool, stir it and strain it over ice cubes into tall glasses.

Aunt Dora's Iced Tea

Aunt Dora Brunk's iced mint tea is best made from her own curly variety of spearmint, a hybrid apparently produced by bees along the Warwick River in Virginia. It has a wide reputation, and many people have tried to imitate it, but it never tastes the same as it does at her house, where you drink it while the tide comes in. MAKES 3 PINTS

1 small handful spearmint leaves   6 ounces sugar
2 ounces pekoe tea or 1 family-size
  pekoe tea bag

Bring 1 pint of water to a boil in a nonaluminum pan. Drop in spearmint, and boil for several minutes. Add tea in a tea ball or tea bag, and steep for 3 minutes. Strain, stir in sugar, and add ice and water to make 3 pints. Pour over more ice to serve.

Basil Pesto

Cold Minted Cucumber Soup

Lydia Mattar Titcomb, a friend who gave me this recipe, says that every time she makes this soup "it comes out a little different." You too can vary the amounts of herbs and acidity. It's a refreshing cold soup for summer, served with pita for lunch, or as an appetizer at dinner. SERVES 4

2 or 3 small cucumbers   1 tablespoon finely chopped mint
2 cups yogurt   leaves
1 teaspoon olive oil   1 teaspoon chopped dill leaves
1 teaspoon white vinegar (optional)   Salt and white pepper to taste
Juice of ½ lemon

Wash cucumbers well (if all you can get is large waxed ones, peel and seed them). Grate or slice thin and place in a colander to drain.

Stir yogurt with a whisk or fork until completely smooth, then stir in remaining ingredients until well mixed. Check seasoning, then gently stir in cucumbers. Chill for at least 2 hours before serving.

Lemon Mint

Pickled chutneys Sweet

Mint and Crab-Apple Jelly

Plain mint jelly is drab brown because cooking changes the color of the leaves; it becomes an artificial bright green if you add food coloring. When you combine mint with crab apples, a beautiful natural pink color and a pleasantly tart balance of flavors result. You can also add some mint infusion as part of the liquid in many other jellies for an intriguingly different flavor. If you want to make jelly with mint only, delete crab apples below and double the amount of mint and its liquid. Try combining all the different mints you have. Label jars with all their names and present mixed-mint jelly as a gift. You can substitute an equal weight of tart apples for crab apples in this recipe. MAKES ABOUT 7 CUPS

3 pounds crab apples
2 cups roughly chopped mint leaves
Juice of 1 lemon

7 cups sugar
6 ounces (1 bottle) liquid pectin

Wash crab apples, remove stems, and place in a large saucepan. Add 3 cups of water, bring to a boil, and simmer, covered, for 15 minutes. Mash lightly to break skins, then drain in a jelly bag or several layers of cheesecloth. Measure out 2½ cups of juice.

Place mint leaves in a large saucepan. Crush them with a wooden spoon. Add 2 cups of boiling water, return quickly to a boil, cover, and steep 10 minutes. Strain into a very large saucepan, mashing mint to extract all the juices possible.

Add crab-apple juice and lemon juice to mint infusion. Stir in sugar until well mixed. Bring mixture to a rolling boil, stirring constantly. Stir in pectin and continue stirring until jelly has boiled hard for 1 minute. Skim off foam, pour jelly into sterilized jars, and seal or cover with paraffin.

NASTURTIUMS

Tropaeolum species  annual

Even if nasturtiums didn't have a pleasantly peppery flavor and a high vitamin content, summer wouldn't be summer for me without their brilliant flowers. It's hard to say which I like best: to eat them, to smell them, or to look at them.

Many times I've forgotten all about work while I gazed out the window above my desk at the sprawling mounds of nasturtiums. Their gleaming flowers seem to float like thick clouds above the foliage. Then it's time to leave manuscripts and go pick a big bouquet, with leaves to eat and flowers to smell. The unusual fragrance of nasturtiums is sweet but not cloying, spicy, reminiscent of childhood summers at Grandma's house.

You can get trailing or vining or compact nasturtiums. The flowers, whose colors range from creamy white through various yellows and oranges to deep crimson, may be single, semidouble, or double. They are usually shaped somewhat like a flaring funnel with a long spur. Leaves are kidney-shaped and bright green.

One of the easiest-to-grow flowers, nasturtiums aren't particular about soil or light or water. If the soil is too rich, however, they'll produce more foliage and fewer blooms, and seedlings especially need adequate moisture to get going. But you can plant them just about anywhere. Among spring-flowering bulbs is a good place, since they'll quickly fill in bare spots when bulb foliage dies down. Nasturtiums adapt well to planters and hanging baskets. The climbing varieties can be grown among cucumbers and squash, and I recommend it: nasturtiums add color to the garden, and they may have other benefits.

There's no doubt that nasturtiums are trap plants for aphids, which gather on the stems and undersides of leaves in clusters that are unsightly but do little harm. The scent of nasturtium leaves reputedly repels whiteflies and squash beetles. However, nasturtiums are susceptible to a wilt that also lives on tomatoes, eggplant, and potatoes; if the leaves wilt and turn yellow, there's nothing to do but plant nasturtiums elsewhere, since the disease remains in the soil.

Some people try to get an early start by planting nasturtium seeds in pots indoors a few weeks before the time to set them out. There's little point in it, since they grow fast from seeds planted outdoors as soon as the soil warms up. The seeds are large, and I just poke them into loose soil with my finger to the depth recommended on the packet. Check seed package directions for the distance to space the plants; it varies considerably, depending on variety.

I made a couple of mistakes when, unable to bear the thought that frost would soon kill my beloved nasturtiums, I potted up and dragged into the house one especially huge trailing plant loaded with blooms. It struggled to live, but I sadly watched it yellow and weaken, and after a month I put it out of its misery. Dwarf varieties of nasturtiums are best in the house, and they should not be transplanted. Start them in a fairly large pot with lean sandy soil. Add fertilizer if you want to encourage leaves rather than flowers. You can leave them outdoors to grow healthy over summer, then wash them thoroughly before bringing them into the house and giving them all the sunlight possible or putting them under plant lights. Watch diligently for black aphids; wash them off, or break off leaves on which they're clustered. Many nasturtiums are perennials in warmer climates, and the plants will go on for years if you never let them freeze. Especially for apartment dwellers who don't have room to grow other greens indoors, a compact nasturtium is a good source of variation for salads.

If you've never tasted nasturtiums, nibble one of the young leaves. They taste like mild pepper and are a bit salty at the same time—something like watercress and similarly high in vitamin C. Although a salad of nasturtium leaves only might be too much, they're most pleasant mixed with other greens, perhaps with a few nasturtium flowers on top for decoration. Buds and flowers are edible, too, but wash them carefully to get rid of any lurking insects. The best part of nasturtiums, the little tender leaves, can be used in sandwiches or chopped fine to add to salad dressings or to scatter over food as a pepper substitute.

When nasturtium petals fall off, seed pods appear in their place. You can pickle them when they're about the size of capers. The easiest way is to pick a handful of pods (leave a bit of stalk attached) every time you gather a bouquet. Just keep adding them to a jar, covering with vinegar each time. When the jar is full, refrigerate it and let the nasturtium "capers" marinate for at least two weeks before using. Or you can make up a whole batch by a different method: soak pods in cold salt water, changing the brine daily for three days; drain, pack in jars, and add a mixture of vinegar, sugar, and herbs as you would for your favorite pickles. Use pickled nasturtium pods as you do capers, to sprinkle on salads, add to sauces, or eat as is.

Nasturtium and Radish Cheese Canapés

When you serve this cheese spread, everyone is intrigued. It has bright red and green flecks, a crunchy texture, and a peppery flavor. Try making it also with a triple-crème cheese, such as Boursault. The nasturtium leaves will get bitter and the radishes lose their texture if it's made ahead, so have everything ready to fix at the last minute—it doesn't take long to put it all together.

MAKES ABOUT 1 CUP OF SPREAD

1 bunch or handful small red
   radishes
1 tablespoon finely chopped
   nasturtium leaves
1 teaspoon lemon juice

8 ounces cream cheese, at room
   temperature
Thinly sliced pumpernickel or rye
   bread
Small whole nasturtium leaves

Wash radishes thoroughly and remove tops and roots. Slice a few radishes very thin to reserve for garnish; coarsely grate the rest. With a fork, quickly blend grated radishes, chopped nasturtium leaves, and lemon juice into cream cheese. Spread immediately on bread. Top each canapé with a whole nasturtium leaf, then a radish slice, and serve right away.

ONIONS

*Allium species
annual or
perennial*

The all-purpose globe onion you buy in a net bag at the grocery store is to its family what parsley is to other herbs: unglamorous but essential. Many onion family members—including leeks, shallots, and garlic—are more distinguished or interesting, and I've discussed them separately. A cook could probably manage without them, however, whereas it would be difficult to prepare many meals without the predictable "1 chopped onion" for everything from hamburger to salad to sauces and soups.

When I put "onions" on the grocery list, I realize it's not quite as simple as any old bag of yellow or white onion balls. Globe onions are sometimes described as either American (the pungent ones) or foreign (the mild types, such as Bermuda or Spanish), but ordinary all-purpose onions vary considerably in texture and pungency, depending on variety and age. It's a pleasure to experiment with all the varieties: purple and brown, large and tiny, mild and biting, oval or flattish or elongated, wild and cultivated. Grow as many as you have room for in your gardens. For a start, check seed catalogs for the many varieties, their characteristics, and their adaptability to your area.

Your growing season has much to do with how you plant onions. Most onions can be started from seeds, seedlings, or sets (small dried bulbs). In short growing seasons, seeds will not produce large onions before frost, since they take some five months to mature, and sets or seedlings are advisable if you want to harvest big bulbs.

I plant onion seeds, which are inexpensive and take up less space than sets. Because my growing season is brief, I don't try to grow enough big onions for winter. Rather, I concentrate on growing lots of scallions or bunching onions that I can use in salads, gazpacho, and many other summer dishes that are compatible with a gentle onion flavor. Bunching onions become elongated rather than round and can be planted more closely than globe varieties; you can put them in the herb bed or along the edges of the asparagus bed.

Start onion seeds in early spring as soon as the ground can be worked. Thin seedlings to the distance recommended on the packet, using thinnings as scallions or transplanting them to moist soil.

To plant onion sets, cover the bulbs with just enough soil so that the top still sticks out. If they are covered too deeply they may rot before they sprout. Space them far enough apart so that they will have room to mature; this depends on variety, but 6 inches in each direction should be adequate even for large sweet Spanish onions.

Onion seedlings can be purchased by mail or often at local nurseries. You can start your own indoors about 2 months before the ground warms up in your area. Sow seeds thinly in rich soil and give the seedlings all the light possible, preferably from overhead plant lights. You can move them to the coldframe when they are a month old. Plant onion seedlings in damp soil.

Onions prefer rich, loose soil, well drained but moist. It's important to keep them weeded; weeds use up moisture and prevent onions from swelling. Mulch between the rows but not too close to the plants—they like to push up out of the ground as they mature. Break off any flowers that appear; they divert energy from the bulbs.

Although often planted as a pest deterrent, onions are subject to a good many pests themselves. Onion maggots, tiny larvae of the onion fly, burrow into the stems and young bulbs. Onion thrips suck the leaves. Organic gardeners recommend rotenone or a spray of oil and soap to control these creatures, and mothballs scattered along rows deter them. Scatter onion plants in different spots around your gardens, and keep them healthy by giving them good care. Often insects will attack one section of the garden, working their way down the row, while they spare a group of the same plants elsewhere, and they tend to pick on weak, neglected plants.

When onion leaves start to yellow and fall over, the bulbs are nearly ready to harvest. Speed their ripening by gently bending the leaves over with your heel or the back of a rake. When the leaves are withered, pull the onions, dry them in the sun or a well-ventilated area, shake off all the earth possible, and store them in a cool place. Or braid the stems of a dozen or so together and hang them.

In addition to my problems with a short growing season, ordinary globe onions are so easily available (though increasingly expensive) that I prefer to use my garden space and my energy for more unusual varieties. One of these is the Egyptian onion (*A. cepum viviparum*), also called tree onion because it produces clusters of bulblets at the top of its round hollow stems. These tiny onion bulbs are first green; then they turn brownish red. They are hard-textured and too

Planting Onion Sets

small to use in quantity, but they have a good strong flavor that's fine to add to cucumber pickles or tie in a bag and add to soups or stock. I add handfuls of them, unpeeled, to tomato sauce that is eventually sieved (see recipe). Egyptian onions have a pleasant habit of reproducing themselves: they fall over by their own weight, then sprout. You can also pull off the bulb clusters, separate them, and lightly cover them with soil. They're extremely hardy—I've often brushed away snow to gather them—and I use the young foliage as I do chives. The bulbs store well.

Wild onions are confusing only in their nomenclature. The taste of what is variously called wild onions, wild garlic, and wild shallots is unmistakably garlicky. I well remember the flavor of the milk our cows produced after eating *A. vineale* or *A. canadense* when I was a child. I've since wondered if some delicious garlic cheese might not have been made from that spring milk we threw to the pigs. What we called wild garlic resembles a miniature, young Egyptian onion. Its leaves grow from a single bulb in early spring and look somewhat like thin young scallion shoots. Purple heads form in summer; they have a few flowers along with dozens of tiny bulbs about the size of a grain of wheat. Dig the bulbs to use as you do garlic, raw or boiled, chop the young stems as a substitute for chives, and pickle the seed heads.

Other onion varieties include perennials such as multiplier onions and the hardy Welsh onion (*A. fistulosum*), or ciboul, which has tubular, fat leaves. If you appreciate the subtle (and some not so subtle) flavors of onions, try to collect some of these rarer versions.

Giving examples of what to do with onions is like explaining how to use parsley. Spanish or Bermuda onions, because they are sweet and usually mild, are good raw in salads and sandwiches. All-purpose globe onions retain their more assertive flavor better in soups and stews that are simmered for a long time. But much is a matter of taste and experimentation. All onions can be made into good soup, and all are enjoyed raw by someone somewhere. Their uses range widely: a mild seasoning for stock, baked onions stuffed with meat, deep-fried onion rings with a cornmeal batter, a thick slice of pungent raw onion on buttered bread.

Throw out the onion salt if you've ever possessed such a substitute for real onions, and try some of the many varieties that taste and smell like real onions—varied but all good.

Hearty, Thick Onion Soup

Some onion soups are simmered until the onions practically melt. Some are cooked so briefly that they lack depth. I worked out this recipe to combine the best in taste and texture. It's based on Julia Child's method of bringing out the rich flavor of onions and my memories of the tender but firm onion slices in the delicious soup served at the Four Seasons restaurant in New York. Along with a big crisp salad, it is hearty enough to make a meal in itself. SERVES 4

> 1½ pounds (4 to 5 medium) onions
> 1 tablespoon butter
> 1 tablespoon olive oil
> ½ teaspoon sugar
> 3 cups beef broth or 2½ cups
>   broth and ½ cup dry wine
>
> 4 slices (1 inch thick) French
>   bread
> Salt and pepper
> 1 to 2 cups grated Gruyère or
>   Parmesan cheese

Slice the onions about ⅛ inch thick. Cook them in butter and olive oil over moderate heat in a 2-quart covered saucepan for 15 minutes. Shake pan occasionally. Remove about half the onions and reserve them.

Stir sugar into remaining onions and cook them uncovered over moderate heat, stirring frequently, for 30 minutes. (Don't take shortcuts here. The heat should be high enough so that you *have* to stir frequently to prevent browning. Find something to do nearby—read a cookbook—so you can keep watch and end up with onions of a deep golden color.)

Pour beef broth or broth and wine into saucepan, and bring to a boil. Simmer partially covered for 40 minutes. Meanwhile place bread slices in a roasting pan and bake them in a 300° oven for 30 minutes or until they dry out and brown lightly.

Return reserved onion slices to saucepan, and simmer for 5 minutes. Season to taste, but remember you're going to add salty cheese. If you used salted broth, the soup may be salty enough—just add a few grinds of pepper. The soup can be made to this point, set aside (or frozen), and reheated just before serving.

To serve, dip a ladleful of soup into each of four heatproof bowls. Sprinkle a bit of the cheese into each bowl. Fill bowls with remaining soup. Place a slice of toasted bread on top of each bowl, and sprinkle with remaining cheese. Place soup bowls under broiler until cheese is bubbling and lightly browned.

6 stripps of baccon

Grandma Ziegler's Onion Pie

Our grandparents' warm kitchen was a favorite spot when we were young. While Grandma rolled out pastry and sliced schnitz, Grandpa peeled apples with his magic knife. We watched amazed as he went round and round, taking off the peel in one long spiral so thin we could see through it. We thought Grandma's onion pie a bit strange (pies were supposed to be sweet), but we liked the slight crunchiness of the onions and bacon. You can make this descendant of the honorable Swiss onion tart richer by using cream instead of water and sprinkling grated cheese on top, and I like it with a layer of spinach in the bottom, but this is Grandma's version. SERVES 4

Pastry for one 9-inch crust
2 cups thinly sliced onions

Salt and pepper
6 strips bacon

Line pie pan with pastry, fill with onions, and season generously. Sprinkle 2 tablespoons of water over onions, and place bacon strips on top. Bake at 350° F. for 30 to 35 minutes, until bacon is crisp.

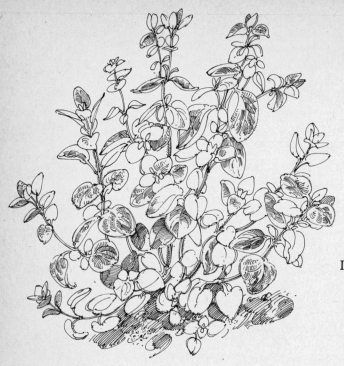

OREGANO

Origanum vulgare
🌿 *perennial*

If you like a hot spicy pizza with a rich tomato sauce flavored by dried oregano, try ripe tomatoes, warm from the garden, sprinkled with freshly snipped oregano leaves. Grow your own, and you can have both. As with marjoram, I grow oregano to use fresh in the summer, then dry it for winter dishes.

In the section on marjoram I discuss how it differs from oregano. These two related herbs confuse many people, but you won't have any trouble if you keep your perennial and annual herb beds separate. Whereas marjoram must be treated as an annual in most climates, oregano is a very hardy perennial that will last for years.

Oregano is also known as wild marjoram, at least partly because of its weedy habits—and indeed it does go wild in some areas. When herbs are as good as oregano, however, I don't care if they behave like weeds and spread and self-seed. And I find oregano attractive with its sprawling stems and its dark-green bowers of rounded leaves. It bears purplish-pink flowers in late summer, and their fragrance compensates for the straggly appearance they give the plant.

My last seed packet of oregano contained a thousand seeds. As usual, I couldn't resist planting them all, and too thickly, because they're so tiny (someone should invent a seed planter that forces people like me to sow thinly). Oregano takes about two weeks to germinate, and weeds are much more efficient than that, so by the time I found the seedlings among the grass, merely rescuing them from suffocation forced me to thin them to the proper 1 foot apart. Oregano should be sown barely covered with fine soil after the ground has warmed up. Put it where it can get all the sunlight possible, but just about any soil will do, and fertilizer is unnecessary.

Oregano plants can be obtained from root divisions or stem cuttings. Be cautious if you get plants from a nursery that doesn't specialize in herbs. Because there are so many *Origanum* species (and marjoram is often known as *Origanum majorana*), you might get a form that doesn't have the pungency you want. Or maybe you'll find a milder kind you do want—some people think *O. vulgare* really is vulgar, that it's just too strong for refined tastes. Its fragrance is often described as thymelike, and that's the most accurate comparison I can come up with when I nibble the fresh leaves. When dried, however, oregano develops a smell all its own, with a bit of sweetness, a slight bitterness, and that pervasive aroma that makes a southern Italian restaurant evident a block before you see it.

Oregano can be grown indoors, but it's not very happy when confined. Leave it outdoors, where it can sprawl, and grow dittany of Crete (*O. dictamnus*) in the house. Dittany is a species of oregano that is small, pretty, and easy to grow, and its fresh flavor is indistinguishable from that of common oregano.

Cut oregano branches to dry as soon as they are big enough to hang, then place them upside down in a shady, airy place. Be sure they're crumbly dry before you crush them into jars—any moisture left will cause a musty flavor. Make an Italian herb mixture by combining dried oregano, marjoram, thyme, rosemary, savory, and perhaps basil and sage. Arrange these fresh herbs in an Italian bouquet for a friend, or use it as a centerpiece for a spaghetti dinner. To preserve some of the summer flavor of oregano, finely chop the leaves into olive oil, refrigerate it, and use it to sprinkle over the top of pizza or pasta.

Italian, Spanish, and Mexican cookbooks have numerous recipes for using dried oregano. Try the following ones for a wonderful fresh dimension.

Marinated Mushrooms and Onions Oregano

Oregano is sometimes known as the mushroom herb in Italy. Of course almost all herbs and greens go well with mushrooms, and you might substitute purple basil for a variation in color or nasturtium leaves for a peppery flavor. Try oregano with wild mushrooms—morels or shaggymanes—and a mixture of chopped wild greens such as dandelion, cress, and purslane. MAKES 2 CUPS

½ pound small fresh mushrooms
1 lemon
½ pound tiny white onions
¼ cup vinegar

¾ cup olive oil
1 clove garlic, minced
¼ cup finely chopped oregano
  leaves

Clean mushrooms, remove stems, and place caps in a saucepan. Squeeze juice from lemon over them. Peel onions and add them to saucepan. Cover with water, and bring to a boil. Turn down heat and simmer for 5 minutes. Drain well, then toss in a bowl with remaining ingredients until well mixed. Marinate unrefrigerated, tossing occasionally, for several hours. Refrigerate up to a week if you like, but the oil will congeal, so bring to room temperature before serving.

Ripe Tomato and Green Oregano Pizza

We lay on the warm grassy bank and inhaled the smell of hay drying on the field below after we'd eaten this pizza al fresco. With all its fresh ingredients, it was quite unlike any pizza we'd had before: it made us feel satisfied but not satiated. It's the best late-summer luncheon I know that combines good things from the gardens. You can add other fresh herbs to it—basil, marjoram, parsley—or your favorite pizza meat, or you can use all white flour, but just like this it's both light and nourishing. SERVES 4

1 package active dry yeast
2 cups all-purpose flour
1 cup whole-wheat flour
Salt
4 tablespoons olive oil
4 to 5 firm ripe tomatoes
4 large mushrooms
2 tablespoons chopped oregano
   leaves

½ pound mozzarella cheese, grated
   or sliced
½ cup grated Parmesan cheese

Measure 1 cup of lukewarm water (105° to 110° F.), and stir the yeast into it until dissolved. Place the flours in a large bowl, make a well in the center, and add about 1 teaspoon salt and 1 tablespoon of the oil. Work yeast water into the flour with your fingers a little at a time until it is all used up. Turn dough out onto a floured surface and knead until it is elastic and shiny. Place in a well-oiled bowl, and turn to coat the surface with oil. Cover, set in a warm spot, and let rise until doubled in bulk.

Brush a large round pizza pan (at least 13 inches in diameter) or a 15-by-10-inch jelly-roll pan with about a tablespoon of oil. Turn the dough out onto a floured surface and shape it into a ball. Roll it thin into the size of the pizza pan. Place in the pan and stretch with your fingertips to touch all edges. Brush dough with oil, and put it in a 500° oven for 5 minutes to bake slightly.

Slice the tomatoes about ½ inch thick. Slice the mushrooms thin. Take the pizza crust out of the oven (but leave oven on) and cover it with tomato slices arranged in an attractive overlapping pattern. Arrange mushroom slices on top. Sprinkle with oregano, season to taste, and scatter any remaining oil on top. Cover with mozzarella and sprinkle Parmesan on top. Bake on lower shelf of oven about 15 minutes or until cheese is bubbling and slightly browned. Serve immediately.

PARSLEY

Petroselinum crispum and hortense

🌿 *biennial*

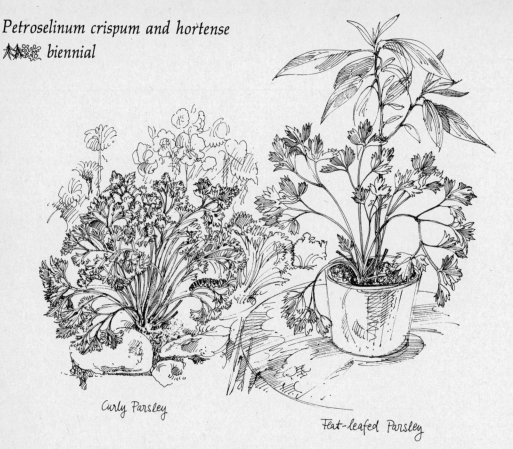

Curly Parsley

Flat-leafed Parsley

Can you imagine life without parsley? From breakfast omelet to luncheon platter decoration to sauce for dinner, it's the herb practically everyone eats in one form or another. Unfortunately, it is often relegated to a mere aesthetic position.

It's appalling to think how much parsley garnish restaurants must throw away; if it were chopped into the food it would add flavor as well as nutrients. Only one freshly minced tablespoon of parsley adds considerably to your recommended daily intake of vitamins A (340 International Units) and C (7 milligrams) and iron (.2 milligrams). Maybe that's why it makes you feel peppy and why Peter Rabbit went searching for parsley when he felt rather sick after overindulging in Mr. McGregor's garden.

Three types of parsley are widely available: the familiar curly kind, the flat-leafed or Italian, and Hamburg, grown for its white root. The curly is pretty, the flat-leafed has a stronger flavor, and people who like parsnips generally like parsley root, which can be prepared as you would Florence fennel (see entry). Avoid wild plants that look like parsley; they are called fool's parsley because they smell bad and are poisonous.

Parsley seeds germinate slowly (up to three weeks), and soaking them overnight before planting speeds the process. It's best to plant seed where it is to grow, since the long taproot can be damaged in transplanting. But I've found that even if half the root is cut off, the plant struggles along and usually makes it.

Parsley is a real survivor, hardy through winter even in Vermont, and a self-seeder too. Since it's biennial, it blooms the second year. In the fall I shake the ripe flower heads to scatter the seeds, cover them lightly with straw, and wait for new plants in the spring. Parsley patches can get rather crowded this way, and the plants are supposed to be spaced 6 inches apart, but it doesn't seem to matter much as long as the plants have rich, loose, moist soil.

Curly parsley is so attractive that it is often used as a border in the flower bed. It grows more than a foot high, depending on how much compost and space you give it. Planting parsley on the edge of the asparagus bed is also a good idea, since the soil there should be rich. Parsley does fine in partial shade, though I've found it won't thrive in a completely shaded spot.

Few pests bother parsley. You are most likely to see a handsome green caterpillar with black stripes who can eat her way through many leaves in a hurry. I can't bear to destroy her, since I know that what is called the parsley worm is fattening herself up so she can turn into a gorgeous black swallowtail butterfly—who will, of course, produce more little parsley worms. But if you start with one packet each of flat-leafed and curly leafed parsley, you'll have enough plants to feed all God's creatures in the area.

If you live in a fairly warm climate, you can pick parsley outdoors all winter, perhaps protecting the plants with some leaves or a bushel basket.

Growing it indoors is not difficult. Since markets almost everywhere sell fresh parsley these days, maybe you'd rather use your houseplant space for herbs more exotic, but parsley is attractive, and used so frequently that it's handy to be able to snip just the right amount of your own as you need it.

You can plant seeds in pots, preferably in the spring, leaving the plants outside to grow lush over summer, or plant whenever you like if you have plant lights. I've had good success with carefully digging up both curly and flat-leafed first-year plants outdoors in the fall and potting them in rich, well-drained, somewhat acidic soil. I trim any wilted foliage, wash the leaves well, and water the plants with fish emulsion. Parsley indoors tends to get paler and leggier than outdoors; you can use the softer stems along with the leaves in many dishes. Keep it pinched back. My parsley seems to do best after my plant-eating child does his own efficient trimming job.

Spider mites sometimes attack indoor parsley, especially the Italian kind (or maybe the damage is simply more apparent when the mites suck the plant juices on its flat leaves). I wish I could tell you what eliminates spider mites; all I can say is that my mites seemed to thrive on garlic spray; hot and cold water sprays were ineffective; a vodka bath perhaps slowed them down a bit. Fortunately, mites usually get serious only near spring, so I trim the damaged plants and set them outside, where mites are rarely a problem. It's a good idea to have indoor parsley growing in several containers widely separated, since mites travel from plant to plant. Some of my parsley pots were uninfested while others looked pitiful. Since parsley survives better than most herbs in partial shade indoors, and doesn't mind cool temperatures, you can scatter pots of it all around the house.

Some people think dried parsley is fine, and it is better than none, but if you must preserve parsley, freezing will retain its color and flavor better, and it's simple to pack sprigs loosely in little freezing packets. Silica gel drying (see page 41) works very well: the parsley becomes crisp but stays bright green and flavorful. However, since parsley is so widely available, so easy to grow, why waste time changing its natural fresh goodness? It keeps a long time refrigerated. Just wash it (grocery-store parsley is often gritty), shake it as dry as possible, and store it in a plastic bag in the refrigerator.

An easy way to "chop" parsley is to squeeze it through a garlic press. This releases lots of flavor, because it helps extract the oil from the leaves. So many recipes call for parsley in small amounts that it's difficult to think of it as an herb to use in quantity. But the flat-leafed variety can be added generously to salads (the curly is a bit tough to chew unless finely chopped), and you can use parsley blossoms to make tempura. Parsley stems are rich in flavor; save trimmings to add to your soup pot or court bouillon. Stuff a chicken cavity with parsley sprigs, baste the bird with parsley butter as it roasts, and you'll have a very parsleyed baked chicken. Fried parsley is easy and different. Even though it's cooked it's nutritious, because the frying is done so fast, and people aren't likely to leave it on the edge of their plates. Wash curly parsley heads, dry, and fry, a handful at a time, in deep fat until parsley is crisp—only a few seconds. Drain, sprinkle with salt if you like, and serve immediately.

Look at the following recipes for other ways to use parsley generously. And the next time you're served a big sprig of curly parsley on your salad, send it back to the kitchen to be chopped.

Tabbouleh

Such a splendid combination of textures and flavors and colors deserves to be eaten more often—and tabbouleh is highly nutritious too. Some people prefer to be authentic and chop the parsley very fine by hand. It takes at least an hour to do this properly, and using the blender produces the same flavor, though a slightly smoother texture, in minutes. You can also use a food processor.
SERVES 6

1 cup fine bulgur (cracked wheat)
3 cups roughly chopped parsley
½ cup mint leaves
½ cup lemon juice
½ cup olive oil

1 cup finely chopped scallions or
    green garlic tops or chives
Salt and pepper
1 large tomato
1 cucumber

Place bulgur in a large mixing bowl, cover with water, and let soak for at least an hour or until wheat has softened. Drain, squeeze out all moisture possible with your hands, then spread bulgur on a cloth or paper towels to dry out further.

Put parsley and mint in blender container, add lemon juice and oil, and blend, pressing herbs down with a spatula, until they are all finely chopped.

Return bulgur to mixing bowl and add herb mixture, scallions or other onions, and seasoning to taste. Chop the tomato and cucumber fine, drain them in a colander to remove as much liquid as possible, and add them to the tabbouleh. Refrigerate if you like, but tabbouleh tastes fine at room temperature too.

Parsley and Potato Soup

The possibilities are endless and enjoyable when you start with a simple potato soup—which lacks a certain visual appeal—and consider how to make it more colorful and nutritious. You can cook other vegetables with the potatoes to provide interest, such as carrots to make an orange-tinted soup, but if you add fresh herbs, as in this recipe, you retain their vitamins and get a lovely sea-green color. Using this basic recipe, you might substitute for the parsley: watercress, purslane, lettuces, dandelion greens, chervil, spinach, sorrel—use your imagination, and use it generously. SERVES 4

4 medium potatoes
1 medium onion, chopped
2 tablespoons butter
2 cups chicken stock
2 cups milk or light cream

2 cups roughly chopped parsley
Salt and pepper
4 slices bacon, fried and crumbled
*   (optional)*

Peel the potatoes, cut them into half-inch cubes, and cook them until tender. Meanwhile sauté onion in butter. When potatoes are cooked, drain them, return to cooking pot, and add stock and milk or cream. Heat slowly. Place parsley in blender container, add the onions with their cooking butter, add about half the potatoes with their liquid, and blend until smooth (or use a food processor). Stir blended mixture into the remaining potatoes, add seasoning to taste, and heat. Serve with crumbled bacon on top if you like.

PEPPERS

Capsicum species  *annual*

Some like them sweet, some like them hot, some like them raw, some in the pot—and some of us like all the pepper varieties: green, red, yellow; sweet, mild, hot, fiery; bell-shaped, conical, round, big, little.

All peppers form neat attractive little bushes that adapt well to indoor pots, planters, and the vegetable garden. Their glossy, tapered leaves are pretty even before the colorful fruit forms. Choose the ones most suitable for your tastes and growing conditions, but don't reject any until you've tried them.

Seed catalogs list an array of peppers with descriptions of flavor and the number of days to maturity. Check their versions of these basics:

Sweet bell peppers, the familiar boxy green ones available in grocery stores, are useful in salads, to flavor cooked dishes, and to stuff. The ones you grow at home may be tapered and grooved into various shapes. As they mature they redden (or turn yellow, depending on variety) and turn sweeter. I start picking the tiny ones as soon as possible, although they're slightly bitter, since the season is short in Vermont and rarely is it warm long enough to produce the deliciously sweet ripe red fruit.

Pimiento, with round, red, fleshy fruit that is used for stuffing olives and is often canned, and mild *banana peppers*, which look like their namesake, are other sweet peppers with their own distinctive flavors.

"Chili pepper" is a loose term for many varieties. Their common characteristic is the way they burn your throat, a sensation pleasurable to cognoscenti and sometimes alarming to initiates. Chilies are the source of ground cayenne pepper and commercial Tabasco. Generally, chili peppers are slender and tapered. The fruits stand upright like candles on the tabasco pepper plant. On the cayenne pepper plant, my favorite for indoors, the twisted pods hang thick like ornaments among the bright-green foliage.

Other more or less hot peppers include *jalapeño*, with spicy green upright fruit, essential for many Mexican dishes; *Hungarian wax*, somewhat banana-shaped, first yellow, then turning red; and hot little *cherry peppers*. Gurney's seed company sells a packet of ten varieties of hot peppers—an excellent idea, since most people don't want many plants of one variety and it's interesting to experiment with different types.

Numerous varieties of tiny ornamental peppers are grown primarily as houseplants. If they are members of the genus *Capsicum* (such as Christmas peppers), they too are edible—and very hot.

Peppers are perennial shrubs in the tropics, and cookbooks reveal what an important ingredient they are in cuisines in hot climates. In the North, peppers are an annual so tender that one must take some care to get a good crop outdoors. Even though you grow one of the several early-bearing varieties, it is necessary to set out plants rather than seed directly in the ground, since most peppers require more than three months of hot weather to bear fruit.

Start pepper seeds indoors six to eight weeks before outdoor temperatures average 55°F. If you want only a few sweet pepper plants it's easier to buy sturdy ones at a greenhouse. Plant them at least 3 feet apart.

The ground must be warm when you set out pepper plants. They are somewhat particular about soil too. Peppers do best in well-drained, sandy, sweet soil with adequate magnesium and phosphorus. If soil is too rich, the foliage will be beautiful but the fruit scanty. If it's poorly drained, fruit will not form well, yet peppers need plenty of moisture. When you set out plants, water them well with a liquid fertilizer solution that contains trace minerals. Mulch the plants to preserve moisture.

Most problems with peppers outdoors are caused by inadequate care to the plants' needs. If leaves spot and drop off, the soil probably lacks magnesium. Mosaic virus may appear if soil is too acid or the plants don't get adequate ventilation. To prevent cutworms, sink a cardboard collar in the soil around the plants when you set them out. Aphids and whiteflies should be hosed off or sprayed with a garlic and hot pepper solution (see page 12)—yes, it's homeopathic in a way: you use the plant, in a different form, to treat the disease.

Most hot peppers are excellent houseplants, and if you have plenty of light you can even grow large sweet peppers indoors. Tropical plants such as peppers do well in overheated houses as long as they're watered and misted frequently. Use sandy potting soil and add all-purpose fertilizer occasionally.

If spider mites and whiteflies appear, treat them immediately (see pages 31–2). I put my houseplant peppers outdoors in the summer; they flourish in the sunshine and rain. If you do this or pot up plants from outdoors, wash the foliage very well before you bring plants inside.

Keep hot pepper plants, with their bright, tempting fruit, out of children's reach. Always wash your hands after handling hot peppers; the oils cling, and I can testify that they don't feel good if you rub your eyes with pepper-stained fingers.

Peppers have shallow roots, so cut or break fruit off gently to avoid pulling up the plant. Before frost, pick outdoor peppers and store them in a cool place. Chili peppers can be dried on a screen until they shrivel, then packed in jars. As you use them, save some seeds for planting in the future.

Sweet bell peppers, especially red ones, are very high in minerals and vitamins, especially vitamin C, and low in calories. Red chili peppers, however, are astonishing: 21,000 International Units of vitamin A per 100 grams (spinach has 8,100) and 369 milligrams of vitamin C (many times the recommended daily allowance). Even a small amount, which is all most people can handle when ingesting such a fiery substance, will add appreciably to your nutrient intake. (Chili peppers are often ground and put into capsules for vitamin supplements.)

Hot peppers are not to be used recklessly by the novice. Start by adding a dash of cayenne or liquid Tabasco to cooked dishes instead of salt, or use one of your small chili peppers in a stew, then remove it before serving. As your palate adjusts, go on to other recipes in which the heat of peppers is an essential ingredient, such as Mexican chili.

Stuff sweet peppers, or large hot ones, with mixtures of meat, rice, cheese, and whatever else suits your budget and taste. The basic recipe is simple: cut off pepper tops, scrape out seeds, parboil peppers 5 minutes, drain, place in oiled baking dish, and fill with stuffing ingredients. The filling can be as inexpensive as leftovers bound with eggs and cooked rice or as costly as seafood in béchamel sauce. In general, bake stuffed peppers at 350° F. for about 30 minutes.

My husband adds minced sweet green peppers to frittate, omelets, macaroni and cheese, and every other egg and cheese dish he can. I often find that the peppers he uses so generously dominate other flavors, and I tend to be more cautious (but then I'm the one who puts too many hot peppers in chili for many people's taste). I like green and red sweet peppers as a vegetable in themselves: sautéed with garlic oil until barely al dente, threaded on skewers for shish kebab, slivered in mixed green salads, pickled like cucumbers. Test for yourself: try peppers minced and chunked and whole, raw and cooked, and see which you like best. Maybe you'll find, as I do, that they're best of all when you snitch crunchy pieces as an appetizer while you're preparing the meal.

Sauce Pipérade

You can add more tomatoes to this basic fresh-tasting sauce and use it to dress pasta, make chili sauce by adding hot peppers to it, thin it with mayonnaise to make salad dressing, or stir beaten eggs into it for a fluffy pipérade. Use it just as it is with roasted chicken, on grilled fish, or as a dip for fresh vegetables. It freezes well. MAKES ABOUT 1 QUART

2 cloves garlic
2 large onions
½ cup olive oil
4 large sweet green or red peppers
   (or a combination)

4 large ripe tomatoes
½ cup diced cooked ham
1 tablespoon chopped basil
Salt and pepper

Mince the garlic. Cut onions in half, then slice thin. Heat the oil in a large skillet, add garlic and onions, and sauté over moderate heat, stirring frequently, for 10 minutes.

Remove and discard seeds and membranes from peppers. Slice peppers into thin strips. Peel and core tomatoes and chop them coarsely. Add peppers and tomatoes to skillet, cover, and cook over low heat for 30 minutes.

Uncover skillet, add diced ham, and cook over moderately high heat, stirring with a wooden spoon, until sauce thickens a bit, about 15 minutes. Stir in basil and season to taste.

Deviled Crab or Clams

Visits to the seafood market in Richmond, Virginia, were exercises in overindulgence: oysters cracked open at the bar, hot spicy shrimp to shell and eat on the way home, and a boxful of deviled crabs to reheat for "dessert." Now, when I recall that piquant fresh crab mixture, I sigh and open a few cans of clams to make a good substitute. SERVES 4

2 cups crabmeat or two 6½-ounce
   cans minced clams
4 tablespoons mayonnaise
1 egg, lightly beaten
½ teaspoon finely crushed hot red
   pepper, Tabasco, or cayenne
   pepper

½ teaspoon dry mustard
1 cup fine dry bread crumbs
Salt and pepper
2 tablespoons melted butter
1 tablespoon minced parsley
Lemon wedges

Combine crabmeat or clams, mayonnaise, egg, red pepper or Tabasco, and mustard. Stir in half the bread crumbs, season to taste, and mix well. Heap mixture in crab shells, clam shells, or other small ovenproof containers.

Toss remaining bread crumbs with melted butter and parsley. Sprinkle on top of seafood mixture, patting lightly with your fingers to make crumbs adhere. Bake in a 350° oven about 15 minutes, until crumbs have lightly browned. Serve immediately with lemon wedges.

Southern-Style Barbecues with Hot Pepper Sauce

To do this right, you need a whole pig—about 70 pounds will do—and a pit with oak coals. We like barbecued pork on buns so much that we've simplified the recipe considerably. We sometimes cook the pork on a spit or roast it in the oven, basting it with the chili-pepper mixture. The hot pepper sauce is essential; if you can't make it from scratch, substitute Tabasco, but it's not quite the same. You can make up a big batch of this sauce and refrigerate it for whenever the barbecue munchies strike. Or add it to chopped clams and bread crumbs for delicious deviled clams. MAKES ABOUT 24 BARBECUES

4 pounds pork loin
2 cloves garlic, chopped
2 onions, chopped
10 hot red chili peppers, fresh or dried
1 cup vinegar

1 cup tomato sauce
3 tablespoons white or brown sugar
1 tablespoon black pepper
24 hamburger buns
1 pint cole slaw

Place pork in a saucepan, add garlic and onions, and nearly cover with water. Bring to a boil, cover, turn down heat to a brisk simmer, and cook at least 3 hours, until meat is falling apart.

Meanwhile, remove stems and seeds from chili peppers. Save seeds to plant, if you like, and place chilies in blender container with vinegar. Blend at high speed until peppers are finely ground. Strain through several layers of cheesecloth. Add tomato sauce and sugar, and stir to dissolve sugar.

When pork is tender, drain off cooking liquid and let meat cool uncovered until you can easily strip it from the bones with your hands. Chop meat

gleaming purslane leaves

fine with a knife, shred it with your fingers, or put small amounts at a time in the blender and chop coarsely. Place in a saucepan, add black pepper and about a tablespoon of water, and steam gently to heat through.

Heat buns, then fill them with pork. Serve cole slaw and pepper sauce in separate dishes for each person to top barbecues.

makes good nibbling while you garden weed

PURSLANE

Portulaca oleracea ❀ annual

Purslane, with its vinegary flavor and crisp texture, makes good nibbling while you weed the garden. Its vitamins and texture are an asset to salads and stews. Purslane also taught me some lessons about weeds and their proper place.

"You'd better get that purslane out," my father advised when he viewed our first vegetable garden in Vermont. "If you let it spread you'll never get rid of it."

"Oh, no, we're encouraging it," we replied with all the smugness of innocents who've just absorbed the *Stalking* books. "Euell Gibbons says it's good in salads and to thicken stews and it has lots of nutrients and . . ."

Thank you, Daddy, for not saying, "I told you so." By the next summer gleaming purslane leaves had spread a fat carpet over the vegetable garden.

leaves had spread a fat carpet over the garden

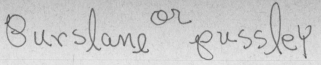

They're practically impossible to pull out: when you grab them they just break off in segments, leaving the roots intact.

We now use a newspaper and hay mulch on the garden, but that doesn't mean the purslane stays beneath it. I'm convinced it gathers strength under cover, then creeps out one moonlit night. You awake in the morning to find the carrot seedlings strangled.

But purslane has more nutrients than carrots, so maybe it's just as well to lose some of the carrots and eat purslane instead. It has three times the calcium and vitamin C of raw carrots, and five times more iron. It doesn't have as much vitamin A, but its 2,500 International Units per 3½ ounces is generous—about half the recommended daily amount.

Purslane, or pussley, as it is sometimes called, grows only about 2 inches high, but its green and reddish succulent leaves spread on mucilaginous stems for more than a foot. The plants look much like those of the flowering portulaca, a showier relative. Purslane has insignificant pale-yellow flowers. They open briefly in the morning when it's sunny, then hasten to turn into seed pods that pop open, scatter, and self-seed as reliably as johnny-jump-ups.

Varieties of purslane grow and are used in cooking in many parts of the world. The leaves have a pleasantly acidic flavor that complements milder greens in salads, and purslane is used in many cuisines as a potherb because its mucilage thickens soups and stews. Boil a mess of leaves the same way you do any cooked green, or put them in casseroles. Purslane can be frozen after parboiling. You can make crispy pickles from the stems just as you would pickle green beans, and the seed pods can be dried and powdered into flour. Purslane is a traditional ingredient in chivry butter; make it by chopping purslane, chervil, parsley, tarragon, and chives into soft butter. It's delicious with a leg of lamb.

I have found purslane plants, with all the water they contain (some 90 percent), to be a splendid addition to the compost pile. If you start a garden, watch for this useful plant to appear. Purslane has an intelligence network that is uncannily tuned to the sound of soil being cultivated. I've never seen it growing in lawns or fields, but start a vegetable garden and the purslane plants in your neighbor's garden will confer in anticipation: which of us gets to be the infiltrator this time? It's hard to believe that people cultivate purslane, but if you decide to, I pass on this advice from Maude Grieve in her classic herbal: "Keep the plants clear from weeds."

ROCKET

Eruca sativa ❀ annual

arugula

Rocket,
also known
as roquette, arugula,
rugula, rocket cress,
and garden rocket,
has a distinct flavor. It's been described as mushroomy, turnipy, and mustardy, but nobody calls it delicate. It's so robust that you might be advised not to overdo it when you first try rocket.

As I did. I'd read so much of the joys of rocket that I profligately heaped it in the salad bowl after I'd thinned the seedlings. Later I read in *Larousse* that rocket is used as a "seasoning" in salads, and that is how I recommend you start using it. Then maybe you'll become so fond of its flavor that you'll relish whole bowlfuls of it, the way many Italians do.

Rocket has toothed, spear-shaped leaves that resemble large field cress. Seeds germinate and grow rapidly in practically any soil. Thin the plants to 6 inches apart, and start using them as soon as you can pick leaves a few inches long. Pale purple, white, or variegated rocket blooms are sometimes called vesper flowers because they have a pleasant fragrance in the evening. They appear when the rocket plants are about 3 feet tall, far past the time for harvesting. By midsummer the plants have gone to seed and have perhaps reseeded themselves.

Leafhoppers ate lots of tiny holes in my rocket seedlings, and since I wasn't overly fond of rocket—it *is* an acquired taste—I was grateful that the leafhoppers congregated on the rocket instead of on my lettuces. If you want unholey rocket, try a garlic spray (see page 12). Rocket also attracts cabbageworms, since it's a member of the mustard family; covering the seedlings with cheesecloth or nylon netting will deter the butterflies whose larvae eat the leaves.

Be careful not to bring in pests if you pot plants for indoors. Wash the foliage carefully.

Rocket can be an herb, greens, or an aromatic, depending on your taste. Use its small leaves as you would parsley to accent a salad. Cook it with other greens, such as collards and dandelions. Blend it with melted butter for a pleasantly sour flavor that goes well with seafood, potatoes, and pasta.

ROSEMARY

Rosmarinus officinalis
🌿 *perennial*

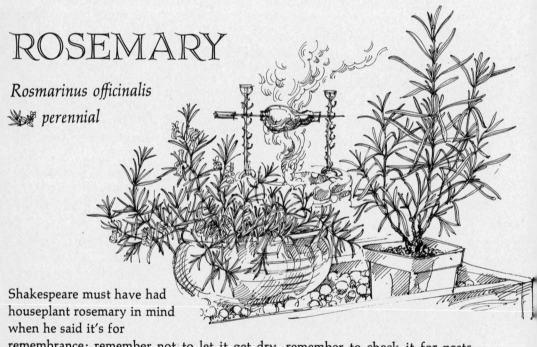

Shakespeare must have had houseplant rosemary in mind when he said it's for remembrance: remember not to let it get dry, remember to check it for pests, remember to keep it pinched back, remember to keep a constant watch on it—and it may be happy if it's a mind to. None of my herbs has given me more grief, or greater rewards.

First, the rewards. Rosemary is an attractive plant, with its leathery deep-green leaves that resemble pine needles on a little shrubby tree. They grow about an inch long and are silvery underneath and evergreen where there's no severe freezing in winter. And rosemary has a wonderfully pungent resinous odor. You can smell it when you walk into the herb garden, and the piny flavor comes through when rosemary is used in cooking.

Rosemary stems quickly get woody. The plant grows up to 2 feet or more in warmer climates, where it is perennial. Its flowers are pale blue or white or pink, and they rarely produce seeds. Some species, and there are many, include Corsican (*R. corsicus*), with narrower leaves and deep-blue flowers, and prostrate (*R. prostratus*), a spreading rosemary that grows only up to a foot tall and makes a good houseplant. Many rosemaries can be trained as bonsai.

As in its native hot climate, rosemary thrives on all the sun it can get and prefers well-drained alkaline soil. Use some lime if your soil is acid, and fertilize sparingly. In cold climates one must treat the plant as an annual—it won't survive temperatures below zero—but sometimes rosemary will make it through winter if it's covered with hay and a basket.

Rosemary seeds should be lightly covered with soil when all danger of frost has passed, or you can start seeds indoors about six weeks before the soil warms up. Although mature plants should be grown at least a foot apart, I let the seedlings grow much more thickly than that. Plants remain small the first year anyway, so I transplant some into pots that I'll later bring indoors, use others generously in cooking, give a lot away, and let the rest form a mass in tight space, since they'll die when winter comes anyway. When the first frost comes, I trim back the plants and use some of the branches on the barbecue grill, either right on the hot coals or as a bed under quickly cooked foods like fish and squash.

But my rosemary packets contain a thousand seeds, and you may not want even a fraction of the plants that their poor germination produces. Greenhouses often sell rosemary even if they carry few other herbs, and you can select a healthy, well-shaped plant. Remember that nursery purchases may harbor insects, so keep the plant quarantined for a few weeks, and replant it if the roots are coming out the bottom of the pot.

Rosemary can be propagated by cuttings or layering. For cuttings, take a 4-inch branch of new growth, strip the leaves from the bottom, place it in moistened sphagnum moss and sand, and cover it with a plastic bag. It may take months to root. Layering is easy if you already have outdoor plants. Bend down a rosemary branch until you can secure it to the ground with a small rock or a hairpin. Cover the grounded part with soil, and keep it moist until roots form, then cut the branch from the main stalk and plant the new roots.

Now the grief. After I thought I'd had all the ten rosemary plagues, I discovered mealybugs on my indoor plants. I've composted so many dead rosemaries that I've lost count, and I'm now convinced that their greatest need is consistent moisture to their leaves and roots. Some herbs neglected indoors will wilt but revive with watering, but once rosemary leaves dry out, there's nothing to do but strip off the dried leaves for cooking, then discard the plant. Give the plant good drainage, but never let the soil dry out. Frequent washing or misting of the leaves seems to be what keeps my plants going now. It helps get rid of pests such as mealybugs and red spider mites, and it keeps the leaves moist. If leaves turn yellow, the pot may be too small for the root system or the plant may not be getting enough light. Pinch off pale growth at the tips of the branches; these pallid leaves tend to wither anyway, and they are mild and soft enough to add to salads.

Drying rosemary is simple, and it's an herb that retains much of its flavor when dried. Hang branches until you can easily strip leaves off, or spread sprigs on a screen until they are thoroughly dry, then pack leaves in jars. When using dried rosemary in cooking, it's often best to grind it to a powder with a mortar and pestle, since the whole leaves, even when cooked, are a bit tough to chew.

For fresh rosemary, one of the best and easiest ways to extract flavor while eliminating the "pine needles" is to lay branches or sprigs on top of roasts and vegetables while they cook, then remove before serving. Fresh or dried rosemary is assertive in flavor, so it goes well with game, strong-flavored fish, and robust vegetables such as beets and cabbage. It's also good with lamb. Make slits in grilled meat or roasts and push rosemary and garlic slivers into them before cooking. Stuff a hen with rosemary leaves before roasting, and use leaves in poultry or pork stuffings. To make rosemary vinegar (good in a salad of strong greens, such as dandelions or spinach), add several sprigs or a handful of rosemary leaves to a jar, pour cider or red-wine vinegar over to fill, and set on a sunny windowsill for a few weeks. Rosemary wine to use for basting or in cooking can be made the same way. Rosemary butter for brushing on fish or steaks is easiest to make by blending a stick of melted butter with about a half cup of rosemary leaves until the leaves are finely chopped.

Remembering to care for rosemary plants may be a problem, but remembering to use the leaves in cooking never is.

Rosemary Pickled Beets

You can use canned beets for this, and I do in winter, often substituting rosemary vinegar for the fresh rosemary. Leftover beet vinegar can be used to pickle onions or hard-boiled eggs. Hot buttered beets and Harvard beets are also good with rosemary. MAKES ABOUT 1 PINT

*1 pound fresh beets (preferably
    tiny new ones)*
*3 rosemary sprigs or 1 tablespoon
    chopped leaves*

1 cup vinegar
½ cup sugar
Salt

Cut tops off about 2 inches from beets, but leave roots on. Save tops to use in salad or cook as greens. Scrub beets well. Cook them in a pressure cooker or steam or boil them just until they are done. Time will depend on size of beets, but for beet pickles they're best crunchy-tender.

Rinse cooked beets in cold water until you can handle them, then cut off roots and stems and rub off skins. Leave tiny beets whole; if they're large, slice, julienne, quarter, or dice them. Pack warm beets in pint jar.

Place rosemary in a saucepan, pour vinegar over, and stir in sugar. Add salt to taste. Bring mixture to a boil, stirring, and pour it over beets. Cover jar, let cool, then refrigerate at least a week before eating.

Rosemary Venison Steaks, Swiss Style

Rosemary's piny flavor goes perfectly with meat from the woods. We like venison well cooked, but you could sauté these steaks after marination and serve them rare, reducing the marinade separately to make a sauce. Wild rice and watercress salad are good accompaniments to venison. SERVES 4

4 venison round steaks, cut 1 inch
  thick
¼ cup rosemary leaves
2 onions, sliced
2 cups sliced carrots
1 cup chopped celery
2 cloves garlic, minced

½ teaspoon pepper
2 cups dry red wine
¼ cup vinegar
Flour
½ cup olive oil
Salt

Place steaks in a nonaluminum bowl or heavy leakproof plastic bag. Add rosemary, onions, carrots, celery, garlic, pepper, wine, and vinegar. Place in refrigerator for 24 hours.

Remove steaks, reserving marinade. Pat steaks dry, dredge them in flour, and sauté in olive oil in a Dutch oven until brown on both sides. Add marinade with its vegetables, bring to a boil, cover, and simmer gently for about 2 hours. Remove meat and reduce sauce further if you like, or thicken it with a bit of flour blended in water. Add salt to taste.

RUE

Ruta graveolens 🌿 *perennial*

People have been known to drink rue tea, and in some countries rue leaves are added to salads, but I include it in my perennial herb bed because of its attractive gray-blue-green foliage. Frost seems to intensify its color in the fall, and rue is one of the few plants in Vermont already going strong when the snow melts.

Rue's strong, acrid odor repels many insects—and it repels me if I get too close to it for too long. (Some people are even allergic to the plant and develop a skin rash after handling it.) The leaves, which taste very bitter, look a bit like

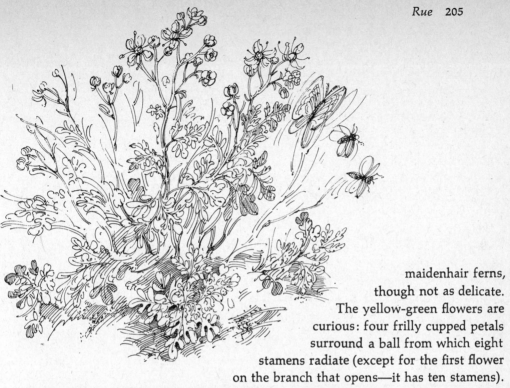

maidenhair ferns,
though not as delicate.
The yellow-green flowers are
curious: four frilly cupped petals
surround a ball from which eight
stamens radiate (except for the first flower
on the branch that opens—it has ten stamens).
Nevertheless, when the plant blooms, it's a disappointment: one expects something more stately than the huddled flower clusters. Much more elegant are the white airy masses of wild meadow rue flowers that I let seed themselves in the herb garden because the name, if not the family, is the same.

Rue grows from 2 to 3 feet high and is usually propagated by seeds, although cuttings can be rooted in spring. It often self-seeds, and the hardy plants survive in almost any soil for at least five years. They should be grown a foot apart. Rue makes an unusual dwarf hedge. Its foliage contrasts nicely with such white flowers as baby's breath and petunias, and the colors combine just as well in herb bouquets.

Rue can be dried to use in tea or ornamental dried arrangements. If you want to keep leaves green for winter, cut the branches and bury them until needed. Rue is supposed to repel flies and is more handsome than most herbs, so you might like to try it as a decorative houseplant.

SAGE

Salvia officinalis 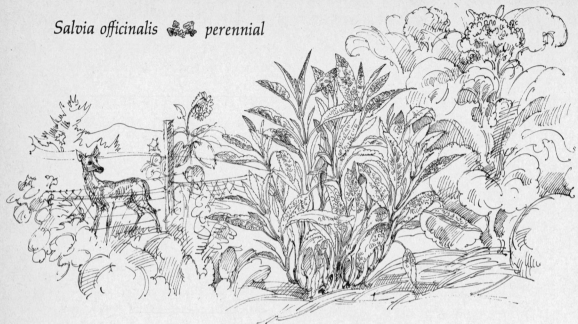 perennial

When sage is fresh, it has a mild zest unlike the strong flavor of dried sage. Grow at least one plant in your perennial herb bed if you can, and grow one indoors during the winter in cold climates, where sage is smothered by snow. It is evergreen in warmer climates.

Common sage leaves look like pebbly gray-green tongues. The flowers are violet-blue spikes. A very hardy perennial, sage can be propagated by seeds, layering, cuttings, or root division. Many varieties of sage are mutants whose seeds will revert to the ordinary kind. Some have leaves variegated with white and purplish red; some have yellow variations on the edges of the leaves. Clary sage (*S. sclarea*), a biennial, is often grown for its fragrant flowers, which bloom the second season on greenish-white or pinkish spikes. Pineapple sage (*S. rutilans*) is a tender perennial with scarlet flowers; it is good in punch and tea because its fresh leaves smell slightly like fresh pineapple. Dwarf forms of sage make attractive edgings for flower beds.

If you start sage from seeds, use restraint in sowing or ruthlessly thin the plants to at least a foot apart. Sage grows 2 to 3 feet tall and branches out into a small bush. After about five years, it gets woody, and it is time to lay down some of its branches, cover the stems with soil, and start rooting new plants. You may discover that some branches have already adventurously bedded down and rooted all by themselves. All you have to do is snip the stem to the mother plant, dig up the new roots, and set them in fresh soil. Destroy the old plant. Sage doesn't seem to be particular about soil as long as it is well drained and gets plenty of sun.

Sage, I've been told repeatedly, repels cabbageworms. For years I've been picking cabbageworms off the broccoli that touches the adjoining sage leaves. I plant sage in the vegetable garden for a purpose not mentioned by organic gardening manuals. Deer don't like sage, and after they've eaten off all the broccoli, the interspersed sage plants grow vigorously and the row doesn't look so bare.

Dried sage can be very good, with a flavor and fragrance much stronger than fresh leaves. But it gets musty if leaves aren't dried thoroughly, so hang sage branches in a well-ventilated area until they are crumbly dry—but don't crumble them into jars. Leave them as whole as possible, and crush them just before you use them to retain their best flavor. I keep branches hanging and pull off leaves as I need them.

For indoor plants, I pot up small sage bushes that have spent the summer in the vegetable garden. I prune them to a compact shape and wash them well. Sage is a member of the mint family, and it attracts all the same pests. You can discourage red spider mites by washing the foliage with sudsy water, then rinsing well, and this takes care of most other pests. The most disgusting creatures to attack indoor sage are mealybugs; see page 32 for some ways to attempt to eradicate them. Wash or mist sage often indoors, and give it as much light as possible. Pinch back the shoots so the plant doesn't get scraggly. The leaves will be smaller and their flavor won't be as pungent indoors, so you can add the little ones from pruning to salads. Be sure the soil has good drainage, and don't overwater or overfertilize; sage does best in fairly dry and neutral soil.

If you haven't had luck with ordinary sage as a houseplant, it may not be your fault. Hardy common sage, like most big herbs and greens, simply prefers the outdoor environment. Indoors, my sage plants always reflect my winter cabin fever by getting woody-stemmed and pale-colored, but they perk right up when they're set back outdoors. Look for compact varieties imported from warmer climates; they adapt better to indoor conditions. Several mail-order herb companies specialize in sages (see Sources of Seeds and Plants, page 251).

Toward the end of summer, when the sage bushes in the garden are large and spreading, we cut branches to lay on top of the charcoal when we cook outdoors. Food cooked over the coals is flavored with sage—or maybe it just seems to be because the air is filled with sage aroma.

Sage has generous quantities of vitamins A and C, and some people nourish themselves by chewing or smoking the leaves. One is often cautioned to use sage with discretion, because it has such an assertive character. I'm inclined to use fresh sage generously in foods that it dominates in a pleasant way (such as breads and potatoes) and even more lavishly with aggressive ingredients (such as pork and sharp Cheddar cheese). Instead of bay leaves, try spreading fresh sage leaves over a roast while it cooks.

A bouquet of sage leaves provides a nice backdrop for flowers of almost any color, but purple and violet flowers combine handsomely with sage sprays and spiky purple sage flowers. Use them as a centerpiece when you serve the following recipes.

Sage and Cheddar Biscuits

Cheese makes ordinary baking-powder biscuits rich and moist, and sage gives them color and piquancy. Serve them hot for best flavor. We sometimes substitute other herbs or greens and cheese: tarragon with Gruyère, watercress with Roquefort, and dill with Parmesan are just some of the possibilities.
MAKES ABOUT 12 BISCUITS

2 cups flour
1 tablespoon baking powder
4 tablespoons butter
½ cup grated firm Cheddar cheese

2 tablespoons finely chopped sage
  leaves
About ¾ cup milk

Sift flour and baking powder into a mixing bowl. Use your fingers to blend butter and cheese into flour until mixture is in crumbly fine particles. Add sage. Stir milk in with a fork, adding just enough to make a soft but not sticky dough. Knead lightly for about 1 minute on a floured surface, then pat out to about ¾ inch thick for fluffy biscuits, about ¼ inch for crusty ones. Cut with floured biscuit cutter, and place on an ungreased baking sheet; space biscuits closely for soft texture, separated for crispness. Bake in preheated 425° oven for about 15 minutes.

Veal Scallops with Sage

Fresh sage leaves used this way provide just the right balance between delicate veal and salty ham. Evan Jones, an authority on cheeses and American food, provided this recipe. He was inspired by the Tuscan use of fresh sage.
SERVES 4

8 thin veal scallops (about 1½ pounds)
Flour
2 tablespoons cooking oil
3 tablespoons butter
Salt and pepper

8 pieces thinly cut prosciutto, trimmed to size of veal scallops
16 large sage leaves
⅓ cup dry white wine
½ cup veal or chicken stock

Dredge the veal lightly in flour. Heat the oil and 2 tablespoons of the butter in a large skillet until sizzling, and sauté as many of the veal scallops as the pan will hold without crowding them. Cook only about 1 minute on each side, add another tablespoon of butter, and cook the rest. Salt lightly (Italian ham is salty), and grind fresh pepper over. Toss the prosciutto in the skillet just enough to heat through. Place two sage leaves on each scallop, cover with a piece of prosciutto, and fold over, securing with a toothpick if necessary. Pour the wine into the skillet, boil hard, and scrape up brown bits from the pan, then add the stock and reduce the juices by about a third. Put scallops back into pan and turn once in the hot juices, remove to a hot platter, scrape any remaining sauce over them, and serve.

Pork Chops with Sage Dressing

A favorite at our house whenever we can find very thick pork chops. Wayne's mother got us in the habit with her deliciously pungent pork stuffing. At first, it tasted to me as if it combined two parts sage to one part bread crumbs, but I came to love it. This is a variation of her recipe, and you can use less sage if you like, or more if you're as reckless as we are. A sauce or gravy could accompany this dish, and fried apples are traditional. SERVES 4

1 large onion, finely chopped
1 clove garlic, minced
4 tablespoons butter
1 cup chicken broth
2 cups dry bread crumbs
4 tablespoons finely chopped sage
  leaves

Salt and pepper
4 thick (about 1-inch) lean pork
  chops
Sage sprigs

Sauté onion and garlic in butter until translucent, then pour in broth and heat briefly. Pour mixture over bread crumbs, add chopped sage, and season to taste. Mix thoroughly. Spread some stuffing mixture against one end of a small loaf pan, place a pork chop against it upright, add more stuffing, and continue process until pork chops are used up, filling in with stuffing. Cover tightly with foil, and bake in a 400° oven for about 1½ hours, or longer if you like the pork to be falling-apart tender—it won't dry out with all that moist dressing around it. Serve each pork chop with its share of stuffing, and add a few sage sprigs for garnish.

Hot Sage Sausage

This is not the sort of sausage you normally eat for breakfast, although I've known southerners to down it readily with grits and scrambled eggs and biscuits to soften the blow. If you can't take it straight, you might use it in pizza or add it to stuffing or combine it with hamburger in a meatloaf. It's wonderful in sausage bread, but however you use it, plenty of refreshing liquid should accompany it. Fatty pork fries better, but we like the sausage a bit lean to save calories. Reduce the amount of seasoning if you want a blander sausage.

MAKES ABOUT 1 POUND

1 pound ground pork
4 tablespoons finely chopped sage
   leaves

1 teaspoon black pepper
1 teaspoon crushed hot red pepper
   or Tabasco

Blend all ingredients well in a mixing bowl. If you use your hands to mix, and they work best, wash them carefully afterward to remove traces of hot peppers. Form sausage into patties or fill casings. Refrigerate at least 24 hours for flavors to blend. To cook, place sausage in a cold skillet and fry slowly, turning several times, for about 30 minutes.

SAVORY

Summer Satureia hortensis  *annual*
Winter Satureia montana *perennial*

Summer Savory

Winter Savory

The bean herb, it's called, and for a good reason. Lentils, favas, soybeans, limas—all are enhanced by the flavor of savory. But the best combination is the first small green beans steamed simply and briefly with a few sprigs of delicate summer savory as the only seasoning. That's why I plant the annual summer savory among the beans in the garden, and no basket of snaps comes to the house without a bouquet of savory on top. Winter savory stays in the perennial herb bed, as decorative as it is useful for a stronger flavor with dried beans and meat.

The two most familiar of the many varieties of savory have similar leaves and flavor, but their growing habits, soil requirements, and appearance are quite different.

Summer savory grows up to 2 feet tall, with branchy stems and sparse, almost scraggly foliage of slender leaves about half an inch long. Its flowers are small, a light pink. You can start seeds indoors, but there's no good reason to: if you plant it when you put the beans in, you'll have plenty by bean-picking time. Sometimes I make breaks in the bean row and drop in a few savory seeds, and sometimes I make a row between the bean rows. Seedlings should be thinned to about 6 inches apart—use them, stems and all, to flavor your first dish of peas. Summer savory likes moist soil, the richer the better, and it grows quickly. Its fragrance is lighter, sweeter, and more pleasant than winter savory. It will self-seed if the season is long. If you want to dry it (and it's good dried), pick the branches and hang them just before they start to bloom. When they're thoroughly dry, strip the leaves off and store them in jars.

Winter savory, with its bright-green, glossy leaves, makes a handsome little evergreen shrub that grows up to a foot high and spreads out to 2 feet across. The base of the stems is woody, the leaves a bit tough and half an inch long. In June or July tiny white or pinkish flowers appear like stars scattered over the bush. Sow seeds outdoors in well-drained ordinary soil; rich, moist soil encourages the sort of soft growth that doesn't winter over well. Better, find a local source to supply you with some slips or root divisions, since you probably don't need all the plants that will sprout from a packet of seeds. Once you get plants going, they're no problem. Just trim them back in the spring to encourage new growth (throw trimmings on the charcoal when you grill hamburgers), and divide plants every few years to share with friends. Compared to summer savory, winter savory tastes sharper, spicier, more resinous, so less of it is needed to flavor food. You can dry it just like summer savory, but it takes longer to dry thoroughly.

But savory is such an obliging year-round herb that you shouldn't have to dry it unless you like it that way. The annual produces far more than you can use fresh in the summer, so freeze or can it along with your beans or other vegetables. The perennial is always there as a backup: through winter in warmer climates you can gather its leaves, and it makes a fine houseplant. Treat it as you would rosemary (see entry). Summer savory is not a good indoor plant—it just gets scragglier—but winter savory in the house loses some of its pungency and becomes more like summer savory in texture and taste.

When you use either kind, remember that the mature stems are tough. Savory is a handy herb for cooking on top of vegetables or in the soup pot: you can throw in some whole branches and retrieve them before serving. If you're using savory in salads or blended into a dish, strip off the tender leaves only. Because they're rather small, they're hard to wash, so savory plants should be kept mulched to prevent mud from splashing on them when it rains.

Savory is a wonderful salt substitute. The leaves are kind of salty and slightly peppery too; I think they provide all the seasoning needed with vegetables. Savory adds flavor to stuffings, sausage, and bouquets garnis. Make savory butter (good on biscuits) by spinning a handful of savory leaves with a stick of melted butter in the blender. Pour warm vinegar over savory sprigs, steep it for a week, and use it in making a dressing for bean salads that is savory in every way.

Savory Bean Salad

This can be a one-bean or a ten-bean salad. I combine as many different beans as I can gather from the garden—limas, yellow and green snaps, fava beans—and add canned garbanzos and kidney beans, cooked soybeans, navy beans, lentils, and split peas, to make a medley of colors, textures, and flavors. The fresh savory is what makes the beans special, so you can use one kind of bean only. Or pair resinous winter savory with the "heavier" dried and canned beans and use lighter summer savory with fresh legumes. SERVES 4

6 cups cooked beans (see above)
4 tablespoons chopped savory
* leaves*
1 onion, chopped
1 sweet green or red pepper,
* chopped*

¼ cup olive oil
¼ cup vinegar
¼ cup sugar
Salt and pepper

Place beans, savory, onion, and chopped pepper in a mixing bowl. Combine oil, vinegar, and sugar, and mix until sugar dissolves. Pour over beans, toss, and season to taste. Cover and chill at least 24 hours for best flavor.

Green Beans in Savory Sour Cream Sauce

Tiny green beans cooked with savory until barely tender are good in their simplicity. For a richer dish, perhaps with more mature beans, try this. SERVES 4

1 pound fresh green beans
2 cups thinly sliced onions
2 tablespoons butter
2 ripe tomatoes, peeled, seeded, and
  chopped

2 tablespoons chopped savory
  leaves
1 egg
1 cup sour cream
Salt and pepper

Trim beans, drop them in boiling water, and cook until crisply tender—5 to 10 minutes, depending on their size. Run cold water over beans, and drain them in a colander.

Sauté onions in butter in a large skillet until soft. Add tomatoes and cook over high heat, stirring, for 10 minutes. Add green beans and savory, and heat.

Beat egg into sour cream, and stir gradually into beans. Heat gently, add seasoning to taste, and serve immediately.

Beans Baked with Savory

Dried beans need not be ordinary. Lots of fresh savory and some inexpensive meat can turn them into a nourishing dish that is delicious enough to serve guests, especially on a cold winter night. This is a simplified, scaled-down version of cassoulet, that rich and delicious (but time-consuming) French way of preparing baked beans. Any kind of dried beans—navy, Great Northern, haricot, lima—will do, and a combination is even better. SERVES 6

2 cups dried beans
1 bay leaf
1 onion, chopped
1 clove garlic, chopped
1 carrot, sliced
6 peppercorns
About 2 ounces salt pork

1 pound cubed pork butt and/or
   lamb shoulder
1 pound hot Italian sausages
2 tablespoons olive oil
½ cup chopped savory leaves
Bread crumbs

Prepare beans for cooking according to package directions (you may have to soak them overnight, or not as long if they're the quick-cooking type). Place them in a large Dutch oven and add enough water to cover. Tie bay leaf, onion, garlic, carrot, and peppercorns in cheesecloth, and push the bag into the liquid. Simmer until beans are tender—at least an hour—and add more water, if necessary, to keep them covered.

Meanwhile, chop the salt pork, pork butt and/or lamb, and sausages, and sauté them slowly in oil until well cooked.

When the beans are done, discard the cheesecloth bag. Stir the meat mixture and the savory into the beans, mixing well. Sprinkle a generous layer of bread crumbs on top, and bake about 1 hour at 350°F.

SHALLOTS

Allium ascalonicum 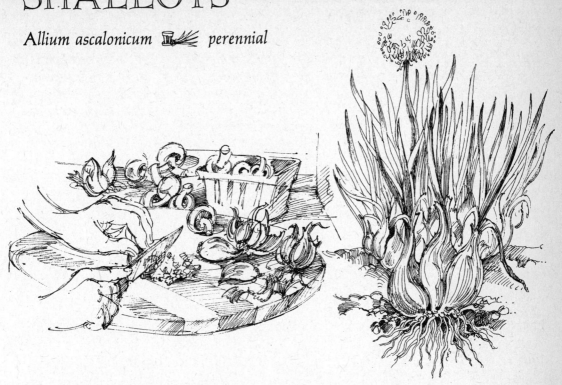 *perennial*

Not many years ago, when I walked into markets in New York City and asked for shallots, a bunch of green scallions would be thrust at me. In New Orleans they still call scallions shallots (and vice versa), but in most parts of the country the shallot, or échalote, which has long been essential to French cooking, has finally been "discovered" and is called by its proper name. Numerous seed catalogs now offer shallot bulbs or seeds, and my local grocery store sells tiny plastic bags of shallots. They're dreadfully overpriced, and sometimes shriveled or sprouting, but I'm grateful that they're there at all, since I used to have to order them by mail.

Shallots look somewhat like garlic, but the cluster of bulbs, or cloves, isn't as tightly enclosed as garlic. So-called Welsh shallots have golden-brown skins and a milder flavor than the French-Italian variety, whose skin is brownish red. Peeled shallot cloves are a delicate ivory tinged with purple. Once you've seen and tasted shallots, nobody can fool you by trying to pass off such ordinary creatures as scallions or onion sets.

It is said that shallots are between onions and garlic in flavor, but that's not quite true. Shallots are delicate yet aromatic, sweet yet bity, and so distinctive and addictive that once you start using them you will skip certain dishes if you can't get shallots for them.

Shallots need a long growing season—about 120 days—to mature. My disappointment was profound at the end of that first summer in Vermont. I had planted a whole costly pound of shallot cloves, planning to get a good winter's supply when they all multiplied and divided into fat heads. They multiplied all right, but each bulblet in the cluster was as slender as a spice clove—difficult to peel for most uses. Fortunately, I missed some bulbs in my sad digging, and they wintered over to produce halfway decent-sized heads next summer. I now plant shallot cloves, especially when I have some that are starting to sprout, in the asparagus bed and let them develop at their own pace. I don't try to grow enough for all our needs, since I can buy fresh shallots at the store, but it's nice to have a standby source, and the green tops can be clipped to use like chives.

If you live in a climate warmer than mine, you can grow shallots, most profitably and in little space, from bulbs in one season. Barely cover shallot cloves set at least 6 inches apart in well-drained soil in either fall or early spring. Or try shallot seeds, which take two seasons to mature into edible heads. The plants grow to about a foot tall. As the bulbs mature they push up out of the ground. Don't try to cover them; you'll slow down their growth. When the tops brown and wilt, pull up the bulbs and dry them in the sun or an airy spot for a few days. Clip the tops before storing them in a cool, dry place.

When you buy shallots at the store, pick plump ones and squeeze them to be sure they're firm. If any of the cloves turn soft and sprout, plant them right away, even if you have to keep them going indoors in potting soil until you can stick them in the ground when the snow melts. Shallots, however, aren't really an indoor plant, and you won't get much of a crop from potted ones.

Because we still consider shallots a rather elegant indulgence, we use them sparingly (So why do we run out of them so often? Well, let's say we use them with greater discretion than we do onions and garlic). Potato salad is no longer the same without minced shallots, and they must go into sauce Béarnaise and flaming pork chops. If you have a big pile of shallots you can make hot spiced English pickles or stuff a whole chicken with shallot cloves as you would with garlic cloves (see recipes).

Eat shallots, however you have to obtain them. Grow them, however long it takes. If we all work together, maybe they'll become so common that the price will come down.

Rosemary Pickled Shallots à la Rosemary

Rosemary Arnold's spicy pickled onions are so good to crunch along with Myers and Coke at her house that one is almost full before the Yorkshire pudding (to say nothing of the tipsy parson) arrives. She inspired me to try pickling shallots instead of onions. This is my recipe, in honor of Rosemary's good English meals, and I should note that she insists the malt vinegar is essential. MAKES ABOUT 1 QUART

2 pounds shallots
1 tablespoon salt
1 cup vinegar (preferably malt vinegar)

1 tablespoon sugar
2 hot red peppers, fresh or dried
¼ cup rosemary leaves

Peel shallots, cover them with water, add salt, and soak for 2 days. Drain, and place in nonaluminum pot. Add vinegar, sugar, peppers, and rosemary. Boil 5 minutes, let cool, and place in a quart jar. Cover and refrigerate at least a month before serving.

Oysters with Mignonette Sauce

A fresh oyster requires little dressing: a squeeze of lemon juice is adequate. Shallots, however, provide a perfect balance between the delicate oysters and the acidic lemon. The classic sauce mignonette is usually made with vinegar. Good red-wine vinegar has an appealing color, but I think lemon juice tastes better. This recipe allows a dozen medium oysters per person, with a cup of sauce for dipping. Serve more or fewer oysters, depending on the appetites of your guests and whether the oysters are large or average or tiny Olympias.
SERVES 4

⅓ cup finely chopped shallots
⅔ cup lemon juice
3 teaspoons coarsely ground black
   pepper

48 medium-sized unshucked oysters

Combine shallots, lemon juice, and pepper, and chill for several hours. Open oysters, trying to retain their juice (see *From Julia Child's Kitchen* for how to do this properly). Discard top oyster shells, and arrange curved bottom shells containing oysters on a big platter of crushed ice. Divide chilled sauce into small bowls for each diner to sprinkle on oysters.

Flaming Pork Chops with Shallots

Shallots are essential in this dish. Craig Claiborne, on whose recipe it is based, says the mustard is the fillip. Perhaps, but the shallots are the essence. Serve these chops with green noodles (see page 103) or mashed potatoes.
SERVES 4

8 thick (preferably 1-inch) pork
   chops
Flour
8 tablespoons butter (preferably
   clarified)
½ to 1 pound mushrooms, thinly
   sliced

¼ cup minced shallots
3 tablespoons cognac
1 tablespoon Dijon mustard
½ cup heavy cream

Trim pork chops of excess fat and bone them, holding small pieces together with toothpicks if necessary. Or leave chops whole if you prefer. Dredge lightly in flour. Heat half the butter in a skillet large enough to hold the pork in a single layer, and brown on both sides. Remove to a platter.

Add remaining butter to skillet and sauté mushrooms and shallots 5 minutes, stirring to cook evenly. Return pork to skillet.

Heat cognac, pour over pork, and quickly light with a match. Mix mustard and cream thoroughly, and stir mixture in around the pork. Bring to a simmer, cover, and cook about 45 minutes, turning pork and stirring occasionally, until it is very tender.

brimms with flavor

SORREL

Rumex species  *perennial*

Before my editor urged me to grow sorrel, I thought it was just a weed. It can be, but it's much more.

Why is sorrel so little known in this country? It brims with flavor and vitamins, and is very easy to grow. Because it's a perennial, once you plant a few

areas .

to the same plant in different

Various folk names have been applied

Sour dock

Pleasant

Since members of genus Rumex are numerous and similar in appearance

seeds you have plenty of greens year after year. A few handfuls can be quickly turned into a piquant soup that causes people who have lived in Europe to get teary-eyed with memories of bistros and country inns.

Sorrel comes in so many varieties that I can't be dogmatic about which is called what. Since members of genus *Rumex* are numerous and similar in appearance and taste, various folk names have been applied to the same plant in different areas. The common denominator is "sour": sourgrass, sourweed, sour-dock—and here more confusion. *Rumex* also includes the wild docks, with their varying leaf shapes and flavors and names, including burdock. When I moved back to the country with vague recollections of all that Mother taught me about nomenclature of plants, the docks and sorrels became as confusing as they seem to be to the botanists, who assign changing names at a staggering rate.

All sorrels *are* sour, a pleasant sour that can be described as lemonlike or vinegary, because of their tartaric acid, oxalic acid, and potassium content. They contain almost as much vitamin A as dandelions and almost as much vitamin C as green peppers—in other words, a lot. Sorrels range from cultivated French or garden sorrel (*R. scutatus* and other species) to numerous wild sorrels (*R. acetosella* and many others). They are considered an indication of acid soil, where they do grow happily, but they thrive in rich, moist soil. Their leaves vary, depending on species, but are generally oblong, arrowhead-shaped at the base, and from several inches to more than a foot long. Whether wild or garden variety, sorrels make nutritious eating. They are good food for people who want to avoid salt—sorrel provides all the seasoning needed.

If you want to eat wild sorrel, it's not hard to find in the country. It's that plant with roots that creep along, under and around everything, sending up bursts of lance-shaped leaves, then reddish-brown flower spikes. You pull up a clump only to discover that it's part of a thin root necklace with sprouts that seems to have no end. You can use the leaves of wild sorrel just as you do garden sorrel, but they are small and thin and usually quite dirty, so it's a job to prepare enough of them for soup. Toss a few into salads, but plant the more succulent cultivated variety to make soups and purées.

French sorrel seeds are now available from a number of mail-order companies in this country. I planted only a 6-foot row, which provides plenty of greens for family and guests. You may want to plant sorrel in a bed apart from

R. scutatus and other species

your annual vegetable garden. It's attractive enough so that you could put it in a perennial flower bed or at one end of your asparagus bed. It will grow in partial shade.

The first year, sorrel sends up a rosette of pale-green tender leaves that grow up to 2 feet long. The second year a seed stalk appears with small flowers. Cut it off to encourage leaf growth, or, if you prefer, let it flower and dry it for arrangements.

Since a little sorrel flavors a lot, it's a good green to grow indoors, especially if you have plant lights. Start it from seeds or pot up a small plant from outdoors. Keep it well trimmed.

You can use sorrel leaves as soon as they are a few inches long. Tear a few small ones into a mixed salad or cole slaw. Use them instead of lettuce in sandwiches. Mature leaves are excellent for soup; try also cooking them with cabbage or sautéing them with lettuce for a tangy flavor. Add chopped sorrel leaves to potato soup or any cream soup, and you won't need to add salt. Use big leaves for dolma. Mince sorrel into cream cheese for bagels with lox. Purée leaves with water in the blender, freeze, and use to make soup or add to dishes during winter.

Sorrel Soup   French Sorrel

Variations on sorrel soup are as endless as your imagination. This recipe is piquant, and if you'd like it less sour you can substitute lettuce, watercress, or spinach for some of the sorrel. You can add other herbs, more potatoes, carrots, almost anything you like. The sorrel will dominate in almost any case—and you won't need to add salt. SERVES 4

4 tablespoons butter
½ cup chopped onion
2 cups finely shredded sorrel
2 large potatoes, thinly sliced
2 cups chicken or vegetable stock

1 cup milk
1 tablespoon chopped chervil or
  dill
Croutons

to numerous wild sorrels
(R. acetosella and many others)

Heat butter in a large saucepan. Add chopped onion and cook until it wilts. Set aside a small handful of sorrel and add the rest to the pan. Add potatoes and stock, bring to a boil, and cook until potatoes are tender. Pour mixture into blender container, and blend at high speed until puréed. Return to saucepan, and stir in milk and chervil or dill. Reheat slowly to serve hot, or refrigerate to serve cold. Top each soup bowl with reserved sorrel and croutons.

Shad Stuffed with Roe in Sorrel Sauce

Sorrel and shad aren't always in season at the same time, but if you're lucky you can combine them splendidly around May. This recipe is the invention of Judith B. Jones, my editor, and she suggests you use canned sorrel if your crop isn't ready when the shad are. SERVES 4

2 pairs shad roe
2 tablespoons butter
2 tablespoons chopped scallions
   or shallots
¾ cup dry white wine or vermouth
Salt and pepper

2 boned shad (¾ to 1 pound
   each)
1 teaspoon cornstarch
1¼ cups heavy cream
⅓ tightly packed cup cooked,
   puréed sorrel

Sauté roe briefly in butter with scallions or shallots in an enamel frying pan or saucepan, turning them once. Pour the wine over and simmer 10 minutes. Remove the roe with a slotted spoon, break up with a fork, season liberally, and stuff into the cavities of the two shad. Generously butter a pan just large enough to hold the fish, place the fish in it, and cover loosely with foil. Bake at 375° F.

While the shad is baking, prepare the sauce by boiling down the pan juices from the roe, reducing them by one-third. Dissolve the cornstarch in a little of the cream, and add along with the rest of the cream to the boiling juices. Simmer until the consistency is that of a thin cream sauce. Add the sorrel, mix well, and heat long enough to exchange flavors.

After 30 minutes test the shad to see if the fish flakes easily. If so, it is done (if you like it a little drier, bake another 5 minutes). Remove to a platter, pour some of the hot sorrel sauce over the fish, and serve the rest in a sauceboat.

SPINACH

Spinacia oleracea and Tetragonia expansa annual

Whether used simply
in a crisp salad or
elegantly in a lobster
quiche, spinach is
versatile and delicious.
It's also nutritious—
higher in iron, calcium,
and vitamins
than most cultivated greens.

Elsewhere in this book I've recommended lamb's-quarters as an excellent spinach substitute and suggested using dandelion greens instead of spinach to make green noodles. But I grow both true spinach and New Zealand spinach in addition to foraging for wild substitutes. Mixed summer salads would be incomplete without the color and tang of spinach leaves, and I like to have them handy in the garden for many other dishes.

True spinach (*Spinacia oleracea*) forms a bunch of broad, usually crinkly, dark-green tender leaves. It's definitely a cool-weather crop. When daily temperatures go above 70° F., spinach goes to seed in a hurry. In the North you should plant it as early as you can work the soil, and if you plant it late in fall, just before the ground freezes, you'll get an early spring crop. Southerners can often grow spinach over winter.

Sow spinach seeds in rich, neutral soil—not too sweet or too sour. Make successive sowings every few weeks if you want a continuous crop. Thin seedlings to at least 3 inches apart, and give them a side dressing of nitrogen-rich fertilizer. I water spinach with a fish-emulsion solution. It must have plenty of water to produce succulent leaves. A mulch close to the plants will help retain moisture and prevent rain splatter (if you've ever eaten gritty spinach you'll appreciate the importance of mulching).

When spinach leaves touch the seedlings next to them, thin them again, removing every other plant. These thinnings should be big enough to use in salads or cooking. From now on, use outer leaves or whole plants as you like. When flower buds appear, pinch them off to encourage lateral growth, but plan to use up the crop soon. Freeze the cleaned leaves if you wish: scald them about a minute, chill them in ice water, drain, chop if desired, and pack in freezer containers.

Spinach aphids can be pests, and as they spread spinach yellows. If you see little holes in the leaves or if they are turning pale, spray the undersides of the leaves well with a garlic and red pepper solution (see page 12). Crowded spinach plants bolt faster and are susceptible to molds and mildews. Space the plants as directed for sturdy, fungus-free growth. Check seed catalogs for varieties resistant to disease, and choose those recommended for your growing area.

Grow spinach plants indoors if you have space; it's nice to pick a few leaves to add to winter salads. Give the plants rich soil and cool temperature. They grow best under plant lights, but will manage with less light than many herbs.

New Zealand spinach (*Tetragonia expansa*), a relative of beets and Swiss chard, has a mild spinach flavor. A spreading plant that grows up to 2 feet tall, it has abundant, light-green, tender but brittle leaves. Unlike true spinach, it is heat-resistant—just what you need to have on hand when the regular spinach bolts. New Zealand spinach also withstands cold and is practically pest-free. Since its leaves grow on thick stems well above the ground, they're usually so clean that they don't need washing. The plant thrives when it's cut back, so you can keep picking and picking.

Altogether wonderful greens, good in salads or cooked. If you have some space, do grow New Zealand spinach, whatever your climate. The seeds look like beet seeds: they're big, and each one produces several plants. They germinate slowly. The first time I planted them I was about to sow something else in the row when the fleshy sprouts finally appeared. Soak the seeds overnight in warm water before planting if you want faster germination.

Start seeds indoors or sow them in a furrow as soon as the ground can be worked. Plants should be spaced at least 2 feet apart; thin the weakest seedlings. When New Zealand spinach is about a foot tall you can start pinching off the succulent tips. The plant will keep producing until well after frost.

Cook and freeze the leaves as you would true spinach. New Zealand spinach is very watery and thus low in calories. You can steam the leaves slowly for 5 minutes without adding any liquid.

Malabar spinach (*Basella alba*) is a good vegetable to grow if you have limited space, since it's a climbing plant that can be trained on a trellis or fence. It's not a true spinach, but its large glossy leaves look like smooth spinach leaves. It tastes much like New Zealand spinach and thrives in hot weather. Malabar spinach is as pretty as ivy; grow it as an edible ornamental plant.

All spinaches are good simply steamed with the water that clings to them after you've rinsed them. You can quickly braise them in butter or oil. I like cooked spinach with a dash of vinegar only, but it can be enhanced with crumbled bacon, chopped hard-boiled eggs or onions, or lots of butter—spinach will absorb enormous amounts of butter, and the sweetness of butter complements the acidity of spinach. After you've cooked spinach, you can spin it in the blender or food processor with milk or cream and herbs and seasonings to make a good hot or cold soup.

Cooks around the world know spinach is a perfect foil for pasta. Summer and winter, we work spinach into all sorts of dishes using macaroni, linguine, and manicotti. Its bright-green color immediately makes pale pasta more interesting. People who wouldn't touch spinach by itself find it most palatable when it's combined in imaginative ways with other foods. And the nutritional value of spinach is good enough reason to use it however you can.

So add chopped raw spinach to green mayonnaise, salads, and herb butters. Add chopped cooked spinach to omelets, frittate, scrambled eggs, stuffings, pâtés, and meatloaves. Mash it with potatoes, or use it in a rice ring. These are fairly simple ways to add color, flavor, and vitamins to your diet. Some more elaborate recipes for spinach follow. Plain or fancy, spinach is good, and good for you.

Spinach and Lobster Quiche

Quiches are so elegant, especially this one, that people often think they're complicated to make. Actually they're as easy and foolproof as pie. This recipe uses a rich but simple crust; substitute your favorite pastry if you like. And try it with other seafood: shrimp and crab also go well with the colorful spinach. Quiche is good hot or at room temperature. SERVES 6

7 tablespoons butter, at room
  temperature
3 ounces cream cheese, at room
  temperature
1½ cups flour
Salt
3 tablespoons minced shallots

2 cups chopped fresh spinach
White pepper
4 eggs
1 cup lobster meat
1 cup heavy cream
½ cup grated Gruyère cheese

Mix 4 tablespoons of the butter thoroughly with the cream cheese, then sift in flour and ¼ teaspoon salt. Mix with your hands until smooth, wrap in plastic, and chill for 1 hour.

Cook shallots in remaining 3 tablespoons butter until wilted. Stir in spinach, and cook, stirring, for about 5 minutes. Season to taste. Mix in blender or food processor with eggs. Combine with lobster and cream.

Roll out pastry to fit a 9-inch quiche pan. Place pastry in pan, and prick it all over with a fork. Either butter the bottom of another pan the same size and place it inside the pastry, or use buttered foil to make a lining to cover the pastry. Weight lining with dried beans. Bake at 400° F. for 8 minutes. Remove lining and beans, prick pastry again, and bake about 3 additional minutes.

To serve quiche puffy hot, turn oven to 375° F. about 45 minutes before serving. Pour filling into crust, and sprinkle cheese on top. When oven is hot, bake quiche about 30 minutes, until puffed and lightly browned.

Crepes à la Florentine

Don Pellman presented this to us on a frigid Vermont evening, and it was such a spectacular gateau, with its layers of filling and crusty-brown top, that I almost hated to see him cut it apart to serve it. Crepes—merely thin French pancakes—are glorified when prepared this way. The dish can also be inexpensive if you use leftovers (ham, asparagus, bits of overripe cheese) or wild plants (lamb's-quarters, dandelion, or violet greens) as substitutes for the fillings listed below. And chopped herbs or shallots vary the fillings. SERVES 4

CREPES

2 cups flour	*4 tablespoons melted butter*
4 eggs	*3 tablespoons cooking oil*
2 cups milk	

Sift the flour into a blender container or bowl. Add the eggs, milk, and butter, and blend for a minute or beat with a wire whisk until thoroughly mixed. Refrigerate for at least 2 hours.

Heat a crepe pan or a skillet with a bottom diameter of about 7 inches. Brush it with oil, heat until almost smoking hot, and pour in 2 tablespoons of the batter. Immediately tilt the pan so the batter spreads all over the bottom. Cook about 1 minute, turn the crepe, cook about 30 seconds, and slide the crepe onto a plate. Repeat process with remaining batter, greasing pan lightly each time.

FILLINGS

3 tablespoons butter	*2 cups chopped cooked spinach*
3 tablespoons flour	*Salt and pepper*
1½ cups milk	*1 cup chopped cooked chicken*
1 cup grated Gruyère cheese	*1 cup cottage cheese*

Melt butter in a 2-quart saucepan, stir in the flour with a wire whisk, and cook slowly for about 3 minutes. Meanwhile bring the milk to a boil, then beat it quickly into the flour and butter. Keep stirring until the mixture returns to a boil. Reduce heat to a simmer, stir in Gruyère cheese, and beat until it melts and is smooth.

Add about ½ cup of this sauce to the spinach, and season to taste. Add another ½ cup sauce to chicken, and season. Mash the cottage cheese, and add salt and pepper.

Now everything is ready to be assembled. Place a crepe in a round, shallow baking dish, and spread it with a layer of spinach mixture. Press another crepe on top, and spread it with chicken mixture. Add another crepe, and spread cottage cheese over it. Continue to alternate crepes and fillings until crepes are used up. Cover the mound with the remaining cheese sauce. Bake in a 350° oven for about 30 minutes.

Lasagne with Spinach

Making a lasagne with good things from your garden is an act of love. It takes time and care to do the fresh tomato sauce and prepare fresh spinach, and this special lasagne should be reserved for special people who appreciate your effort and the rich combination of flavors.

Some tips and notes regarding lasagne:

People usually eat more lasagne than most recipes specify.

Don't try to cut down this recipe. A pound of lasagne noodles is a convenient amount, so make the whole thing and serve a crowd. Any leftovers are good reheated, and lasagne freezes well.

If you don't make your own herby tomato sauce, spin fresh herbs in the blender or food processor and add them to whatever tomato sauce you have.

Use 2 packages of frozen spinach if you can't get fresh.

Substitute homemade sausage (see recipe) if you like.

Make your own green lasagne noodles with spinach, lamb's-quarters, or dandelion greens. Follow the recipe on page 103, cutting pasta dough into wide strips.

Make a good vegetarian lasagne by omitting the meat and substituting extra cheese, more spinach, and perhaps eggplant slices.

For variation, roll the filling in the lasagne noodles and bake the rolls covered with sauce and cheese. SERVES ABOUT 12

1 pound hot and/or sweet Italian
  sausages
2 tablespoons olive oil
1 large onion
2 cloves garlic
1 pound lean ground beef
1 pound mushrooms
2 pounds fresh spinach

3 eggs, lightly beaten
1 pound ricotta cheese
Butter
1 pound lasagne noodles
1 pound mozzarella cheese
½ pound Parmesan cheese
2 quarts tomato sauce (see page
  59)

Place sausages in a large skillet with about ½ cup water. Bring to a boil, cover skillet, and cook slowly for about 15 minutes. Remove sausages, cool, slice thin, and set aside.

Wipe out skillet and add olive oil. Chop onion, mince garlic, and sauté them in oil for a few minutes. Add ground beef and stir it to crumble as it cooks. Clean and slice mushrooms and add them to skillet, stirring until they wilt. Set skillet and contents aside.

Wash spinach if necessary, remove stems, and chop leaves coarse. Combine in a bowl with eggs and ricotta cheese. Set aside.

Butter the largest, deepest baking dish you have—15 by 10 by 5 inches is perfect for this big lasagne, but you can improvise with smaller pans, determining the number you need as you layer ingredients.

Cook lasagne noodles until they are barely tender, 8 to 10 minutes. Put them in a colander, run cold water over them, and drain.

Slice the mozzarella thin and grate the Parmesan.

When noodles are cool enough to handle, spread a thin layer of tomato sauce in the bottom of the baking dish. Add a layer of noodles, barely overlapping them. Spread on a layer of the spinach mixture, smoothing it with a spatula. Add a layer of ground beef mixture, then some mozzarella, then some sausages, then a sprinkle of Parmesan. Cover with tomato sauce and repeat layers until all ingredients are used up. Just be sure the top is covered with plenty of sauce and cheese.

Cover baking pan tightly with foil or a lid, and bake lasagne for 30 minutes in a 350° oven. Remove cover and continue baking until cheese is lightly browned, about 15 minutes. Let lasagne cool and settle a bit before serving—it will be easier to cut.

TARRAGON

Artemisia dracunculus 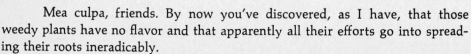 *perennial*

After loving dried tarragon in chicken dishes for many years, I was overjoyed to find a flat of healthy-looking plants labeled tarragon at a market. What's more, they were cheap—79 cents for six plants. They flourished in my perennial herb bed, and soon I was sharing root divisions with friends.

Mea culpa, friends. By now you've discovered, as I have, that those weedy plants have no flavor and that apparently all their efforts go into spreading their roots ineradicably.

What I bought was Russian tarragon (*A. redowski*), which does bear some resemblance to true French tarragon, but not much once you've seen them growing together. And I do view them side by side now every year, because I can't get rid of that bastard tarragon, despite the great heaps I've torn out. Once, when I potted up one of my real tarragons to bring indoors, it didn't take well to the move. As its leaves died down, what to my horrified eyes should appear but little arrogant shoots of Russian tarragon springing up around it.

Be very suspicious when you obtain tarragon plants, and *never* accept seeds. Expect to pay more for real tarragon plants than you do for most other herbs. French tarragon is propagated by some living part from the plant; only the wrong kind sets seeds. But it can be difficult to determine whether the roots or small plants will be the real thing.

First, get your tarragon plants, cuttings, or roots from a reliable source: a local greenhouse with personnel who know what you mean when you ask if it's Russian or French tarragon; a mail-order nursery that specializes in herbs (sending packaged plants over a distance is treacherous, but it may be the only way you can obtain them); a friend who grows herbs—but beware of novices such as I was.

Second, crush a tarragon leaf and sniff it. Real tarragon smells like licorice, anise, camphor—an odor as indefinable as that of most herbs but strong and tangy, yet sweet. Fake tarragon smells like little more than lawn grass.

Finally, if you're still in doubt, observe the appearance of the full-grown plant if possible. French tarragon grows up to 2 feet high on delicate woody stems, and its dark-green slender leaves are about 2 inches long with pointed tips. The tarragon you don't want has slightly rough light-green leaves that are more rounded, thicker, and longer. Real tarragon waves in the wind like a tiny twisted bamboo; the other sort, hereinafter not to be mentioned, develops fattish stems and unsightly foliage that with sullen defiance sprawl across everything within 6 feet.

Now that you've got your real true French tarragon, give it the care it deserves. It likes plenty of sun, a limy, well-drained soil, and constant moisture. Water on the leaves is beneficial, so turn on the sprinkler during dry periods, especially if you see the leaves curling up. Don't overfertilize tarragon; as with most perennial herbs, this causes the plant to become juicily tender and thus susceptible to winter kill. When frost comes, trim the plants back and bank them with soil or cover them with a mulch. It takes some time for leaves to develop in the spring; don't get discouraged if the plant looks dead for a while.

Because tarragon needs a period of cold rest, it doesn't do well outdoors in frost-free areas. For plants indoors, you can pot up a small tarragon, but you must leave it outdoors for a couple of weeks of freezing temperature or put it in the refrigerator for a month or so. The same cool-weather treatment should be applied annually to tarragon plants bought from nurseries or propagated in other ways.

You can root tarragon cuttings by snipping off several inches of top growth in midsummer and putting them in water, or you can layer plants by pushing a branch onto the ground and covering a few inches of the stem with a rock until new roots form. Check mature plants for small side shoots from the main roots; these can be cut out carefully and potted.

Tarragon is a temperamental houseplant. Watering is a problem. If tarragon is overwatered the roots rot, but inadequate water causes the leaves to curl and dry. Add sand to the soil to help drainage. Fertilize tarragon occasionally with a weak fish-emulsion solution. If the plant appears to be expiring, with wilting and yellowing leaves, cut it back severely, put it in the refrigerator for a week, and you may get new growth. Give tarragon all the light and air circulation possible, and wash the leaves frequently to remove dust and bugs.

The flavor is not lost when you dry tarragon, but it is definitely changed. I think dried tarragon is just as good as fresh tarragon, so I don't despair when my indoor plants fail: I've dried a lot just in case. Home-dried tarragon, used within six months, is dark green; it retains much of its fresh anise flavor yet develops a delicately sweet taste and a distinctive aroma when used in cooking. Tarragon is easily dried by hanging branches in an airy place out of sunlight. But check it often and don't let it get too dry; as soon as you can easily strip the leaves off, pack them in jars.

You can also freeze tarragon sprigs in plastic bags, blend chopped leaves with oil or butter (wonderful for basting fish or chicken), make tarragon mustard by mashing leaves with dry mustard and a bit of water, or pound tarragon with butter and egg yolks for a sauce for hot foods or cold hors d'oeuvres.

My favorite way of preserving tarragon is to put sprigs into rice-wine vinegar. Any other mild vinegar will do, but rice vinegar is delicate and straw-colored, so beautiful with tarragon leaves trailing through it that someone should devote a haiku to it. I avoid using it for ordinary things because it's such a pleasure to look at the full bottles, but I use it for salad dressing over mild greens like Boston lettuce and in a vinaigrette for special vegetables like asparagus.

Tarragon, fresh or dry, has such a distinctive flavor that I don't like to mix it with other herbs (although it's an essential ingredient in *fines herbes*). Its dominant but reserved taste enhances such mild-flavored foods as chicken and fish and very fresh young vegetables. It's the aristocrat of herbs.

Creamy Tarragon Dressing

Chef Gusti Iten, at the Common Man restaurant in Waitsfield, Vermont, is a master of parsleyed rack of lamb, lemony pork piccata, and a crisp romaine salad tossed with a tarragon-curry dressing. It's a tangy, surprising combination, even though I don't usually like to mix fresh herbs with spices. This is my variation of Gusti's recipe, and it's good even if you omit the curry. MAKES ABOUT 2 CUPS

*1 generous tablespoon chopped
  tarragon leaves
2 cloves garlic
1 teaspoon curry powder*

*1 cup mayonnaise
½ cup milk
2 tablespoons vinegar
¼ cup oil*

Place ingredients in blender container in order listed. Blend at high speed until very smooth. Refrigerate at least 2 hours for flavors to blend.

Béarnaise Sauce

Serve Béarnaise—basically hollandaise with tarragon and shallots—with châteaubriand, filet mignon, tournedos, a double cut of prime ribs, poached eggs, fish, or asparagus. Such foods would seem to be perfection in themselves, but Béarnaise can actually elevate them. MAKES ABOUT 1 CUP

*1 tablespoon minced tarragon
  leaves
1 teaspoon minced shallots
3 peppercorns, crushed
¼ cup vinegar*

*¼ cup dry white wine or vermouth
3 egg yolks
1 cup melted butter
1 teaspoon finely chopped mixed
  tarragon and chervil or parsley*

Place minced tarragon, shallots, peppercorns, vinegar, and wine in a small saucepan, and simmer until the liquid is reduced to about 1 tablespoon. Cool to lukewarm.

In the top of a nonaluminum double boiler, stir the egg yolks with a whisk or fork over low heat (do not let the water in the bottom of the double boiler boil or touch the top container) until the eggs begin to thicken. Strain the herb liquid into the eggs, and stir well. Begin adding melted butter slowly, almost a drop at a time, stirring continuously, then add butter in increasing amounts, continuing to stir, until you are pouring in a very thin stream as the sauce thickens. Depending on the freshness of the egg yolks, the sauce will be as thin as pancake batter or as thick as mayonnaise.

Stir finely chopped tarragon and chervil or parsley into the sauce. It will hold for up to 20 minutes over hot water.

Rémoulade Sauce

A traditional sauce for shrimp, rémoulade is also delicious with a platter of cold raw or crisp-cooked summer vegetables. Squeezing the herbs and garlic through the press releases a lot of their flavor, and this rémoulade can become powerful if it's stored more than a day. You can mince the herbs and garlic instead for a milder flavor, or use a food processor. I use leftover rémoulade as a salad dressing by thinning it down with oil and lemon juice.

MAKES ABOUT 2½ CUPS

*1 tablespoon chopped tarragon
  leaves
1 tablespoon chopped parsley
1 large clove garlic*

*2 hard-boiled eggs
1 teaspoon Dijon mustard
½ teaspoon anchovy paste
2 cups mayonnaise*

Push all the tarragon leaves you can into a garlic press, and squeeze out all the juice and bits of leaves possible into a mixing bowl. Rearrange what's left in the press, add any remaining tarragon and the parsley, and continue the process. Add garlic last, and squeeze and rearrange residue until most of the herbs and garlic are pressed out. Chop the eggs fine into the mixing bowl. Stir in mustard, anchovy paste, and mayonnaise. Chill for a few hours before serving.

Chicken Tarragon with Mushrooms

Dried tarragon is also excellent in this recipe—use half as much and crush it into the wine. I love every variation on chicken tarragon that we've tried: using sour cream instead of heavy cream, dry sherry in place of white wine, sliced mushrooms if only large ones are available. Serve this over green noodles (see page 103) or rice or with a piping of mashed potatoes, with a few tarragon sprigs as garnish. SERVES 4

2 whole chicken breasts, boned,
*   halved, and skinned*
Flour
6 tablespoons butter (preferably
*   clarified)*
½ pound button mushrooms
1 tablespoon minced shallots
¼ cup dry white wine
½ cup chicken broth
1 heaping tablespoon chopped
*   tarragon leaves*
¼ cup heavy cream
Salt and white pepper

Dredge chicken breasts lightly in flour. Heat butter in a large skillet, and sauté chicken quickly until brown on both sides. Remove chicken to a platter. Clean mushrooms, slice off stems, and sauté caps until lightly brown, then remove to platter. Sauté shallots for about a minute, pour wine over them, and cook over high heat, stirring, until wine is nearly evaporated. Add a tablespoon of flour and stir in for a minute, then stir in chicken broth and tarragon. Put chicken and mushrooms back in skillet, cover, and cook over low heat for 30 minutes or until chicken is tender. Remove chicken to a hot platter and keep it warm while you stir the cream into the sauce. Season to taste, heat gently, then pour sauce over chicken.

Frogs' Legs Tarragon

My high-school boyfriend never caught many bullfrogs when he went gigging with me in Grandpa's pond. I held the flashlight for him, and I averted my head in horror whenever he stabbed. I never minded eating the frogs, of course, and now that I can buy the legs and avoid the slaughter, I enjoy them even more. Frogs' legs, often compared to chicken drumsticks, are more delicate but richer in flavor, tenderer yet with a more interesting texture. Tarragon gives them just the right accent, but you can use chervil, parsley, or basil instead. Use any size frogs' legs you can get, freshly gigged or frozen, domestic or imported. Serve little ones for an unusual canapé or appetizer. SERVES 4

3 pounds frogs' legs
Milk
2 cups fine dry bread crumbs
4 tablespoons minced tarragon
  leaves

Flour
2 eggs, beaten
Butter or oil
Lemon wedges
Salt and pepper

Soak frogs' legs in milk to cover for about 1 hour. Meanwhile toss bread crumbs with tarragon in a shallow bowl. Remove frogs' legs from milk, roll them in flour, dip in beaten egg, then dredge in tarragon bread crumbs. Place on a rack to dry for about 15 minutes.

Heat enough butter or oil to cover the bottom of a large skillet, and quickly sauté frogs' legs, turning them gently with two forks, until they are lightly browned and cooked through—5 to 10 minutes, depending on size. Serve with lemon wedges, and let each person season to taste.

THYME

Thymus species 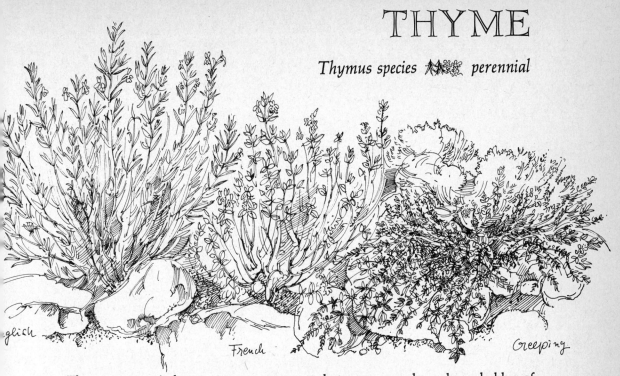 *perennial*

glish   French   Creeping

The varieties of thyme are so numerous that some people make a hobby of collecting and propagating them. Thymes are versatile: you can use some kinds for a small hedge, grow many others for flavoring, plant creeping thyme on paths, where it releases its fragrance when stepped on, and grow it indoors to trail in hanging baskets.

The thyme most often used in the kitchen comes from *T. vulgaris*, an upright little shrub, 8 to 10 inches high, with woody stems and oval, dainty leaves about 1/8 inch long. So-called French thyme has purplish, narrow leaves; broader-leafed gray-green English thyme has a similar flavor. Flowers are pink or light purple, and the plants are very hardy.

T. serpyllum, creeping or wild thyme, has many horticultural forms. It can be used for flavoring but is more often grown as a ground cover. It forms a mat a few inches high, and flowers may be crimson or purple or white, depending on the variety.

And the variety seems endless. The common names of some of the creeping thymes suggest their flavor and appearance—lemon, orange, caraway, woolly, silver—and you'd best have plenty of space for them to crawl if you want to specialize in them. In some parts of the country thyme has escaped and returned to the wild, and how I envy anyone who has a whole field of fragrant wild thyme to make love in.

All the thymes like lots of sun and good drainage. They prefer somewhat limy soil, but they're not fussy. The seeds are very small and need warm soil to germinate. If you want to get an early start, plant seeds indoors, then set seedlings outside at least 9 inches apart. Upright thyme gets scraggly after a few years, and the easiest way to start new plants is to bend branches over, cover the stems with soil, then separate and replant the new roots that form. It's even simpler to pull up and separate roots for new plants of creeping thymes.

Mulch around thyme plants that you'll be using for eating so the dirt doesn't splash up when it rains—it's hard to clean thyme's tiny leaves. Cover plants with a light protective winter mulch in cold climates; despite thyme's hardiness, the plants can be damaged by ice. Diseases and insects seem to ignore thyme; I'm not sure why, but it's nice.

Indoors, thymes still want lots of sunlight. Upright thyme makes a handsome houseplant, but keep it compact by trimming. Creeping thymes trail and adapt well to hanging baskets. Add some lime to the potting soil. Thyme leaves are small outdoors, and in the house they stay smaller yet, so it's hard to get much of a crop. I prefer to use dried thyme in the winter and save my plant space for those fresh herbs I can't do without.

Dry thyme by cutting branches to hang just before they bloom. When the leaves feel crisp, strip them off just as you do fresh thyme: hold the stem in one hand and run your other finger and thumb against it from the top down. You can also freeze the fresh leaves or add them to butter, vinegar, or oil.

Nobody seems to be able to describe the flavor of thyme. Some call it mintlike, others clovelike, but everyone seems to agree it's pungent. Winter savory and thyme are known as the herbal substitutes for salt and pepper, and thyme is best used as you use pepper—with some discretion. Creole cuisine uses thyme generously, many people consider it essential in New England clam chowder, and it's an important ingredient in bouquets garnis, stuffings, and stock. Add fresh thyme leaves to salads sparingly. Only the leaves should be used for cooking. Add the tough stems to the soup pot, throw them on the barbecue coals for a pleasant aroma, or compost them. Some people like thyme jelly and thyme tea, and lemon thyme is good in both.

Thyme Creamed Onions

Cooked onions, with their sweet yet distinctive flavor, combine well with the aggressiveness of thyme, and the green flecks of the herb add color to an otherwise pale dish. SERVES 4

24 small white onions
4 tablespoons butter
4 tablespoons flour
2 cups milk or cream

2 tablespoons chopped thyme
leaves
Salt and pepper

Boil onions in their skins about 20 minutes, or until tender. Drain and cool them while you make a roux: melt the butter in a large pot, stir in the flour until blended, and cook gently a minute or two. Bring the milk or cream to a boil, add it all at once to the flour-and-butter mixture, and stir with a whisk over medium heat until sauce is smooth and thick.
Peel onions, add them to sauce, stir gently, and reheat. Stir thyme into pot, season to taste, and serve.

Thymely Summer Squash

When the squash crop has become so prolific that you're ready to compost it all, it's time to trim the thyme bushes. Aunt Esther Fisher learned to appreciate cooking with thyme in Haiti, and I love this recipe of hers for its simple goodness and its utilization of two ingredients that I always have in abundance around August. Vary amounts according to your crop and appetites.

Yellow summer squash or zucchini
Butter
Dry bread crumbs

Chopped thyme leaves
Grated Parmesan cheese

Slice squash about half an inch thick, and boil or steam gently until barely tender. Drain and place in one layer in a shallow buttered baking dish. Brown bread crumbs in a little butter, stir in a generous amount of thyme, and scatter mixture over squash. Dot with butter, cover with as much cheese as you like, and bake at 350°F. until cheese is browned.

Pot Roast with Thyme

A variation of Jamaican pot roast. West Indian countries use thyme in a great many dishes as the predominant herb. Like sage, thyme can sometimes be added with a fairly heavy hand in hearty foods, and it can liven up cheaper cuts of meat. You can add carrots or potatoes to this pot roast. SERVES 6

3 pounds beef chuck or rump roast
Flour seasoned with salt and pepper
4 tablespoons cooking oil
1 onion, chopped
1 clove garlic, minced

2 cups beef broth
6 ounces tomato paste
1 tablespoon chopped thyme leaves
Thyme sprigs

Trim the beef of as much outside fat as possible. Dredge in seasoned flour. Heat oil in a Dutch oven, brown meat all over, and remove to platter. Brown onion and garlic lightly in same oil, and remove them with a slotted spoon. Discard any remaining oil. Place beef broth, tomato paste, and thyme leaves in blender, and whirl until thyme is finely chopped. Return meat to Dutch oven, scatter onion and garlic over it, then pour in mixture from blender. Place in a 325° oven and cook for about 2 hours, basting the meat occasionally. Remove cooked roast to a serving platter, and thicken the broth if you like. Slice roast, decorate platter with thyme sprigs, and serve with sauce.

VIOLETS

Viola species  *perennial or annual*

Oh, that first spring
in Vermont after
we'd escaped the city!
Spring in Central
Park was nice, but here every day
brought new discoveries as the snow receded
into the roaring brook. Catkins appeared on the wild willows, dark-green heads
of field cress pushed through the slush, trout lilies and trilliums bloomed along
the banks. And violets were everywhere: tiny yellow violets in the marshy field,
lavender-blue ones in unexpected corners, white ones spreading into the new
lawn.

Violets seduce and then possess. I succumbed to their charm and began
digging them up and putting them along the edges of my flower beds. It
wouldn't have been necessary to transplant them, I've since discovered, and I
would have been well advised to eat them instead. Violets, which are pretty and
tidy when they bloom, become spreading weeds when they're offered rich soil.
Good weeds, though, and I still can't bear to destroy them. I carry baskets of

them out to moist spots in the field and give them a blessing. I want them to survive, but not at the expense of my other herbs and flowers.

Of the numerous violet species, the ones that are likely to volunteer in your flower beds have purple or white and blue flowers. These showy blossoms are not fertile. The inconspicuous fertile flowers come later and never open. They turn into pods containing many seeds which go flying in all directions when the pod pops open.

Violet leaves contain incredible amounts of vitamins: just half a cup of the greens has as much vitamin C as four oranges and more than the recommended minimum daily requirement of vitamin A. The flowers are also rich in vitamin C, and although I doubt that children have nutritional intuition, my one-year-old gobbled them with all the enthusiasm of a sailor threatened with scurvy.

Young violet leaves and buds have a mild flavor with a hint of white pepper and are good mixed with other spring greens in salads. Older leaves get darker green and tough, but you can finely shred them and boil them in a small amount of water for about 15 minutes. Serve them with crumbled bacon, chopped hard-boiled eggs, and a dash of vinegar. They taste somewhat like spinach but are bitier. Because of their mucilaginous quality (violets are sometimes called wild okra), they can be used to thicken stews.

Many pests, including slugs, attack violets, but they generally turn up after the plants have bloomed, and by then you have so much foliage that they can't damage it all.

Purple violet flowers make beautiful syrups and jellies. Euell Gibbons and Alta Bauman provided me with this recipe for violet syrup: gather a jarful of purple violet flowers without stems, cover them with boiling water, put a lid on the jar, and steep for 24 hours. Strain the bluish infusion into a measuring cup. For each cup of infusion add 2 cups of sugar and the juice of half a lemon (which will turn the liquid purple). Bring mixture to a boil, stirring, then pour it into a jar, seal, and refrigerate. This violet syrup is tartly sweet, good on pancakes or stirred into new-fallen snow to make lavender snow cream. Or add it to club soda and ice and top it with a violet flower.

Candied violets are pretty and a better candy than most, since they do have vitamins. Make a special dessert by topping homemade ice cream with violet flowers rinsed in water, dipped in superfine sugar, and dried until brittle.

WATERCRESS

Nasturtium officinale  *perennial*

When I murmur "watercress, watercress," it's almost like a mantra. I am mentally transported on a warm breeze to a clear stream. Birds twitter softly, cows low, and I dip my feet serenely into a pool fringed with watercress, then fill my straw basket with glossy sprigs.

My "mantra" is a blessing, since my watercress crop is erratic. When I carefully sank peat pots with watercress seedlings along the brook, my Brownie troop discovered them. They were so excited—"Mrs. Owen, Mrs. Owen, these wild plants grew their own pots!"—that I couldn't reprimand them for jerking up my cherished seedlings. We had watercress sandwiches.

The next time, I tried transplanting watercress from my mother's stream. The Brownies, I then discovered, had performed a rescue operation. Watercress needs fresh water, but its shallow roots won't withstand the floods that wash out my brook whenever the snow melts or hard rain falls. I hope somebody downstream is enjoying my watercress as much as I do for brief periods.

Look along slow-moving streams for foliage that is bright green and lobed like the watercress sold in grocery stores. They're the same species, although wild watercress is usually smaller. It creeps along the water's edge and forms a shiny dark-jade mass of leaves. Pinch off the tender tips. Succulent young stems can be eaten along with the leaves, but the plant becomes bitter after its tiny whitish flowers form.

It's a shame that this caution is necessary: exercise your usual judgment about wild plants. If there's any reason to believe watercress is growing in polluted water, you'd better content yourself with admiring its stamina. Or you might pull some roots, wash them, and transplant them to a stream you know is safe.

Most commercial watercress is grown in greenhouses; they provide special conditions of light, water, and nutrients that are difficult to duplicate in the home. But if you take some care you can grow watercress successfully indoors. The potting soil must be humusy to hold adequate moisture but sandy to drain it before it gets stale. Provide rich soil, high in nitrogen, for dark-green growth, and add some limestone.

I've grown watercress from seeds and from rootings. The easiest way is to pull up some wild plants and pot them, but rooting is also quick. Save some of the healthiest-looking sprigs from the bunch you buy at the store, put them in a glass of water, and change water daily until roots form—it usually takes only a few days—then pot them and water well.

Watercress does best in cool temperatures indoors, and it needs only partial sunlight. Its roots must have constant moisture; set the pot in a deep saucer of water and keep the saucer filled. Unlike most plants, watercress prefers to keep its feet wet. Cut off the tops to use as you need them. They will have a milder flavor than the often bity wild watercress.

Eat watercress raw to enjoy all its high vitamin and mineral content. It's notably rich in calcium, has twice the vitamin C of spinach, and contains considerable vitamin A. Many people associate watercress with dainty tea sandwiches—a few leaves pressed between pale wafers of buttered bread. Watercress is better heaped on hearty meat sandwiches made with slabs of dark homemade bread. Its mustardy crunch is perfect with salami and corned beef.

Mixed green salads always benefit from watercress, and so do many other salads. Chop the leaves into chicken, bean, and potato salads just before serving. Add slivered watercress to cole slaw. Blend watercress with melted butter, chill, and spread it on bread or add dollops to soup. Make healthful beverages in the blender with tomato juice, watercress, and herbs.

Watercress can be boiled or added to a mess of greens. Try stir-frying it briefly with vegetables to retain its vitamins and texture. Use watercress to make green noodles (see page 103), and add piquant flavor to vichyssoise by combining soup with raw watercress puréed in the food mill or food processor.

Get your watercress along a babbling brook, out of pots on your windowsill, or at market, but get it. Catharine Osgood Foster tells of a priest who went about planting watercress in wet spots. I respect that good father even more than Johnny Appleseed.

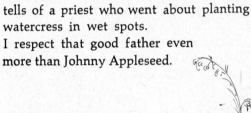

WORM-WOOD

Artemisia absinthium
perennial

One of the essential culinary herbs it's not— for me, at least. Wormwood, a scraggily attractive gray bush, can serve as a hedge, a background in flower beds, and a novelty in the herb garden. Some people find other uses for it as well.

Wormood

Plant wormwood only if you have space for it to spread. It grows up to 5 feet tall and twice that wide. You can trim it to keep it compact, but its strong underground roots go deep and far, no matter what the soil or light conditions, and it will readily go wild.

Wormwood has been touted as a pest deterrent, probably because of its very bitter taste and acrid odor, but aphids thrive on my wormwood, and cats, dogs, and skunks cuddle up under its drooping branches. I wouldn't think of planting it near the vegetable garden, as is sometimes recommended to keep out animals. I'm sure it would be even more destructive of my carrots than purslane and pigweed are, and furthermore it's a very hardy perennial.

Wormwood grows easily from seeds planted in spring, then thinned to at least 2 feet apart. Unless you want a hedge, you probably won't need all the plants a seed packet produces, so get a plant from a nursery or a layered or rooted branch from a friend. Wormwood's soft thin leaves, irregularly spaced and divided, are up to 3 inches long, with a silky-furry texture. Inconspicuous pale-yellow flowers appear on the ends of the branches in midsummer, and this is the time to cut and hang them for dried bouquets or tea.

I find it best to trim wormwood to the ground when frost comes, using the branches as a winter mulch for more delicate perennials. If you don't trim the stalks, the lower branches have a tendency to root-layer themselves.

You can grow wormwood indoors and trim it like bonsai. You can also, I'm told, use it to concoct potables, intoxicating, debilitating, or enervating, and make "absinthe" by adding wormwood sprigs to Pernod. Since I've grown wormwood only for the pleasure of looking at it outdoors and for cutting branches to add a pleasing gray contrast to bright flowers in bouquets, I can't advise you on culinary uses, but having nibbled wormwood leaves, I'd suggest you start ingesting them in small doses.

Euell Gibbons, in *Stalking the Healthful Herbs*, calls wormwood "a truly noble herb." With his usual enthusiasm for weeds, he makes wormwood cordial sound almost like ambrosia. One of these days, I'm going to have a glass in loving memory of all he's taught me about wild herbs and greens.

SOURCES OF
SEEDS AND PLANTS

INDEX

SOURCES OF SEEDS AND PLANTS

To compile this list, I sent letters with a questionnaire to more than a hundred companies. Ordering by mail involves hazards: companies go in and out of business and they change their catalogs and prices, but the majority of the companies who replied to my letter were prompt and wrote notes that indicated they care about pleasing their customers. The following list is based on their responses, my personal acquaintance with their products, and my perusal of their catalogs.

Unless a price is noted, catalogs are free. Larger companies generally mail with no charge catalogs that offer a wide range of the most common greens, herbs, and aromatics. Smaller companies that charge a fee for their lists are often the best sources for more unusual plants and seeds.

W. Atlee Burpee Co., Warminster, Pennsylvania 18974; Clinton, Iowa 52732; Riverside, California 92502 (write to the location nearest you). For years I've ordered herbs and vegetables from this reliable company, and I highly recommend their products. Seeds and plants.

Borchelt Herb Gardens, 474 Carriage Shop Road, East Falmouth, Maine 02536. More than 200 varieties of organically grown herbs. Enclose stamp for list. Seeds only.

Carroll Gardens, Westminster, Maryland 21157. Many thymes and mints. Seeds and plants.

Comstock, Ferre & Co., 263 Main Street, Wethersfield, Connecticut 06109. Good general selection of seeds.

Cottage Herb Farm Shop, 311 State Street, Albany, New York 12210. Even have pokeberry seeds. Catalog 25¢. Seeds only.

J. A. Demonchaux Co., 225 Jackson, Topeka, Kansas 66603. Specialize in French products: different varieties of leeks, corn salad (mâche), Welsh onions, sorrels, shallots, chervil. Seeds only.

Greene Herb Gardens, Greene, Rhode Island 02827. Oldest commercial organic-herb growers in this country. Send stamped self-addressed envelope for introductory offer on kitchen garden, handbook, and listing. Seeds only.

Gurney Seed and Nursery Co., Yankton, South Dakota 57078. Charming catalog, with unusual varieties of greens and aromatics. Seeds and plants.

Chas. C. Hart Seed Co., 304 Main Street, P.O. Box 169, Wethersfield, Connecticut 06109. Very good overall selection of the herbs, greens, and aromatics mentioned in this book plus many more. Seeds only.

Hemlock Hill Herb Farm, Hemlock Hill Road, Litchfield, Connecticut 06759. Catalog (50¢) lists excellent selection of perennial plants, with instructions on growing.

Howe Hill Herbs, Camden, Maine 04843. Onions, mints, thymes, and much more. Catalog 35¢. Seeds and plants.

J. L. Hudson, Seedsman, P.O. Box 1058, Redwood City, California 94064. Catalog 50¢. Seeds only, but what an array of seeds—practically everything mentioned in this book and a wide range from wild to exotic, since Hudson collects from all over the world.

Le Jardin du Gourmet, West Danville, Vermont 05873. Specialists in shallots, other French aromatics, greens, herbs. Nice people, as I've learned from corresponding with them. Catalog 25¢. Seeds and plants.

Joseph Harris Co., Inc., Moreton Farm, Rochester, New York 14624. Especially good selection of lettuces, onions. People who care about pleasing you. Seeds and plants.

Ledoar Nurseries, 7206 Belvedere Road, West Palm Beach, Florida 33406. Mints and unusual varieties of thymes, plus many other herbs. Catalog (50¢) is interesting and informative, and its cost is refunded with your first order. Seeds and plants.

Logee's Greenhouses, 55 North Street, Danielson, Connecticut 06239. Unusual herbs in addition to all the basics. Very attractive catalog is $2. Plants only.

Lounsberry Gardens, P.O. Box 135, Oakford, Illinois 62673. Ferns, some herbs. Catalog 25¢. Plants only.

Mincemoyer Nursery, County Line Road, Jackson, New Jersey 08527. Ferns, other wild plants, some herbs. Catalog 25¢. Plants only.

Nichols Garden Nursery, 1190 North Pacific Highway, Albany, Oregon 97321. Extensive list of herbs, greens, garlics, unusual plants and seeds. Wonderful catalog, with notes and advice in addition to its impressive list. Seeds and plants.

Geo. W. Park Seed Co., Inc., Greenwood, South Carolina 29647. Nice catalogs, nice people to order from, and a nice idea: they offer mixed collections of herbs, lettuces, and hot peppers. Seeds and plants.

Penn Herb Co., 603 North 2nd Street, Philadelphia, Pennsylvania 19123. Huge selection of dried herbs and some seeds.

Putney Nursery, Inc., Putney, Vermont 05346. Ostrich ferns, some herbs. Plants only.

Rocky Hill Herb Farm, P.O. Box 707, Lake Wallkill Road, Sussex, New Jersey 07461. Plants only.

The Rosemary House, 120 South Market Street, Mechanicsburg, Pennsylvania 17055. As the name indicates, specialists in rosemary, but many other herbs too. Pleasant catalog for 35¢, with good herb gift ideas. Seeds and plants.

Sunnybrook Farms Nursery, 9448 Mayfield Road, Chesterland, Ohio 44026. Huge selection of thymes, sages, mints, alliums, rosemary, others. Catalog 50¢, deductible from first order. Plants only.

Taylor's Herb Garden, Inc., 1535 Lone Oak Road, Vista, California 92083. Many organically grown mints, thymes, rosemary, sage—and pokeweed and more. Catalog 25¢. Plants only.

Thompson & Morgan, 401 Kennedy Boulevard, Somerdale, New Jersey 08083. You no longer have to order T & M's wonderful array of seeds from England. Do send for their beautiful, informative catalog, which even lists the nutritional content of vegetables.

The Tool Shed Herb Farm, Turkey Hill Road, Salem Center, Purdys Station, New York 10578. Good general selection. Catalog 25¢. Plants only.

Vick's Wildgardens, Inc., Box 115, Gladwyne, Pennsylvania 19035. Specialize in wild flowers, including violets, ferns, milkweed, but sell familiar herbs too. Catalog 25¢. Seeds and plants.

White Flower Farm, Litchfield, Connecticut 06759. For $4 you get two catalogs with three interim publications of gardening "notes"—gorgeous and worth the price, although herb selection is limited. Plants only.

The Wild Garden, Box 487, Bothell, Washington 98011. An extraordinary list of thymes and wild plants. Catalog ($1) is worth far more for its fascinating prose. Plants only.

(rezembles Gomphrena
a
INDEX G. globosa,
brillant Amaranthaceae
purple globe amaranth
Shocking Pink clover)

chivry butter, 198

in a cock-a-leekie page 141
leeks shallotts

Marrubium vulgare, 132
marsh marigolds, 157
mayonnaises, 48, 49
mealybugs, 32
Melissa officinalis, 144
Mentha species, 165
mezze, 47
mice, 16
mildew, 31
milkweed, 163–165, *illus.* 163
Mint and Crab-Apple Jelly, 172
mints, 165–172, *illus.* 165
mirepoix, 79
mister, plant, 27
mites, 31
mold, plant, 31
moles, 16
mulches, 9–11
mushrooms, 57, 161, 184, 237; wild, 35
mussels, 87
mustard greens, 129
mustards, herb, 42

N

Nasturtium officinale, 173
Nasturtium and Radish Cheese Canapés, 175
nasturtiums, 173–176, *illus.* 173
nematodes, 14, 33
Nepeta cataria, 80
nettles, 36
New Zealand spinach, 225
noodles, 103
nutrition. *See* specific plants, minerals, and vitamins.

O

Ocimum basilicum, 70
oils, herb, 42
onion pie, 181
onions, 58, 176–181, *illus.* 176, 184, 241
onion soup, 180
orange mint, 167
oregano, 182–185, *illus.* 182
Origanum majorana. See marjoram.
Origanum vulgare, 182
ostrich fern, 117
outdoor plants, 3–16
Oysters with Mignonette Sauce, 220

P

parsley, 186–190, *illus.* 186
Parsley and Potato Soup, 190
pasta, 73, 103, 230
peas, 97
Pellegrini, Angelo, 72
pennyroyal, 166
peppermint, 166
peppers, 191–197
pesticides, 13, 30
pesto, 72
pests: indoor, 30–33, *illus.* 31; outdoor, 12–16, *illus.* 13
Petroselinum, 186
pickles, 111, 184, 203, 219
pie, 181
pigweed, 136
pimiento peppers, 192
pineapple sage, 206
pizza, 184
plant lights, 24–26

A NOTE ABOUT THE AUTHOR

Millie Owen was born in Newport News, Virginia, and was graduated from Eastern Mennonite College in Harrisonburg. She worked for the Rodale Press in Pennsylvania and for New York publishers as an editor and copy editor until she and her husband moved to Vermont. There, in addition to raising a young son, they cultivate herbs and aromatics and preserve the fruits thereof. Mrs. Owen continues to work as a free-lance copy editor, with the result that most of the distinguished cookbooks of the last decade have had the benefit of her careful eye.

A NOTE ABOUT THE TYPE

The text of this book was set on the Linotype in Palatino, a type face designed by the noted German typographer Hermann Zapf. Named after Giovambattista Palatino, a writing master of Renaissance Italy, Palatino was the first of Zapf's type faces to be introduced to America. The first designs for the face were made in 1948, and the fonts for the complete face were issued between 1950 and 1952. Like all Zapf-designed type faces, Palatino is beautifully balanced and exceedingly readable.

Designed by Gwen Townsend